The Money Masters

Onno de Beaufort Wijnholds

The Money Masters

The Progress and Power of Central Banks

palgrave
macmillan

Onno de Beaufort Wijnholds
Washington, DC, USA

ISBN 978-3-030-40040-8 ISBN 978-3-030-40041-5 (eBook)
https://doi.org/10.1007/978-3-030-40041-5

This Palgrave Macmillan imprint is published by the registered company Springer Nature Switzerland AG.
The registered company address is: Gewerbestrasse 11, 6330 Cham, Switzerland

To Chris

Preface

Firemen and central bankers have a lot in common. Fire stations are usually quiet places, its occupants irregularly called upon to put out local fires and perform rescue operations. Central banks often also experience little serious action over extended periods of time, mostly keeping occupied by monitoring economic developments and making modest adjustments in monetary policy. But just as firemen respond aggressively to major conflagrations such as the devastating wildfires in California and Australia, central bankers act resolutely when a major financial emergency, such as the world-wide financial crisis of 2007–09, unfolds.

As I described in my book *Fighting Financial Fires* (2011), central banks in a large part of the world were acting like firemen in those years, fortunately with success, although serious damage had been done to the financial system. Moreover, in the wake of the narrowly avoided disaster, a deep recession, lasting for years, plagued the world economy. Once more, the monetary authorities had their work cut out for them. In their efforts to get their economies up to speed again, they broke new ground by introducing unconventional tools.

This book has been written to provide a better understanding of how central banks have progressed over time to become powerful players in the world economy. Relatively anonymous for a long time, they have in recent years been the subject of increased political scrutiny and criticism, including at the highest level. In addition to countering the arguments of politicians eager to undermine central banks' independence in favor of their own power over monetary policy, there is a need to educate a wider audience on the why and how of central banks' activities. My colleagues who have contributed to this book and I firmly believe that managing money is best left to the non-political experienced technocrats at central banks. We fully subscribe to the view expressed by Paul Tucker, former Deputy Governor of the Bank of England, that '[h]olding public office is an enormous privilege. It requires doing, thinking, planning, managing, and perhaps most crucially today, explaining' (Tucker 2018, X).

A product of close collaboration between the main author and experts on important segments of central banking, we hope that our collective backgrounds have enabled us to write a book which adds to the knowledge of the practice and theory of central banking.

Washington, DC, USA — Onno de Beaufort Wijnholds
2020

References

De Beaufort Wijnholds, Onno: *Fighting Financial Fires: An IMF Insider Account*, Palgrave Macmillan, Basingstoke, 2011.

Tucker, Paul, *Unelected Power: The Quest for Legitimacy in Central Banking and the Regulatory State*, Princeton University Press, Princeton and Oxford, 2018.

Acknowledgments

This book has greatly benefited from contributions by the following specialists: Benny Andersen on The Global Financial Crisis (Chap. 11), Marco van Hengel and Paul Hilbers on Maintaining Financial Stability (Chap. 13) and Jeroen Hessel on the European Central Bank: A New Power (Chap. 10). The other chapters have been written by me and I take full responsibility for their content.

Benny and Paul are former colleagues from my days at the Netherlands Bank and the International Monetary Fund, while I got to know Marco and Jeroen, both from the Netherlands Bank, as knowledgeable and diligent scribes. Working with these contributors to produce a coherent overview of the progress and power of central banks and the challenges they may face in the future has been a pleasure.

Special thanks go to Peter Cornelisse, emeritus professor at Erasmus University in Rotterdam, who read the whole manuscript and whose comments and suggestions have made this a better book. Rasmus Rueffer provided up-to-date information on European monetary developments, as George Pineau had done before him.

Of the many central bankers and academics with whom I have discussed central banking over the years, I want to single out Sylvester Eijffinger of Tilburg University, who not only has made important contributions to the literature but also developed a profound understanding of the practice of central banking.

As with my previous books, my wonderful wife, Christine Nicholson, undertook the task of editing the text with respect to language and meaning and who unfailingly supported me in getting the job done.

Contents

Notes on Contributors

Benny Andersen is a former Executive Director at the International Monetary Fund. He served for 30 years at Denmark's Central Bank in various positions, including as Head of Financial Markets Department and Head of International Economics and Relations. He has held different teaching positions at the Economics Department of the University of Copenhagen, Denmark, including on monetary policy issues.

Onno de Beaufort Wijnholds is a former Executive Director of the International Monetary Fund and former Representative of the European Central Bank in the United States. During his 40-year career, which began at the Netherlands Central Bank, he was closely involved in dealing with monetary issues and international financial crises. Previously, he was Professor of Money and Banking and has published widely in this area.

Jeroen Hessel is a senior economist in the Financial Stability Division of the Netherlands Bank (DNB), where he specializes in macroprudential policies and European financial integration. He previously worked in the Economics and Research Division, and is an expert in various aspects of the Economic and Monetary Union (EMU). Having studied Economics and Law, Hessel is currently completing a PhD at the University of Groningen, the Netherlands.

Paul Hilbers is Director of Financial Stability at the Netherlands Bank (DNB), where he is responsible for systemic risk analysis and macroprudential policies, as well as international financial affairs. Previously he was Director of Supervision Policy at DNB, and he worked at the International

Monetary Fund for over 15 years. Hilbers has also been a part-time professor at Nyenrode Business University in the Netherlands since 2010.

Marco van Hengel is a senior economist in the Financial Stability Division of the Netherlands Bank (DNB), where he specializes in international financial affairs. Before joining DNB, Van Hengel was a senior economist and financial specialist at the Ministry of Finance, specializing in financial sector architecture, fiscal policy and IMF policies. Additionally, he holds a Master's degree in International Economics.

List of Figures

List of Tables

List of Boxes

CHAPTER 1

Introduction

Starting from mostly humble beginnings in the seventeenth century to becoming some of the most powerful institutions in the world of today, central banks' ascendency has been a process of both evolution and planned institution building. This book aims to record and explain this remarkable journey, thereby contributing to a better understanding of an often vaguely perceived policymaker.

Before becoming the true money masters residing in imposing edifices, central banks underwent long periods of relatively smooth evolution interspersed by deep-seated changes. As these shocks mostly resulted in a greater degree of independence from their governments, the power of central banks increased commensurately, save for a limited number of instances where they lost ground to the political branches of government. But such set-backs were almost always reversed over time. For instance, the Federal Reserve (Fed) lacked real influence in the first years after its establishment, but came to play a significant role in fostering the boom of the American economy from the First World War up to the collapse of October 1929. After finding itself in the monetary desert of the Great Depression in the 1930s, partly caused by its policy mistakes, it regained an influential position in 1951 after reaching a landmark agreement with the US Treasury. From then on the American central bank, which had already reestablished its international monetary credentials, was once again an important player on the US economic chessboard. And after slaying the dragon of inflation of the 1960s and 1970s, its place in economic

O. de Beaufort Wijnholds, *The Money Masters*,
https://doi.org/10.1007/978-3-030-40041-5_1

policymaking was never again seriously challenged, despite regular criticism from the more extreme members of the US Congress until recently. However, soon after taking office, the 45th American President became increasingly critical of the Fed to the point that he released an unprecedented barrage of invectives directed at its chairman.

Now the most important central bank in the world, the Federal Reserve was created only after a great number of other central banks had been established, some of which had inspired the founding fathers of the Fed in designing its structure. The first central banks—the Swedish *Riksbank* and the Bank of England—were founded in the seventeenth century. They were followed by France and after a long lag by other Continental European countries, in the early nineteenth century. More official monetary institutions were established after the widespread adoption of the gold standard around 1870, the German *Reichsbank* being the most prominent among these. Three more waves of new central banks followed. The first took place after the ravages of the First World War, actively promoted by the now long forgotten League of Nations. The second wave emerged during the process of decolonization, the newly independent nations emerging on a period of institution building, this time actively promoted by the International Monetary Fund (IMF). Finally, after the implosion of communist Europe, a brief third wave emerged with modern central banks replacing the state banks of centrally planned economies. Here too, the IMF, together with the assistance of Western central banks, played an important role. Thus after a long, sometimes rough journey, the citizens of practically all countries are now served by their own central bank and currency.

The latest chapter in the central bank saga played out during the Global Financial Crisis of 2007–09. Operating in uncharted waters and taking bold action to avert a meltdown of the international financial system, the world's money masters were lauded for their actions, adding to their prestige and power. More recently, the post-crisis recession turned out to be deeper and longer lasting than expected, raising fears of another Great Depression and presenting central banks with another daunting challenge. By introducing new and innovative policies, such as (sub) zero interest rates and quantitative monetary easing, and keeping monetary conditions exceptionally loose, slow but sure success was achieved in returning to satisfactory rates of economic growth in most advanced countries. And in some instances, unemployment fell from high peaks to historically low levels, especially in the United States and Germany. However, monetary policy became overburdened, raising calls for a return to normalcy, meaning letting go of unconventional monetary policy and returning interest rates closer (but still lower than) to historical levels. Moreover, a more active role for fiscal policy, dormant for a long time, is considered by many observers to be overdue.

The economic turmoil of the mid-2010s placed central banks squarely in the limelight, enhancing the perception that these were very powerful institutions. Members of the public, for whom institutions like the Federal Reserve and the Bank of England were largely unknown, have in recent years gained a degree of recognition of what central banks do (they raise interest rates!). All of this has incited renewed questions and criticisms about the proper role of central banks in relation to governments and the economy as a whole. The feeling that (some) central banks are too powerful and need to be reined-in, or in extreme cases, abolished, have taken hold among activist politicians in quite a few countries. As such, increased scrutiny of central banks has become part and parcel of modern democracies. Understanding these needs and to meet the demands of politicians and stakeholders in the private sector for transparency, central banks have over time become much more forthcoming in explaining their actions. While this has led to a better understanding of what goes on in the hushed offices of the world's monetary policymakers, there remains room for improvement, without giving away all the secrets of the temple. In fact there are a limited number of areas within the inner workings of central banks, such as information about intended foreign exchange intervention and the position of individual banks, which have to remain confidential, as is true for government departments such as Ministries of Justice.

But crucial questions remain, such as how powerful central banks have actually become, how did their power accrue over time and how will they operate in the future? These important questions are at the essence of the rise, and sometimes fall, of the influence of institutions managed by government appointed but unelected officials. The history and present state of central banking are crucial for understanding the challenges that official monetary institutions may face in the future. How they will deal with them will help shape the future of national economies and, given the present-day interconnectedness of sovereign nations, the entire world economy. Learning from the past requires an in-depth examination of the path along which central banks became what they are today, taking into account their diversity, not only geographically, but more importantly their stage of development. Advanced economies (as defined by the

International Monetary Fund) generally possess more established monetary institutions and are held to a higher standard than those in developing countries. But considerable progress has been made by the latter, as will be explained in dealing with the more recent history of managing money.

In order to clarify how from their early, modest, beginnings, central banks became major players in the shaping of economic policies, the first chapters of this book are dedicated to their history. For a large part of their existence, the inner workings of central banks remained largely unknown. They were seen as secretive bodies who believed that openness about their activities was undesirable, partly because some of them started off as privately owned entities that did not wish to reveal their business strategies. The mystique of central banking was often cultivated by the institutions leaders, contributing to the notion that conducting monetary policy was more of an art than a science. Writing in 1867 the British economist Stanley Jevons posited that the management of a 'currency is to science what squaring the circle is to geometry and perpetual motion to mechanics' (Jevons 1867, vi). A century later, a former Chairman of the Federal Reserve, Arthur Burns, devoted a lecture to *The Anguish of Central Banking*, stressing the uncertainty that central banks have to deal with (Burns 1979). More recently the Belgian economist Paul de Grauwe observed that despite central banking having been assiduously examined scientifically during the 1980s and 1990s, 'there is still the feeling that, after all, central banking is still an art, and that the success of a central banker depends on such intangibles as feeling the mood of the market' (De Grauwe 2002). And journalist Neil Irwin contributed to the perception of uncovered dark practices by naming his book on central bankers *The Alchemists* (Irwin 2013). However, one of the purported alchemists, Mervyn King, former Governor of the Bank of England, argued in his book *The End of Alchemy* (King 2016) that the mystique of central banking has been largely unmasked. Yet the magnitude of professional private sector *central bank watchers* would seem to suggest that while there is perhaps no more alchemy, the making of monetary policy is not fully predictable and a degree of uncertainty remains.

The history of central banks shows that for most of the time they were considered to be among the least dynamic of financial institutions and government agencies. Chapter 2 relates how in their early days central banks were entities with simple tasks or mandates which only gradually evolved in reaction to new economic and financial developments. Starting with providing loans to the government and issuing banknotes, central banks—the Bank of England leading the way—over time added operations in money markets by buying and selling bills of exchange to their activities. Concerns about financial crises, which erupted from time to time, led central banks to act as lenders of last resort which became an important part of their policies. Increasingly sophisticated open market transactions aimed at influencing conditions on money markets followed. Moreover, the tasks of central banks were drastically altered with the widespread adoption of the classical gold standard between 1875 and 1914 (Chap. 3).

The arrival of the Federal Reserve System in the United States in 1913 injected new ideas and central banking practices, as described in Chap. 4. After the demise of the gold standard in the 1930s, monetary policy became decoupled from the objective of maintaining fixed exchange rates. While initially a period of prosperity, the interwar era was marked by the Great Depression, caused by misguided policies which are analyzed in Chap. 5. How central banks regained prominence in the post-war years with the introduction of the Bretton Woods system of fixed but adjustable exchange rates is the subject of Chap. 6. As related in Chap. 7, the initial success of the new international monetary regime proved to be a shot in the arm for central bank power and prestige. But the dramatic events resulting from the breakdown of the Bretton Woods regime and the widespread surge in inflation of the 1970s complicated the lives of central bankers, especially in the United States where the independence of the Federal Reserve came under siege. At the same time, the now flexible exchange rates allowed central banks to focus monetary policy primarily on domestic economic conditions (Chap. 8). After slaying the dragon of inflation by means of severe monetary tightening in the early 1980s, central banks were on top of their game again, their power and prestige having been restored.

Chapter 9 explains why central bankers enjoyed a relatively easy life between the early 1980s and 2007, a period now known as the *Great Moderation,* during which inflation in the major countries was low and economic growth satisfactory. It was also a time during which important elements of modern central banking were introduced, such as inflation targeting (IT) replacing monetarism and a world-wide move toward greater central bank independence. A further highly significant development was the creation of the single European currency in 1999, adopted by a majority of members of the European Union (Chap. 10). The

European Central Bank which conducts a single monetary policy for the euro area, operated successfully in its first decade, but became entangled in an existential euro crisis during which it had to deploy unconventional monetary tools to restore faith in its currency.

Chapter 11 deals with the unanticipated global financial shock of the second half of the 2000s which drastically ended the tranquility of the long period of moderation. Operating under the threat of a major international financial meltdown, the central banks of the leading economic powers scrambled to provide liquidity support to markets and individual financial institutions. Their comprehensive crisis management also elicited an unusually strong coordination of effort, including joint financial assistance and interest rate actions. While staving off a catastrophe, central banks had to deal with the deep recession following in the wake of their fire-fighting. Fearing a repeat of the Great Depression of the 1930s, the focus of central banks shifted radically from controlling inflation during normal times to stimulating economic growth. Chapter 12 highlights how the persistence of very low inflation, bordering on deflation, swiftly led to a refocusing of monetary policy. Major central banks pumped unprecedentedly large amounts of liquidity into financial markets, known as quantitative easing, having concluded that the effect on economic activity of drastically lowering interest rates was insufficient. In addition, the financial eruption which led to a near collapse of the financial system placed measures to preserve financial stability in the future squarely on the agenda, as explained in Chap. 13. On the domestic front, central banks and governments took measures to tighten the rules pertaining to safeguarding financial stability. At the same time, international cooperation on financial stability issues increased substantially. The host of actions taken to manage the crisis and financial risk significantly bolstered the image of central banks as wielding enormous power, with not only acclaim but also criticism.

In the final chapter (Chap. 14), an attempt is made to look toward the future of central banking. The manifold challenges awaiting the money masters are examined in some detail, ranging from new approaches in monetary policy to the effects of climate change. A main conclusion is that attempts to undermine the independence of central banks are likely to continue and possibly will even escalate. A politically inspired overhaul of their autonomous status will, however, lead to short-termism and an inflationary bias. The end result will be a much weaker overall economic performance, as past experience has demonstrated. Moreover, the authority of central banks with respect to maintaining financial stability will be affected, increasing the risk of financial crises.

Many publications on central banking concentrate on certain periods and activities. As to the history of central banking, excellent studies of the development of the Bank of England and the Federal Reserve and some smaller central banks exist, but they lag many years behind current events. This is understandable, as writing recent official history involving actors still functioning or recently retired is fraught with pitfalls. Some good books about central banking in general date from several years ago but contain little or no information on the dramatic events of recent years or analyses of the political economy of central banks' position and power. This book aims to fill this gap by providing a comprehensive treatment of the evolution of the art and science of these institutions and to provide an up-to-date treatment of the latest approaches in monetary policies and the maintenance of financial stability.

The overriding aim is to provide a thoroughly researched yet easily readable product with a minimal use of technical detail. It is written by a former senior central banker with academic credentials and assisted by former and present high-ranking officials at central banks, combining policymaking experience and academic contributions. For those looking for more theoretical background, most chapters contain a box on monetary theory. These can also serve to illustrate the interaction between theory and practice. But the main focus is on the nature of monetary policy and financial stability measures, while placed against the background of the political economy that is inevitably part of the modern central bankers' mandate.

As interest in central banking has grown, the book may appeal not only to central bankers, officials of other official institutions, universities, academics, politicians, journalists and think tanks, but also to individuals who follow major issues in economics and politics.

References

Burns, Arthur: "The Anguish of Central Banking", *Per Jacobsson Lecture,* Belgrade, October 1979.

De Grauwe, Paul: "Central Banking as Art or Science, Lessons from the Fed and the ECB", Review Article in *International Finance*, Wiley, Blackwell, London, 2002, 129–137.

Irwin, Neil: *he Alchemists: Three* Central *Bankers and a World on Fire*, Penguin Press, London, 2013.

Jevons, Stanley: *Money and the Mechanism of Exchange*, London, 1867.

King, Mervyn: *The End of Alchemy: Money, Banking, and the Future of the Global Economy*, W.W. Norton, New York, 2016.

CHAPTER 2

From War Financier to Bankers' Bank

Early central banks were a far cry from what they eventually became, as described in detail by John Clapham in his comprehensive history of the early history of the Bank of England (Clapham 1944). At the time of the founding of the first 'official' monetary institutions—the Swedish Central Bank and the Bank of England—in the second half of the seventeenth century, economic and financial conditions were vastly different from those in the centuries that followed. Wars regularly ravished the fragile economies of England and the European continent. Since waging war was costly, the belligerents regularly needed to borrow. And to facilitate the procurement of loans, establishing a special financial institution was considered to be desirable. Such was the background against which the Bank of England was established by royal charter in 1694. The new central bank was also granted the right to issue bank notes, thereby bestowing upon it the means to create money. Before this innovation states could only raise money on their own by issuing coins, but there was a cost involved in doing so and counterfeiting and debasement of the currency was common. In England, which was ahead of other countries in matters of money and finances and remained so until into the twentieth century, the Royal Mint was introduced in medieval times to produce reliable coinage. When the famous scientist Isaac Newton was Master of the Royal Mint, he fixed the price of gold at 85 shillings per troy ounce in 1699, marking the beginning of the gold standard. Remarkably, the gold price remained unchanged until 1914.

O. de Beaufort Wijnholds, *The Money Masters*,
https://doi.org/10.1007/978-3-030-40041-5_2

While paper money had existed in earlier times, usually at times of great upheaval such as during the French Revolution, the issuance of bank notes by the Bank of England marked the advent of a reliable means of payment, backed by gold. Since no full monopoly had been granted to the central bank, commercial banks were free to issue their own notes, the quality of which varied significantly. While paper notes put into circulation at that time by fully unregulated banks were supposedly backed by gold, depositors demanding bullion were frequently left empty handed. The convertibility of paper notes became a serious issue and from time to time led to financial crises. (Visitors to Scotland may notice that bank notes issued by the Bank of Scotland are still circulating as legal tender.)

The Need for a Central Bank

Besides serving as a provider of loans to finance costly wars, having a central bank also proved to be useful as a vehicle to centralize a part or all of the rampant and sometimes chaotic issue of bank notes by commercial banks. One way to deal with this unstable situation was to grant a monopoly—full or partial—to issue bank notes to the central bank. In addition, English commercial banks, for reasons of efficiency and safety, started to deposit their gold with the Bank of England. Most of the early central banks were founded on the basis of a government issued charter, usually authorizing the fledgling institution a monopoly to print money. Although government created entities, the new central banks continued to be fully or privately owned and could freely conduct business as if they were a commercial enterprise with a profit motive. Strongly centralized countries, such as Russia, were an exception in that their central banks only conducted transactions for the state. And some central banks that were free to conduct private business were only bestowed with a full monopoly of circulating paper money at a later stage of their development. The Bank of England was not granted a complete monopoly until 1844.

While issuing bank notes is a lucrative business, being pure money creation, the acceptance and use of Bank of England notes by the public, despite being backed by gold, remained limited for a long time. Besides the novelty effect, the cumbersome way the early notes were produced (handwritten) and issued only in relatively large denominations made them suitable only for large transactions. As a result the profits of central banks flowed mainly from their commercial business. But over time, the private sector dealings of central banks were increasingly recognized as implying a degree of conflict of interest. By virtue of internal conviction within the large banks, pressure from governments or legislation, the attitude of those who managed a central bank with private clients changed over time. The propagation of the notion that central banks had to function mainly in the national interest marked the end of their early days. This process was anchored by the nationalization of central banks across a wide range of countries during the twentieth century, the state acquiring full ownership. While there are still a few central banks with private shareholders owning a part of their capital, these wield no influence in practice.

Table 2.1 provides an overview of the main dates in the evolution of the institutional structure of important central banks.

In several cases the founding date of central banks can be interpreted in different ways, as various privately owned institutions functioned in some limited capacity as forerunners. For central banks fully owned by the state at the outset, the date of founding is mentioned under the column nationalization.

The Bank of England and Its Followers

The earliest central bank was established in Sweden, directly as a result of a financial debacle caused by a privately managed bank, enjoying enormous freedom under a royal decree, issuing a flood of banknotes. In order to exercise more government control over monetary matters, a national bank was established under the name of Swedish *Riksbank*, whose history is lucidly described by Klas Fregert (2018). The Swedish innovation was followed 30 years later by England, which had a more advanced financial system. And it was the Bank of England that established the model for many monetary institutions that were created at a (much) later stage. There are early examples of quasi or proto central banks in Europe which are comprehensively described by Ugolini (2017). The most advanced of these, the Amsterdam Exchange Bank, backed and administered by the city council of Amsterdam, was also providing some central bank—like services from 1609 to the end of the eighteenth century. It is sometimes portrayed as the first true central bank, for instance by Quinn and Robers (2007), but this seems a bit farfetched and the Amsterdam bank should rather be seen as a sophisticated settlement institution.

The seventeenth century was a period of many wars among European countries, especially fought as naval battles. As the English navy was often defeated in these clashes, King William III and his government saw an

Table 2.1 Central bank landmark dates

	Established	*Issue Monopoly*	*Nationalization*
Swedish Riksbank	1663	1897	1897
Bank of England	1694	1844	1946
Bank of Spain	1782	1874	1962
Bank of France	1800	1809	1915
Netherlands Bank	1814	1814	1948
National Bank of Austria	1817	1817	1947
National Bank of Denmark	1818	1818	1936
National Bank of Belgium	1850	1850	*
Bank of Russia	1860	1860	1917
German Reichsbank/Bundesbank	1875	1875	1875/1957
Bank of Japan	1882	1884	*
Bank of Italy	1893	1926	*
Bank of China/Peoples Bank	1905	1905	1949
Swiss National Bank	1907	1910	*
US Federal Reserve System	1913	1919	#
South African Reserve Bank	1921	1921	*
Reserve Bank of Australia ^	1924	1924	1947
Bank of Mexico	1925	1925	1925
Central Bank of Turkey	1931	1931	*
Central Bank of Argentina	1935	1935	1946
Bank of Canada	1935	1938	1938
Central Bank of India	1935	1935	1949
Central Bank of Korea	1950	1950	1950
Saudi Arabian Monetary Agency	1952	1961	=
Bank Indonesia	1953	1953	1953
European Central Bank	1998	2000	+

*Minority private shareholders, except South Africa (100%) and Switzerland (55%)

#Federal Agency; regional Federal Reserve Banks have commercial member banks as shareholders

^Initially Commonwealth Bank of Australia

=Established as Government Agency

+Supranational institution

Source: M.H. De Kock (1939), central bank histories

urgent need to strengthen their seafaring capabilities. Its coffers being empty and the government unable to borrow even at high interest rates, it latched on to an earlier plan developed by a Scotsman, William Paterson. The idea was to induce subscriptions to a large loan carrying an interest rate of 8 percent and have the set-up incorporated in the name of The Governor and Company of the Bank of England. Starting life as a financier of war, the Bank of England would gradually become the center of the British financial system in the United Kingdom (including Scotland since 1707). Little change occurred during most of the eighteenth century, with the Bank's charter renewed periodically. But as participating in the Napoleonic wars was depleting the Bank of England's gold stock, convertibility of its banknotes into the yellow metal was suspended and not resumed until 1821.

While during the eighteenth century the Bank of England was still in its infancy as a central bank and its commercial activities were its mainstay, it had already from approximately 1760 on acted as an informal lender of last resort (Kynaston 2017).By the time Adam Smith published his famous book *An Inquiry into the Nature and Causes of the Wealth of Nations* (1776), it had already established a solid reputation. Smith described the Bank as 'the greatest bank of circulation in Europe,' arguing that 'the stability of the bank of England is equal to that of the British government. All that it has advanced to the publick must be lost before its creditors can sustain any loss. No other banking company can be established by act of parliament… It acts, not only as an ordinary bank, but as a great engine of state.'

During the eighteenth century, insight into the fundamentals of money and credit was still rudimentary and the concept of a central bank separate from commercial banks was yet to be developed. However, in the early years of the nineteenth century, Henry Thornton, a banker and politician, developed an impressive early understanding of what should be done to achieve price stability. In his book *Enquiry into the Nature and Effects of the Paper Credit of Great Britain*, published in 1802, he argued that the solution was '[t]o limit the amount of paper issued and to resort for this purpose, whenever the temptation to borrow is strong, to some effectual principle of restriction' (Thornton, 259). The Bank of England should, he averred, let the money stock increase at the rate of production growth. He also saw a role for the Bank as lender of last resort, a concept, as we shall see, was much later more fully worked out by Bagehot. Furthermore, Thornton made a distinction between nominal and real variables, a notion which continued to escape some central bankers right into the twentieth century. Unfortunately his stellar contribution was largely forgotten for over a century.

Bank Note Monopoly

The year 1844 marks a major change in the position of the Bank of England. In an Act of Parliament (known as the Peel Act, so named after the then Prime Minister Robert Peel), the Bank was split into two departments. Having been granted a monopoly in the issue of banknotes, a separate Issue Department was established, authorized to print paper money up to a certain limit. The note circulation had to be backed by gold up to a certain percentage. The Banking Department constituted the vehicle for the Bank's commercial activities, but came to play an important role in influencing general financial conditions through changes in the interest it charged on discounted bills and loans. The Act of 1844 was heavily debated between the supporters of two schools of thought: those who adhered to the *currency principle* advocating a limit on the amount of banknotes outstanding, on the one hand, and adherents of the *banking principle*, who promoted complete freedom of issuance by all banks, on the other. This dichotomy would inform future debates on how to conduct monetary policy by central banks. In the years that followed economists pointed out that the Peel Act rendered the supply of paper money *inelastic*, meaning that as the economy expanded, a rigid limit on banknotes in circulation posed a constraint on its growth. Higher limits were granted by the government from time to time, but always after the problem had become more than obvious. Yet the early recognition that money had to be managed in some way would carry the day in the twentieth century, despite pleas for *free banking*—complete non-intervention in the monetary sphere in the belief that meeting the private sector's demand for means of payments would be best for the economy. In modern parlance: a self-correcting mechanism.

By mid-nineteenth century the Bank of England was playing a dominant role in the London money market, buying and selling bills of exchange at a discount rate that had evolved as the benchmark for the whole banking system. And as London was by far the most important financial center in the world, the *Bank rate* was followed closely abroad as well. The British capital also dominated the international gold market with the Bank playing an important role. While its task as the governments' banker had expanded over time it was also evolving into the banker's bank, with private companies increasingly maintaining deposits with the Bank of England which they could withdraw on demand. Not only was this practice efficient, it also reflected confidence in the financial solidity of the

Bank with its relatively large stock of gold as the ultimate backstop. And so the expression 'as safe as the Bank of England' made its way into everyday language.

In the meantime a number of central banks had been founded on the continent of Europe during the first part of the nineteenth century, in a process succinctly described by M.H. De Kock (De Kock 1939). The most important of these, the *Banque de France*, was established by Napoleon who saw the need for a state bank to extend credit to the government and to deal with the aftermath of the French Revolution during which the printing of an enormous amounts of *assignats* had severely disrupted the financial system. The French central back was highly centralized and lacked the sophistication of its British counterpart. It also did little to develop the private financial system and went on competing with commercial banks much longer than the Bank of England. Another feature of the *Banque* was its infrequent use of its bank rate, preferring to charge a premium on gold sales when there was an outflow of specie. The Bank of England by contrast preferred to react to out-and inflows of gold with changes in its bank rate and did not charge a levy on gold sales.

The central banks of the Netherlands and Austria, in 1814 and 1817 respectively, were set up in the mold of the Bank of England with an important financial contribution of the business sector, but with a greater role of government than in Britain. The Dutch King William I was an enthusiastic supporter of the Netherlands Bank which he called his 'oldest daughter.' The Belgian and Scandinavian central banks also largely followed the British approach. Not so, the Bank of Russia established in 1860. In line with Russian autocratic rule the new institution was highly centralized. The same was true of the Bank of Prussia which in 1875 was subsumed under the *Reichsbank* of a unified Germany. And the Bank of Japan, founded in 1882 as the first of its kind outside Europe, was similarly designed as a true bank of the state. The United States, though a rising economic power, was not among the countries with a central bank until 1913. There had been two attempts at enjoying the advantage of a functioning central bank, but were in both cases—the First and Second Bank of the United States—torpedoed by politics, President Andrew Jackson playing a prominent role. Only after a number of financial panics did the US Congress decide to establish a confidence-inspiring monetary institution.

Lender of Last Resort

In a financial system consisting of a large number of commercial banks, specialized discount and acceptance houses and other money market participants, all operating freely without requiring a license or being subject to some kind of supervision, accidents are bound to happen. In the British context this occurred quite frequently, but these mishaps were of little consequence if those firms that failed were of modest size. However, default by or bankruptcy of an important market participant could well endanger at least part of the financial system. As the system grew, the Bank of England recognized the danger of ignoring the meltdown of a large and interconnected financial institution. It could of course let the crisis burn out by itself, but taking such a course was risky and the Bank was more and more disinclined to follow such a strategy. Yet in earlier times of crisis the central bank was very reluctant to come to the aid of troubled banks. It did continue to perform the task of rediscounting (buying bills of exchange that had been accepted by a solid counterparty) but only to a limited degree and did not provide accommodation through large advances to quell bankers' anxieties. And at the time of the crises of 1847 and 1857, the Bank only lent freely after some pressure by the government. To sugar the pill the Bank was promised that legislation would be passed to indemnify it if its support to the market would result in a failure to maintain a sufficient gold cover. But several years later the Old Lady of Threadneedle Street, as the Bank came to be known fondly, had undergone a change of attitude, now according priority to safeguarding the stability of the vast London money market. And when the next crisis struck, the still privately managed British Central bank reacted with alacrity to avoid a dangerous panic from spreading. This and other crises are vividly described by Professor Charles Kindleberger (1978).

In May 1866 the formerly venerable discount house Overend, Gurney & Company went under, causing a panic in the London money market with reverberations in financial centers abroad. The initially well-run firm had gone public not long before its demise but had made foolish investments in areas such as grain, iron and railroads in which it had no expertise. As these poor decisions resulted in large losses, which only became apparent at a late stage, transparency being virtually absent those days, Overend was sinking fast. Sensing that the panic that broke out could ruin the financial system, the Bank of England immediately provided very large advances (loans) to money market participants. Fortunately at that point the Bank's gold reserves were relatively large, helped by the circumstance that the Bank, sensing trouble, had dramatically raised its discount rate from 3 to 7 percent the previous October, thereby avoiding a substantial drain on its reserves half a year later.

The Bank of England's swift action in extinguishing the crisis of 1866, before it had consulted with the government for which there had been no time, marks its graduation to a mature central bank. Around the same time the Bank of England was also showing itself to be a guardian of the British financial system rather than a profit maximizing entity. This can be seen as a general recognition in the money market that in a panic the Bank of England would be the sole lender. Walter Bagehot, a close observer of the money market, and first editor of *The Economist,* stated that London seemed to experience a major financial crisis roughly every ten years. (Major global financial crises have roughly occurred with the same frequency.)

Bagehot argued that it was the task of the central bank to douse financial fires. And it was Bagehot who first described this crucial central bank function as acting as the *lender of last resort*. In his brilliant book *Lombard Street: A Description of the Money Market*, (Bagehot 1873) he set out the principles that should guide central banks in their lending operations in times of crisis. Starting early in a crisis, a central bank should lend freely to participants in the money market, but at a penalty rate and against sound collateral. These rules are meant to prevent financial institutions that do not need it, to seek loans. This would, in the case of the Bank of England at the time, help to ensure that its gold reserve was not unnecessarily drained. At the same time, all those seeking to borrow from the central bank should put up sound collateral, the monetary authority determining what securities should be accepted. Bagehot emphasized that as the aim is to bring a halt to an ongoing crisis, no money market participant with adequate collateral should be turned away, as this would cause alarm. He also made a distinction between solvent banks and merchants and those who are not would be allowed to fail. Bagehot also emphasized that a central bank should continue to lend until the panic is overcome. Withdrawing at an earlier stage will make things worse.

Acting as lender of last resort could also be undertaken through guarantees provided by the central bank. Moreover, on occasions, the Bank of England felt obliged to call on its foreign sister institutions (such as the French Central Bank) to support it in bail-out operations, who recognized that a crisis in London could easily spill over to financial centers abroad. The reverse was just as common, the French Central Bank from time to time calling on its British counterpart to aid it in putting out a financial fire. Such early examples of cooperation between central banks were a harbinger of a more structured approach in international central bank actions. The crisis in 1890 around the prestigious British private bank, Baring Brothers, is a good example of a lender of last resort operation involving both guarantees and aid from abroad. Barings Brothers had strong ties with banks, inside England and abroad, and rumors that it was in difficulties caused a great deal of unrest. Alert to overly risky activity, the Governor of the Bank of England, Lord Lidderdale, had earlier warned Barings with respect to its purchase of risky Argentinian bills of exchange. A few months later Barings informed the Bank that it was in distress. This time the Governor decided against providing large advances to the money market participants as he feared that the Bank's—at that moment—low gold reserve could well be depleted. And the effect of raising the Bank rate to attract foreign private capital would take too long to materialize in the prevailing circumstances. Since it turned out that Barings was solvent but acutely in need of liquidity, two actions were undertaken. First, the government pledged to increase its balances at its central bank and offered to share any losses the Bank would suffer on paper discounted by the central bank in a limited time frame. In addition, it was decided to put together a large scale guarantee fund that would provide confidence and calm the market, in a joint effort of private banks, commercial banks (at that time known as joint-stock banks) and other financial firms. On top of that, the Russian Government agreed not to withdraw its sizable deposit held at the Bank of England, while the State Bank of Russia and the Bank of France provided loans in gold. An impressive sophisticated and coordinated rescue operation, it served to instill confidence around the world that the British financial system could be trusted.

Bagehot's principles still constitute the basis of the actions central banks take in a crisis. During the first half of the twentieth century—a period in which many new central banks saw the light—the function of lender of last resort was readily accepted. As to be expected, mishaps continued to occur and central bank intervention to save a particular financial institution, or more generally to protect its country's financial system, failed with some regularity. The decision to do all it can to save an important bank at short notice is one of the most difficult decisions a central bank has to make. If it succeeds it is praised effusively, if not it is often made a scapegoat.

Custodian of Gold Reserves

As the banking system in Britain grew, the Bank of England, acting de facto as the bankers' bank, accumulated a sizable stock of gold. This reserve inspired confidence, not only in the Bank, but also in the commercial banks whose clients appreciated that a buffer existed to be drawn upon in times of financial distress. Continental European countries followed along the same path with a lag. In order to be credible, central bank reserves needed to be large enough to be viewed at all times as representing a comfortable level. In other words, they had to be of a size that would allow the general public, as well as commercial banks, to freely convert their banknotes into gold. What could be considered an adequate level of gold held by the Bank of England, and by other central banks became a contentious issue.

A first attempt at controlling the circulation of banknotes came about in 1844 with the Peel Act (mentioned earlier) stipulating that the issue of banknotes should not surpass a certain level and requiring that part to be backed by government securities. Beyond this so-called fiduciary issue, paper notes had to be backed fully by gold. But many observers did not think that such an approach was satisfactory, some arguing that the banknotes in circulation should be backed by some 30 to 40 percent in gold. However, the British Government did not change its position, leaving it to the market to ascertain whether enough reserves were held at the central bank to provide sufficient confidence. In France no official action was taken to link the amount of banknotes to the central banks' gold stock. By contrast, in recently unified Germany the central banks' gold reserve was to remain above a minimum of one third of its banknote issuance, but did not cover deposits outstanding at the *Reichsbank*. The German Government was not alone in not including commercial bank deposits with the central bank in this ratio, but this oversight was later remedied. In due course the so-called proportional system of a minimum gold cover of all of central banks' liabilities was adopted by most newly established central banks. As we will see, the requirement of a minimum reserve cover would have a long life, but would be challenged as less relevant in the future.

An additional question that arose was whether central banks' holdings of foreign exchange should be included as part of its total reserves. Already in the late nineteenth century a number of central banks kept balances in pounds with the Bank of England. The attraction was that instead of gold that bore no interest, deposits in pounds were remunerated. Little is known about this early role of the pound sterling as a reserve currency. The share of foreign exchange in countries' total reserves around 1900 has been estimated at around 15 percent (Lindert 1969). Among the larger holders were Russia (recall its role in the Barings rescue) and the Scandinavian countries. When it became commonplace in the twentieth century to keep part of the national reserves in foreign exchange (in pounds and increasingly in US dollars) they were counted as part of the required minimum cover.

At the turn of the century central banking had come a long way from its modest beginnings. While issuing banknotes and acting as the government's banker were the tasks entrusted to the embryonic central banks, their range of activity expanded significantly during the nineteenth century. The crucial junction for central banks, which started out as privately owned enterprises, was the shift from maximizing profits to institutions that were making the health of the financial system their first priority. Goodhart (1988) places this turning point with respect to the Bank of England in the 1850s. As Kynaston, in his authoritative book on the history of the Bank of England, puts it: 'it was in the 1850s that the Bank started to stop trying to be all things to all men' (2017, 157). As a logical consequence the Bank of England had become the undisputed lender of last resort for the banking industry as a whole and was gradually viewed to be 'a semi-public institution, whose directors are guided in their decisions not by considerations of pecuniary profit or dividends, but by motives of public policy and care for the general interest' (Birnie 1930, 94). Several Continental European Central Banks followed this model. Already at an earlier stage the Bank of England was involved in catering to the normal fluctuations in banks' and bill broker's liquidity needs. As financial systems grew and became more entwined, central banks were increasingly active in discounting bills of exchange (more precisely, 'rediscounting' as they would pay out holders of accepted bills of good quality). Because of the dominant position the British central bank had acquired on the money market, the rate at which it discounted bills that were offered to it (the Bank rate) evolved into the bellwether for the rates market participants charged their customers. The discount rate—the equivalent of an interest rate but calculated up front through a discount on the principal—set by the Bank tended to be above the rate charged by others. This ensured that only institutions in dire need of liquidity would appear at the Bank of England's discount window. In addition, a sophisticated practice to influence conditions in the money market in general was developed by the Bank of England, consisting of openly buying and selling bills of exchange or government securities. This practice, known as open-market operations, has been a mainstay of central bank operations to this day.

While central banking had evolved considerably during the nineteenth century, it did not yet encompass monetary policy as a macroeconomic tool, nor was financial stability an explicit objective of central banks. To the extent there were rules pertaining to the soundness of banks, they were implemented by governments. But central banks of countries in which the banking system was well developed, mainly those of the United Kingdom, France, Germany, Italy, the Netherlands, Belgium, Austria, Switzerland and the Scandinavian countries, were sensitive to the soundness of individual commercial banks, a harbinger of the future preventive role of central banks of prudential supervision. In this sense, financial stability was a tenet of central banking before monetary policy.

References

Bagehot, Walter: *Lombard Street: A Description of the Money Market*, London, 1873.

Birnie, Arthur: *An Economic History of Europe 1760-1930*, Methuen & Co, London, 1930.

Clapham, John: *The Bank of England: A History 1694-1914*, London, 1944.

De Kock, M.H.: *Central Banking*, Macmillan, London, 1939.

Fregert, Klas: "Sveriges Riksbank: 350 Years in the Making" in Rodney Edvinsson et al (eds), *Sveriges Riksbank and the History of Central Banking*, Cambridge University Press, 2018, p 90–137.

Goodhart, Charles: *The Evolution of Central Banks*, MIT Press, Cambridge MA, 1988.

Kindleberger, Charles: *Manias, Panics and Crashes: A History of Financial Crises*, Macmillan, London, 1978.

Kynaston, David: *Till Times' Last Sand: A History of the Bank of England 1694-2013*, Bloomsbury, London, 2017.

Lindert, Peter: "Key Currencies and Gold 1900-1913", *Studies in International Finance* no. 24, Princeton, NJ, 1969.

Quinn, Stephen and William Robers: "The Bank of Amsterdam and the Leap to Central Bank Money", *American Economic Review*, vol. 97 no. 2, May 2007, 262–265.

Smith, Adam: *An Inquiry into the Nature and Causes of the Wealth of Nations*, Edinburgh, 1776.

Thornton, Henry: *Enquiry into the Nature and Effects of the Paper Credit of Great Britain*, London, 1802.

Ugolini, Stefano: *The Evolution of Central Banking: Theory and History*. Palgrave Series in Economic History, Palgrave Macmillan, Basingstoke, 2017.

CHAPTER 3

Central Banks Under the Gold Standard

The history of the pure, or classical, gold standard which served as the lynchpin of the international monetary system from around 1875 to 1914 and from 1925 to 1936 provides important lessons for present day supporters of a return to a system based on gold. The reasons for the demise of this once relatively successful approach to maintaining sound money will become apparent in this chapter and the next.

Adoption of the gold standard by officially expressing the value of national currencies in a certain amount of gold developed unevenly. While the United Kingdom had long since backed the pound sterling with the gold reserves of the Bank of England, France followed its example many years later. Other nations copied the gold regime in the course of the nineteenth century, while it can be said that the United States did so already in 1796 in a limited way. In several cases, among them China and Mexico, countries poor in gold but rich in silver, a silver standard was introduced. But discoveries of the yellow metal in the nineteenth century in California, Australia, Yukon and especially South Africa led to enormous increases in gold production. This plethora of gold enabled a large number of countries to adopt the gold standard, especially in Western Europe, with the notable exception of Spain, but also by the main gold producers. And when Germany officially adopted the gold standard in 1875, the world's main currencies were all linked at fixed quantities of gold. This meant that a system of fixed exchange rates between currencies, generally referred to as the *Classical Gold Standard*, had been established, remaining in place

O. de Beaufort Wijnholds, *The Money Masters*,
https://doi.org/10.1007/978-3-030-40041-5_3

for about 40 years. To distinguish it from later types of gold standard, it is also known as the *Gold Coin Standard*, reflecting that when banknotes were presented to the central bank for conversion, gold coins were paid out. They circulated as a means of payment until 1914. (Such coins later became sought after collectors' items.)

Formalizing the link to gold by law and internationalizing the gold standard meant that currencies were freely exchangeable under the new system. For example, one British pound could always be exchanged for a fixed number of French francs, German marks, US dollars and so on. The repercussions for the functioning of central banks were of great importance.

The operation of the classical gold standard in rudimentary form was described long before it was internationalized in the late nineteenth century. The centerpiece of the working of the gold standard is known as the price-specie-flow mechanism. Its first clear description hails from David Hume, the great Scottish philosopher, in the middle of the eighteenth century (Hume 1752). He explained that when prices were rising faster in one country than those in its trading partners, its citizens would buy goods from the cheaper country. The resulting excess of imports over exports was to be covered by payments in specie (generally gold), other means of payment not being accepted abroad. The outflow of gold would push up prices in the other country, resulting in an outflow of gold on its part. This mechanism would thus automatically ensure a restoration of equilibrium in the respective balances of trade. Implicitly the mechanism was to work instantaneously, but in practice this was not the case, as was recognized at a later stage. The smooth functioning of the price-specie-flow mechanism hinged on complete freedom of international trade and of capital movements. In Hume's day these conditions were generally met and more or less taken for granted.

At the time of the widespread adoption of the gold standard the reigning economic philosophy was precisely a complete freedom of international transactions. This was the period of the doctrine of *laissez-faire*, according to which economies performed best if governments refrained from any kind of intervention and markets were left to their own devices. The underpinning of this philosophy was the theory formulated in 1803 by the French economist Jean-Baptiste Say which held that production would create its own demand. Therefore the size of a country's output would necessarily equal the size of total demand. Also known as the 'law of markets,' Say's theory implied that there could be no excess supply in the economy and therefore no unemployment. Although he did not mention the role of money, Say's law also implied that money was 'neutral' and that no hoarding of money, which would lead to a lack of demand, would occur. Thus freedom of markets would ensure optimal economic results. The general tenet of this theory remained largely unchallenged until John Maynard Keynes explained its flaws (Keynes 1926).

On the basis of the belief in laissez-faire, complete freedom of trade and financial transactions was the mainstay of Western Government economic policies in the era from 1875 to the outbreak of the First World War in 1914. It was accepted that a smooth operation of the gold standard required the absence of tariffs, quotas and capital controls. In addition, informal *rules of the game* were in place to strengthen the adjustment process under the gold standard. Countries that were losing gold had to take domestic measures, such as raising interest rates and other means of tightening credit, to correct the imbalance. Likewise countries receiving gold were expected to lower interest rates and loosen credit. If the rules were carefully followed, adjustment would not have to rely solely on substantial transfers of gold to initiate the time-consuming process of bringing about equilibrium. Playing the game would limit the transfer of gold, allowing central banks to keep smaller reserves than would otherwise be considered a safe buffer to maintain convertibility into gold at home. International capital flows also played an important role as they reacted speedily to changes in interest rates, again rendering the adjustment process much smoother. In addition governments and central banks increasingly strengthened their ties and cooperation with their foreign counterparts, arranging loans to each other to avoid financial strains from getting out of hand and infecting other financial centers.

The classical gold standard, operating under the law of the market, with complete freedom of international transactions and relying on a streamlined price-specie-flow mechanism, was generally hailed as a great success. World trade expanded hugely as the system of immutably fixed exchange rate provided confidence that exporters and importers could be certain that they would receive or pay exactly the amount in their own currency as contracted. There also existed a more or less general expectation that while in the short run prices could fluctuate, in the long run the price level would be stable, giving confidence to traders and investors that in the end that they could expect commodities to hold their value in the domestic currency. Calculations by the Federal Reserve Bank of St. Louis show that during the era of the classical gold standard the price level in the United Kingdom fell on average, but by only 0.7 percent (annual fluctuations during that era were, however, much higher). For the United Sates a similar picture emerges: an average of 0.1 percent, but also with large fluctuations (Federal Reserve Bank of St. Louis Bulletin, May 1981). As a result world production grew considerably more rapidly than before, prosperity among the better-off classes in the Western world becoming quite visible. This was the heyday of the Austrian school of economics, led by such luminaries as Ludwig von Mises, which was for a time the standard bearer of economic liberalism. Their belief in the salutary effects of the gold standard was very strong and the Austrian economists succeeded in convincing academics and policymakers that strict application of gold standard rules rendered superior outcomes in terms of economic prosperity.

The Rules of the Game

Under the gold standard the main task of central banks was to ensure the smooth working of the automatic equilibrating mechanism by guaranteeing the maintenance of a system of fixed exchange rates. The *rules of the game* required that countries take measures to minimize imbalances in international payments (nowadays referred to as the balances of payment), the flow of gold being the ultimate means of adjustment. Movements of gold would take place whenever exchange rates reached the 'gold points,' representing the official rate (or parity) plus or minus the cost of transportation. Gold is a very compact metal and shipping it is therefore relatively inexpensive. For instance, the cost of transportation between London and New York was no more than 0.5 percent. Hence, while the official currency rate between the pound sterling and the United States was fixed at $4.867, the market rate could fluctuate between plus or minus 0.5 percent. Such a narrow band between gold points required central banks to monitor movements in currency rates closely. Losing gold came to be considered a signal of bad policies, like 'the boy who blurts out uncomfortable truths' (Schumpeter 1954, 732). To avoid large or persistent outflows of gold to other countries, central banks' first line of defense was to raise their official discount rates. The effect of such measures was twofold. In the short run higher interest would attract foreign capital and in the somewhat longer run would constrain credit in the private sector, thereby contributing to a slowdown of the economy. If a central bank considered the impact of an increase in its interest rate insufficient, it could, as a second line of defense, conduct open market policies. These would generally consist of selling government bonds to the market at attractive rates, thereby mopping up liquidity in the money market. The Bank of England was, as usual, the most advanced central bank in this type of operations. However, the Austro-Hungarian Bank seems to be the first to make use of intervention in its currencies' forward exchange rate (utilizing the difference between spot and forward rates) between 1907 and 1912. These transactions were also conducted to strengthen the effect of increases in interest rates by influencing capital movements in the desired direction, while maintaining the spot exchange rate within the gold points (M.H. De Kock 1939, 269).

As explained, the overarching objective of central banks under the gold standard was to maintain their currency in a fixed proportion to other currencies, without depleting their gold reserves to levels that endangered convertibility. To this end they would sometimes take drastic measures to achieve that goal. Whenever their currency came under heavy pressure, central banks would be inclined to either start raising their interest rates at an early stage and following up if needed, or in the event of, say, a heavy speculative attack inspired by a low level of the gold reserves push up their rates abruptly to an unusually high level. For instance, when a financial panic in New York in 1907 had a serious spillover effect on the London money market, the Bank rate was increased at short notice from 4.5 to 7 percent. The central bank's swift reaction proved to be effective. That such an action could hurt the domestic economy was not a consideration, operating in accordance with the rules of the game being almost sacrosanct. Neither were short term fluctuations in the general price level considered to be a reason for governments or central banks to consider following another course than sticking to the classical mechanism of the gold standard. However, it was this rigidity that caused some central banks at times to ignore the rules. And it turned out that the supposed automaticity of the gold standard was not as ubiquitous as was (and is) sometimes assumed, as demonstrated by Ragnar Nurkse, in his study on the interwar period (Nurkse 1944).

Monetary policy under the classical gold standard was in principle one dimensional, as we saw in the foregoing, keeping the price of gold fixed and as a result the exchange rate, being the sole objective despite often leading to slower growth and rising unemployment. To the extent economists paid attention to the foundations of unemployment, they tended to attribute it to a lack of flexibility of wages. Nevertheless, whatever the causes, awareness of the problem was growing. Although the average annual level of unemployment under the classical system was 4.3 percent in the United Kingdom and 6.8 percent in the United States, spells of much higher joblessness occurred regularly. As a result pressures for a less dogmatic application of the informal rules led some countries, in particular France and Belgium, to react with less alacrity to support their currencies when they were losing gold. In a process known as *sterilization,* they offset the corresponding decrease in their money supply by conducting open market purchases. But the process could not be continued very long as the resulting loss of gold and the drain of their reserves would become untenable. The Bank of England, while regarded as the conductor of the gold standard system, from time to time allowed its reserves to fall to a level that other countries like France and Germany would consider too risky. The British central bank, experienced some narrow escapes when sizable conversion of bank notes and a large balance of payments deficit occurred simultaneously, by contracting short term loans from commercial and foreign central banks, in situations where raising the Bank rate was not sufficiently effective. Such problems did not affect the French central bank, relying as it did on its large gold reserve and only infrequently resorting to raising its interest rate.

In conclusion, while the classical gold standard continued to enjoy widespread support up to 1914, even if the rules of the game were not always followed slavishly, political pressures increased to change the system in ways that would take into account the social ills of poverty and unemployment. But such forces were still insufficiently strong to bring about reform of the gold standard before the Great War of 1914–18.

Box 3.1 Monetary Theory

Monetary policy became more scientifically based only after 1918. However, in the early twentieth century new academic work foreshadowed a drastic change in monetary thinking. The most influential individual developing new ideas in monetary theory was Irving Fisher, a professor at Yale University. His first important contribution was to distinguish between nominal and real interest rates, explaining that most of the public and policymakers suffered from

(*continued*)

Box 3.1 (continued)

money illusion. They did not realize that part of the level of nominal rate of interest reflected an increase or decrease in prices. The failure by most of the economic profession to recognize the importance of the concepts of the real rate of interest and real wages prevented early monetary policy to attain a higher level of sophistication. But, as Alan Meltzer in the first volume of his history of the Federal Reserve observes: 'Central bankers seem generally to have regarded Fisher as a bright but annoying crank' (Meltzer (2003) would make him famous). The notion of a connection between changes in the stock of money and the level of prices dated from earlier centuries. Classical economists observed that in times of large additions to the world stock of gold (and silver), the level of prices rose and vice versa. However, a full explanation of this phenomenon was lacking. In the early twentieth century, Fisher, by introducing two elements besides money and prices in a formula, succeeded in bringing about a much better understanding of what came to be known as the *quantity theory of money* (Fisher 1911).

In order to explain how money affects the level of economic activity, the velocity of circulation of notes and coins as well as bank deposits (by now recognized as part of the money supply) had to be known. And prices had to be seen as one element of aggregate trade (later expressed as national product). Put together the simple equation reads:

$$MV = PT$$

M is the money supply, V the velocity of money in circulation, P the price level, while T stands for trade or the exchange of goods. The equation is a truism (or in mathematical terms an identity), but captures the relationship between money and prices well, since Fisher holds that V is determined by objective factors such as the habits of households and the development of the technique of payments. When it is assumed that V is constant (a regular occurrence in later years) changes in M explain PT. Additionally, if PT is understood to be nominal national income (Y), changes in the price level can be separated

(*continued*)

Box 3.1 (continued)

from the national product (as became possible with the advent of national accounts in the 1930s). The link between M and P was readily embraced by many economists. Fisher's thinking proved highly influential, and opened the way to statistical measurement of a number of key economic variables, although many interpretations of his concept of velocity led to much confusion rather than clarity. A similar theory, developed by Dennis Robertson (1922), known as the Cambridge (University) approach was based on the propensity of the public to hold cash balances, also called 'hoarding' of money. As we shall see in Box 5.1, John Maynard Keynes modified the cash balance approach significantly in the 1930s in developing his theory of *liquidity preference* (Keynes 1923, 1930).

Other important theoretical breakthroughs occurred during the pre-war period. Some economists developed an improved definition of the money supply, including not only coins (still a predominant part of M at the time) and banknotes, but also demand deposits held by households and businesses with commercial banks. Building upon that insight, the 'discovery' of the process by which money is created by banks through the process of loans, creating deposits which are part of the money supply, initially controversial, was of great significance. It followed that balances held by commercial banks with their central bank were not part of the money supply as they formed the base for money creation by the banks. But this new thinking caught on slowly. As the great Austrian economist Joseph Schumpeter observed: 'As regards central banking, economists enlarged … their conception of central banks, especially the controlling and regulating function of the "lender of last resort". But most of them were surprisingly slow in recognizing to the full the implications of Monetary Management which was … developing under their eyes' (Schumpeter 1954, 1112). Indeed the notion that money could not be fully left alone to its own devices continued to be challenged quite far into the twentieth century by traditional academics and policymakers, yet it proved to be the foundation for more modern approaches to monetary policy.

References

De Kock, M.H.: *Central Banking*, Macmillan, London, 1939.

Federal Reserve Bank of St Louis, *Bulletin*, May, 1981.

Fisher, Irving: *The Purchasing Power of Money: Its Determination and Relation to Credit, Interest Rates and Crisis*, Macmillan, New York, 1911.

Hume, David: "Of the Balance of Trade", *Political Discourses*, Edinburgh, 1752.

Keynes, John Maynard: *A Tract on Monetary Reform*, Macmillan, London, 1923.

Keynes, John Maynard: *The End of Laissez Faire*, Hogarth Press, London, 1926.

Keynes, John Maynard: *A Treatise on Money*, Macmillan, London, 1930.

Meltzer, Alan: *A History of the Federal Reserve 1913-1951*, Volume 1, Chicago University Press, 2003.

Nurkse, Ragnar: *International Currency Experience: Lessons from the Interwar Period*, League of Nations, Geneva, 1944.

Robertson, Dennis: *Money*, Cambridge University Press, 1922.

Schumpeter, Joseph: *History of Economic Analysis*, Oxford University Press, 1954.

CHAPTER 4

The Federal Reserve: A Unique Institution

By 1914 central banking had become widely established and the most advanced among these institutions, whether government owned or not, had developed a number of monetary tools that are in use to this day. However, despite theoretical advances concerning the nature of money and its relation to other economic variables, monetary policy in the modern sense did not yet exist. But drastic change was around the corner, not only as a result of the outbreak of the First World War, but also because the establishment of the Federal Reserve System in the United States created a central bank that would in time eclipse all others in influence and power. Established shortly before the outbreak of the First World War, it immediately had to deal with the consequences of the rupture in the world economy. This proved to be quite a challenge for an inexperienced institution with very little independence from the government, the consequence being that it practically played no role in domestic monetary affairs, except to keep the dollar within the gold points, while America's role in international financial relations continued to be conducted by the US Treasury. But since the United States was the only country that stayed on the gold standard, the Fed could concentrate on ensuring that there was sufficient gold to meet potential demands for conversion. In fact the US gold stock swelled by over $1 billion between the beginning of the war in August 1914 and April 1917 when America entered the conflict. Subsequently in view of the turbulence in the financial world, the United States effectively

O. de Beaufort Wijnholds, *The Money Masters*,
https://doi.org/10.1007/978-3-030-40041-5_4

embargoed the export of gold from September 1917 to June 1919 (Crabbe 1989).

Most of what had been carefully built up in Europe's monetary and financial systems came to a halt when the Great War broke out. Despite holding up appearances in Europe that the gold standard had remained intact, the international financial system was in disarray. The Bank of England, which had maintained a quite modest gold cover against its liabilities before the war, in name maintained domestic convertibility of the pound, but did so by putting in place administrative obstacles and calling on patriotism to discourage demands for gold from the central bank. Gold exports were discouraged due to the difficulty of obtaining insurance for gold shipments when German U boats were sinking a sharply rising number of ships. Later into the war gold exports from Britain were legally restricted. Similar measures were taken elsewhere. A new and blunt instrument to influence financial and monetary transactions, direct controls, became an increasing feature of measures to support the war effort. These ranged from the direct prohibition of certain transactions, such as capital exports, to impounding private gold imports.

The most damaging effect of the war on monetary conditions was the complete transformation of government finances and the manner in which ever increasing budget deficits were financed. As waging a major war requires enormous resources, government expenditure came to hugely outstrip its revenue. Financing the gap by raising taxes by governments was only possible to a limited extent as exposing their citizens to further material hardship became untenable. The alternative, deficit financing through printing money on a gigantic scale, proved to be an equally painful process as it led to runaway inflation. By various means such as price controls—which worked badly—the suffering of the population was delayed somewhat and carried over into the post-war years. Central banks were increasingly drawn into fanning the fires of the inflation machine, by rediscounting short-term Treasury bills and purchasing government bonds at an ever mounting rate, as well as by extending direct advances to the government, sometimes at very low interest rates. Germany went furthest in printing money to finance the war effort, its government pressing the central bank into accepting and discounting an avalanche of Treasury bills (Marsh 1992). Central banks had to fully do their government's bidding under wartime conditions since they lacked the power and independence to resist. At most they could issue euphemistic warnings.

While in theory exchange rates between European currencies and vis-à-vis the dollar were now floating, the desire to avoid strong depreciation which would have a negative impact on the financial system and make desperately needed imports (even) more expensive resulted in a considerable degree of intervention in the markets. In first instance this was done by central banks selling their pound sterling balances to maintain a degree of stability against the still dominant British currency and by raising their discount rates. But since foreign exchange holdings were relatively small, gold movements soon came into play. The gold points lost much of their relevance as currencies such as the French franc fell considerably below their pre-war values. By the end of the war, the United States enjoyed a much increased gold stock, whereas Britain, France, Italy and Russia among the Allies and their enemies, Germany—which had been building up a war chest before the outbreak of hostilities—and Austria, suffered huge outflows of gold. Domestically the public began to lose trust in the future convertibility of banknotes, precipitating precisely what people feared. To protect large payouts in gold to citizens, central banks either legally or by administrative measures suspended convertibility.

The economic and financial legacy of the First World War was enormous. Apart from the massive physical destruction and loss of manpower, trade and financial relations across countries—an attractive feature of the classical gold standard—had been seriously disrupted and would take years to be fully mended. Worse, inflation, spurred by monetary financing by cowed central banks, was completely out of control at the end of the war. And the combination of a gigantic debt overhang and the wish in most countries to maintain the gold coin standard would create serious tensions that would have to be dealt with in peacetime.

A by-product of major wars is deep-seated changes in the international monetary system. However, the post-war negotiations at Versailles did not address the severely disturbed financial conditions in Europe. Moreover, conditions were complicated by demanding reparations from Germany which would prove to be untenable and disruptive. A decisive factor in transforming international economic relations was the advent of the United States as the economic powerhouse of the world and the weakened position of Britain, France and Germany. Not only did the United States hold a large share of the world's official gold which conferred a leading position in global monetary affairs, it had also been the only country able to stay on the gold standard. In addition the United States had moved from being a debtor country to a creditor nation. In line with this development New York's position as an international financial center had been strengthened, challenging the traditional financial center of the world, London. America had as a result of the war morphed from a long term borrower on international financial markets to a global banker, borrowing short and lending long. It was also a boon to the United States that at the end of the war it finally had a central bank, allowing it to have a better grip on monetary conditions and financial disruptions. But before the United States had reached such a strong financial position it had struggled for many decades to bring more stability to its financial system.

America's Struggle Toward Financial Stability

America's first Secretary of the Treasury, Alexander Hamilton, was a champion of financial stability and favored the establishment of a national bank. Despite considerable political opposition, the Bank of the United States, modeled to a large extent on the Bank of England, opened its doors in Philadelphia in 1791. It was a bold initiative taken before most Continental European central banks were founded. However, unlike other central banks, the American institution's life span was short as anti-federalist pressures prevented it from renewing its charter in 1811. A second Bank of the United States, created in 1816, was terminated a mere 20 later by President Andrew Jackson who was fiercely against what was then considered big government. These set-backs contributed to the existence of a chaotic and hugely decentralized financial system in America. The contrast with the increasingly sound financial structure in many European countries was striking, and held back the US economic ascendancy, so striking in other branches of the economy.

The number of banks in the United States grew exponentially in the nineteenth century, because it was easy to start banking by issuing notes, taking in deposits and lending on the money with (very) little capital to absorb losses. Although the United States was on a gold standard there was generally a dearth of gold coins in circulation, and banknotes—supposedly convertible into gold—came in handy in conducting day-to-day transactions. But with around 1000 banks all issuing their own notes whose acceptability was mostly a strictly regional affair, a highly unstable structure emerged. State governments were not blind to the dangers of massive bankruptcies with some of them issuing charters to what they deemed worthy banks and exercising a degree of monitoring of their business. But such oversight was not very effective, given the spate of bank failures that continued to occur. (To this day State chartered banks in America are less rigorously supervised than member banks of the Federal Reserve System.) What was needed was a banking system that crossed state lines, in other words was more centralized.

Change came during the Civil War when legislation was passed enabling the creation of a system of nationally chartered banks. Banks across America could now issue national bank notes which would enjoy a much wider circulation. However, strict limits were placed on the amounts that could be issued: banks were required to hold 20 percent of their liabilities in reserves. Like in Britain at an earlier stage, the note circulation was inelastic, not being able to respond to seasonal needs, such as the need for more cash at harvest time. But the National Banking Act of 1863 was certainly an improvement over the previous situation, particularly as member banks were now subject to federal examinations. And the Act introduced a system of pooling of reserves, in principle allowing for a better use of scarce resources. Yet the way this facility was structured was complicated and inefficient. Foreign observers, impressed by the productive prowess of America's manufacturing, mining and agricultural businesses, were taken aback by what they saw as a primitive financial system. The system was still too decentralized and lacked a lender of last resort. The Treasury tried to help out by placing part of its reserves as deposits with a variety of banks. But such support could not be a substitute for a full-fledged central bank which the United States sorely lacked. Around the turn of the century, enlightened economists, experienced bankers and a handful of politicians, recognizing this shortcoming, began advocating erecting an American central bank along European lines. There was an enormous pushback from anti-federalist quarters based on fears that the government or Wall Street would be granted excessive powers. More than in other countries, America's history had imbued many politicians, especially from the South and West, as well a large segment of the public, with a mistrust of what they saw was a small band of powerful men taking the reins on a matter of cardinal importance. In essence installing a central bank in the United States became a hot political issue. It would take a dangerous financial panic to tilt the balance toward creating an institution that could act as a monetary stabilizer and not leave it to the markets, in a laissez-faire manner, to sort out their own troubles.

The US economy was booming in 1906, fed by large amounts of foreign investment attracted by the promise of excellent returns. Much of these funds originated in Britain as a result of which the pound sterling depreciated against the dollar to its lower gold point. Exporting gold to America now became lucrative. As the drain of the Bank of England's gold reserve—and to a lesser extent of other European central banks—continued apace, the British central bank started to worry. In late 1906 it decided to radically raise its discount rate. The German central bank reacted in similar fashion. In response gold flowed in the other direction, allowing the Bank of England in particular to replenish its depleted reserves. This reversal unsettled the New York money and stock markets, the effect being akin to pricking a balloon. Loan activity shrank as liquidity dried up in an atmosphere of every bank for itself. In the course of 1907, panic broke out on the New York stock market which had grown impressively in previous years and whose participants relied heavily on short-term financing. Banks called in their loans to stock market operators, driving up overnight (call) rates to up to 150 percent. Learning about the unruly state of the market, the public became increasingly afraid that the convertibility of their banknotes and deposits into gold would be suspended, or that the banks would restrict their payments, as had happened during crises in the past. The weakest link in the American financial system were the trusts, non-bank institutions increasingly operating as banks, taking in deposits and lending out money while maintaining low reserve cover as they were not subject to reserve requirements. (Similar institutions are today known as shadow banks.) Soon individuals were lining up at the doors of the trusts to demand cash, producing classic scenes of bank runs, the trusts losing half of their deposits. The smaller commercial banks were also coming under pressure.

The large city banks and the specialized private banks, realizing that the panic could spread further and wreak havoc in the whole financial system, were unsure how to react until John Pierpont Morgan, who headed the eponymous private bank, invited top bankers to discuss the emergency and find ways to douse the fire. Morgan, unofficial doyen of New York's banking community, whose economic and financial interests were widespread (Chernow 2010), commanded enormous respect and practically singlehandedly orchestrated the rescue effort. He decided to let the first trust teetering on the edge to go under, then called upon his fellow bankers to save the next weak link, having concluded that it was solvent. Others followed, receiving bail-out loans shared by the big banks in the form of a syndicate.

The panic of 1907 caused serious damage, not only to the financial sector, but also to the economy as a whole, the national product contracting by an estimated 11 percent. In the wake of the crisis, the proponents of establishing an American central bank stepped up their efforts to convince others of their arguments. The leading light among the group of supporters was Paul Warburg, whose efforts are richly described by Ron Chernow (1993). A successful German émigré banker and financial expert, Warburg fervently argued that a permanent lender of last resort was acutely needed. It was impressive what J.P. Morgan had achieved, but relying on a strongman from the private sector to save the financial system was not sustainable. Banks would in a crisis always tend to pull back loans to save their own hides, but if done on a widespread scale such acts would only make things worse. A central bank, set up along European lines, would react to an impending crisis and lend freely to the market along the rules described by Bagehot, was sorely needed.

In his excellent book on the American Central Bank, Roger Lowenstein notes that 'so pervasive is its influence that America today can scarcely imagine a world without the Federal Reserve' (Lowenstein 2015). For Americans living a hundred years ago, this sentiment was embryonic at best. Not only was it hard to convince the many politicians who were strongly opposed to a role for the government that the absence of a central bank was holding back the modernization of the US financial system, a large part of the public was also opposed to their government controlling the country's money. Fortunately, Warburg and like-minded academics and bankers were able to have Congress agree to establish a National Monetary Commission to study the weaknesses in the banking system and ways to remedy them. Although many of the Commission's members were highly skeptical in the beginning of creating a central Bank (the term was even anathema in most of the discussions), the politicians took their task seriously. They commissioned a large number of studies, including the manner in which the monetary system was managed in Europe. Visits to the central banks of Britain, France and Germany proved useful in educating some of the key players. But it would take many more years and endless political wrangling before a majority in Congress was finally willing to accept a semi-decentralized reserve bank. The Federal Reserve Act, establishing the Federal Reserve System was signed by President Woodrow Wilson on 23 December 1913. The Fed, as it was soon known, was unique in the way it was established: a democratically founded central bank incorporating features that were tailored to the nature of American society. While arriving late on the world scene, the American central bank also benefited from the advantage of the latecomer, avoiding the flaws in the structure of some other central banks, whilst adding new elements to the practice of central banking. The Act of 1913 contained a number of shortcomings, but of which many were remedied by future amendments.

Bringing Order to the Monetary and Financial System

The comprehensive studies in preparation for the new central bank enabled the Fed to be structured in a way that avoided most of the weak elements in the operations of European central banks, such as an inelastic issue of banknotes. The Fed was the only institution in the United States that could issue banknotes, ending the chaotic co-existence of national bank notes and those issued by country (rural) banks. Another important improvement over the previous situation was that the Fed was prohibited to do any commercial business, thus eliminating conflict of interest problems. It was also established that the Treasury should not partake in quasi central banking operations by means of placing deposits with commercial banks. The Treasury surplus would henceforth be deposited with the Fed. As to the organization of the Federal Reserve System, it was established as an arm of the government, thereby avoiding the complication of private ownership which existed among several European central banks. But its independence from the government was not addressed which would later on raise questions of interpretation.

Shortcomings

There were shortcomings too. Being a product of compromise, the System was unnecessarily complicated and too decentral. It consisted of 12 Reserve banks in major cities in the United States. The commercial banks that joined the System (compulsory for National banks, but not for State chartered banks) were shareholders in the regional banks and had to make a contribution to the System of 6 percent of their capital and surplus. At the same time they received a fixed dividend of 5 percent on their shares. The regional central banks were tasked with rediscounting commercial bills and buying and selling gold and government bonds. They were free to set their discount rates on their own. The boards of the 12 regional Reserve banks were made up of local bankers and businessmen. This decentralized construction was checked by the existence of a Board of

Governors situated in Washington. Its seven Governors were appointed by the President, who rewarded Paul Warburg for his enormous input by making him a member of the first Board of the Fed. In the first decade of the Fed it was dominated by the Treasury whose Secretary as well as the head of the Comptroller of the Currency were members of the highest organ of the Fed. This lack of independence would hamper the Fed's policymaking on many occasions. And the absence of full centralization of the new system initially led to severe and unproductive competition between the Board and the Reserve banks (Lowenstein 2015).

A glaring shortcoming of the Federal Reserve System was its vagueness about the new institution's objectives. The Act did not go beyond stipulating that the System was to produce an elastic currency. To some this meant no more than allowing for a seasonal expansion and contraction of the banknote circulation. To others this implied the possibility of an active monetary policy, such as regular open market operations. However, as the Act incorporated the outdated real bills doctrine (only commercial and not financial bills could be discounted), the scope for easing and tightening the money market was quite limited. Another flaw was the freedom of Reserve banks to opt out of lender of last resort operations set in motion by the System. Together with incidental differences in discount rates, such uncoordinated actions contributed to tension between the Reserve banks. Many of these conflicts involved the Federal Reserve Bank of New York which not only dominated the other Reserve banks, but also initially eclipsed the Board in influence.

The Fed's First Years

The Fed's early years coincided with the First World War, precluding any independence that some members of the Board of Governors, especially Paul Warburg, had hoped to achieve. Like central banks in Europe, the Fed was subservient to its Treasury, the demands of wartime financing of the government taking precedence. The result was a policy of keeping interest rates low, the System adjusting its discount policy of charging a penalty rate in order to reduce the cost of borrowing. When gold started flowing to the United States as a result of the War in Europe, the Fed refrained from taking action. After a while inflation developed as the Fed was increasingly financing Treasury bond sales. In the course of the War gold continued to flow to the United States in huge quantities, resulting in a jump in the American share in the global gold stock from 19 percent in 1914 to 35 percent in 1918. This inflow caused the monetary base, which constitutes the banks' power to create money under a fractional banking system to expand greatly. Holding considerably more reserves than required under the law, banks' lending caused the money supply to expand at a rapid pace. But in comparison to the runaway inflation in much of the European countries, the annual increase in the price level in the United States never exceeded 20 percent during the war years. Overall, the United States came out of the War not only victorious but also economically stronger, with much better prospects than the war-torn Europeans and in the financial realm challenging the supremacy of London's dominant position.

References

Chernow, Ron: *The Warburgs,* Random House, New York, 1993.

Chernow, Ron, *The House of Morgan: An American Banking Dynasty and the Rise of Modern Finance,* Grove press, New York, 2010.

Crabbe, Leland, "The International Gold Standard and U.S. Monetary Policy from World War 1 to the New Deal", Federal Reserve *Bulletin,* June, 1989.

Lowenstein, Roger: *America's Central Bank: The Epic Struggle to Create the Federal Reserve,* Penguin Press, New York, 2015.

Marsh, David: *The Most Powerful Bank: Inside Germany's Bundesbank,* Times Books, New York, 1992.

CHAPTER 5

From War to War: 1914–1939

During the war years European central banks' role, which over previous centuries had become more prominent, was significantly reduced as the deployment of monetary policy instruments gave way to the overriding exigencies of the war effort. On the basis of their knowledge of markets and technical matters, the monetary institutions continued to act as advisors to and administrators of their governments. Generally this process took place without major incidents, with one exception. In 1917 the Governor of the Bank of England, Lord Cunliffe, overplayed his hand when on a few occasions he went behind the back of the Chancellor of the Exchequer to give his advice directly to the Prime Minister. Following complaints from the Chancellor and Cunliffe's charge that the Prime Minister, Lloyd George, threatened 'to take over the Bank,' the Governor's days were numbered (Moggeridge 1992, 273–74). As we shall see, the relationship between governments and central banks has from time to time been tense. Although governments, in view of the primacy of politics and their ability to change or revoke central bank's charters or give policy directives, are in principle the dominant power, they cannot count on always emerging as the winner when challenged by the central bank. A positive view of the guardian of the country's money and the innate suspicion of governments can cause embarrassment to the political class and makes it safer to work toward a compromise. During the second half of the twentieth century the question of how, independent of governments,

O. de Beaufort Wijnholds, *The Money Masters*,
https://doi.org/10.1007/978-3-030-40041-5_5

central banks ought to be became a major issue, generally resulting in a strengthening of the position of the money masters.

The interwar years were among the most tumultuous in the life of central banks. Unmoored from the gold standard, the immediate postwar period proved to be highly unstable with hyperinflation raging in Germany and some other European countries. Searching for stability, many countries returned to a modified gold standard, with generally disastrous consequences of depression and massive unemployment. As a result the gold standard was abandoned, currencies floating freely in a chaotic manner. Influenced by economic upheaval, monetary theory underwent far-reaching changes in the 1920s and 1930s (described in Box 5.1), which in turn influenced monetary policy. When the Second World War broke out the modicum of stability that had returned was nipped in the bud.

Central Banking from 1918 to 1928

The first years after the First World War were characterized by volatile business cycles, with recessions and booms developing in rapid succession, while the scarcity of resources and continued central bank financing of budget deficits contributed to high inflation. Depreciating currencies not only made imports more expensive, but also rendered financial markets even more unstable. Stabilizing exchange rates as a way of preparing for a return to normalcy, which for practically all policymakers meant returning to the gold standard, became a major preoccupation. A related issue was whether the national currency should be returned to the pre-war parity or whether it would be allowed to take into account new realities and accept devaluation. In Britain the sentiment tended toward returning to gold at the old exchange rate. For France and Germany such a step was out of the question in view of the enormous changes in their economic situation. But for the United States the rate of the dollar was not an issue, having remained on the gold standard throughout the War. The shift in power toward the United States greatly strengthened its position vis-à-vis its European trading partners who increasingly were confronted with American trade surpluses and the interest rate policies of the Fed. Changes in the discount rate of the Bank of England still produced strong reactions elsewhere, but those of the American Central Bank were equally felt across the developed countries and also in Latin America.

European central banks were entirely dependent on the wishes of their governments, foremost among these was to keep interest rates low. And when rampant inflation struck, especially in France and Germany they were effectively sidelined. Tales of the German hyperinflation abound (buying bread would require a wheelbarrow filled by banknotes). The madness came to an end in 1924 when drastic measures to reduce the budget deficit and a new currency were put in place. The rate between the old and the new currency was based on the prevailing exchange rate of 4.2 trillion marks per dollar. With stability restored, Germany was one of the first countries to return to the gold standard in 1924. At the same time the *Reichsbank* was formally granted autonomy from the government, soon to be headed by Hjalmar Schacht, who fiercely defended his independence (Marsh 1992). While significant, the German central bank's autonomy, encouraged by the Allied victors of the war, was in practice incomplete. But the episode of runaway inflation and the *Reichsbank*'s stronger position laid the foundation for the future German *Bundesbank's* independence and stability orientation. In France, currency stabilization took longer, making Paris a relative latecomer when it returned to the gold standard in 1928. Its central bank never attained a significant degree of independence during the great majority of its existence, one result being a perennially higher rate of inflation than in Germany.

The Federal Reserve soon was no longer constrained by keeping interest low to help the government to deal with its debt overhang. However, it had to take into account the rules of the game of the gold standard and the need to amass enough gold to meet the legal requirement of maintaining a ratio to notes of 35 percent of the yellow metal held by the System (Crabbe 1989). The first consideration was vigorously defended by Benjamin Strong, the charismatic governor of the then dominant Fed of New York (Ahamed 2009, 315), but was in practice hardly adhered to. And the gold cover requirement was seldom a factor, especially when the United States accumulated the largest gold stock of any country in the world. The two requirements were connected, as a relaxed adherence to the rules of the game brought gold to the United States. As a result during most of the 1920s, described by Milton Friedman (Friedman and Schwartz 1963, chapter 6) as the 'high tide of the Reserve System,' the Fed was able to follow a relatively independent course. Understandably it was undergoing a learning process for which the vague formulation of its mandate was partly to blame. The Fed failed its first test in 1920 when during an economic boom the Reserve Banks kept the discount rate low, under pressure from a government that was spending heavily on social policies as a concession to the increasingly strong labor movement. Unchecked by the

Fed, the boom turned into recession as the discount rate was finally raised, followed by a collapse of the money supply and a sharp fall in prices.

When the Fed gained a better grip on the economy and as it was seen as contributing importantly to the prosperity of the remainder of the 1920s, it became more confident and surefooted in its decisions. Although formally bound to playing the automatic adjustment game of the gold standard, the Fed was increasingly redirecting its priorities toward domestic considerations. As a corollary it shifted its monetary operations from mainly changes in the discount rate to open market operations, offsetting (also known as sterilizing) the monetary effects of inflows and outflows of gold. Such transactions were much less visible than changes in the interest rate and therefore harder to detect by gold standard purists. Greater reliance on open market transactions also served to raise the level of sophistication of the Fed of New York closer to that of the Bank of England, which had a long history of buying and selling government and other securities in the London market. However, the increase in market intervention did not sit well with other Reserve banks who wanted a piece of the action. In a compromise the Federal Open Market Committee (FOMC) was established as a forum to discuss monetary policy among the Governors of the Board and the 12 heads of the Reserve Banks. The FOMC has remained the central body of the Federal Reserve System where decisions on monetary policy are made.

A Return to Gold

The general improvement in the global economic situation and the ambition to return to the stability of the pre-war years strengthened the wish among the majority of countries to return to the gold standard. One by one European countries announced that they were once again pegging their currencies to a fixed amount of gold. What that peg would be became a controversial debating point, especially in Britain. In the end the British Government, with Winston Churchill as its Chancellor of the Exchequer, finally reluctantly decided in 1925 to return to the pre-war parity, a decision welcomed by the Governor of the Bank of England, Montagu Norman, who was a staunch supporter of the gold standard throughout his long tenure. By contrast, Germany, which had returned to gold the previous year, had pegged its currency at a greatly devalued rate. Most other European countries had again opted for the pre-war system by the time the French franc was again part of the gold club—at a steeply devalued rate—in 1928. Japan, only modestly integrated in the international monetary system at the time, joined in 1930, but left a year later. (China remained on a silver standard.) With more than 50 countries having chosen the gold standard as their monetary regime, attesting to its reputation as the system best suited to maintain price stability, the adequacy of world gold reserves became a concern. Whereas the demand for monetary gold was rising, production had fallen during the War and not yet returned to pre-war levels. To mitigate concerns about the adequacy of monetary gold, two innovations were introduced. First, the British and French central banks announced that their banknotes could no longer be converted into gold coin, but only in a certain minimum weight in gold bullion. This practically ruled out demand by the general public to obtain gold.

More tellingly, a new version of the gold standard had been devised by British officials with the promise of large savings in gold holdings of central banks and treasuries. The scheme, known as the *gold exchange* standard, promoted the inclusion of foreign exchange deposits as international reserves usable in the settlement of payments between central banks before having to dip into their cherished gold stocks. In addition, the cost of gold transports could be avoided. The obvious candidate for the role of international reserve currency of choice was still the pound sterling which already at the time of the classical gold standard was held—in modest proportions—as part of some countries' reserves. But central banks started to diversify their foreign exchange holdings by opening dollar deposits with New York commercial banks. Besides economizing on gold, the attraction for central banks of the gold exchange standard was that they could earn interest on their deposits with British or American banks, who in turn welcomed the additional attractive source of funding. A large number of countries, some outside Europe, opted for the gold exchange standard, providing a boon to London as a financial center. Although doubts existed about the resilience of the system in some quarters, the renewed convertibility of the pound and its fixed exchange rate initially provided comfort to participating central banks that their investments in the British currency were safe. This would prove to be a serious miscalculation when the pound was devalued in 1931, spelling the end of the short life of the gold exchange standard.

But during the first years of its existence, the modified gold standard was supported by close cooperation between central banks, especially those of the United States, Britain, Germany and the Netherlands. (The

Banque de France was also involved but generally remained more at arm's length, an attitude that continued in the future.) The governors of these institutions developed close personal ties, facilitating their decision-making on interest rates and other central bank business. They also successfully arranged financial support operations for Britain and some smaller European countries in the 1920s. But in 1928 a turning point was reached, often attributed to the succession of Benjamin Strong as president of the New York Federal Reserve Bank by the less personable George Harrison. Another, more objective, explanation is that the United States had become a gold sink, with France a close second, creating some resentment in countries that were having difficulty in adding to their uncomfortably small gold stocks. And it was indisputable that these two countries could only have attracted so much gold by not playing by the rules of the gold standard. Among critics of the policies of the United States during the 1920s, William Adams Brown, who wrote an in-depth study on the gold standard, remarked that through its policy of sterilization '[t]he United States was dragging its golden anchor' (Adams Brown 1940, 286). Figure 5.1 shows that the accumulation of gold during the 1920s and early 1930s by the United States and France stood in stark contrast to the puny and stagnant reserves of Britain and Germany. And their combined share in global

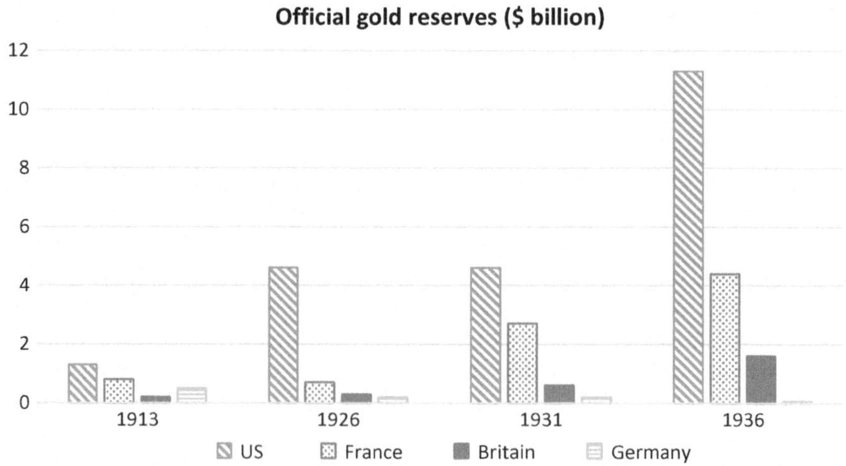

Fig. 5.1 Official Gold Reserves ($ billion). (Source: Board of Governors of the Federal Reserve System 1943)

monetary gold rose to 58 percent by 1931. Such a maldistribution did not augur well for the stability of the international monetary system. It is also telling that the French central bank possessed a sizable portfolio of foreign currency deposits (mainly pounds sterling, but also US dollars) amounting to the equivalent of $1.3 billion at the end of 1928, constituting one half of the total for all European central banks.

A Brief Episode of Prosperity

The 1920s were a period of impressive economic growth and mild inflation on average. While the gold standard had been re-adopted by virtually all of Europe by 1928, its rules had not been strictly adhered to. Bending the informal rules was driven by domestic considerations, governments and central banks increasingly unwilling to automatically adjust their policies to achieve external balance which could lower growth and bring higher unemployment. Straying from the path of the rigidity of the gold standard generally turned out to be beneficial for continuing prosperity. Still the belief in the blessings of the gold standard was almost religious among the more conservative minded. And as long as the official goal was to maintain the gold standard, the objective of central bank policies had to be to support the prevailing monetary system. But monetary debate in the United States had progressed apace, stimulated by economic research at the Fed (European central banks lagged behind in establishing research and statistics departments) and the recently introduced process of Congressional hearings on monetary policy. Central bank officials had to appear regularly before the House and Senate to explain their policies (here too the United States was ahead of other countries). Recognizing the ambiguity of the Fed's role as described in the act that established it, a debate developed seeking to clarify the issue. Despite considerable support for spelling out that the American central bank should seek to achieve and maintain price stability, no Congressional action was taken to amend the Fed's mandate. Part of the argument against change was that the Fed had no appreciable control over the money supply and that the way to achieve economic and price stability was to prevent credit-fueled speculation. The failure to clarify the Fed's goal(s) was a missed opportunity and, according to Allan Meltzer (2003, 192), could have avoided the policy mistakes of the Fed in 1928 and 1929, a cardinal cause of the Great Depression of the early 1930s.

Box 5.1 Monetary Theory

During the 1920s the quantity theory of money remained controversial although it still enjoyed considerable support among academics. Much of the discussion focused on the interpretation of the velocity of money, without leading to a consensus view. Another issue that remained unsettled was the direction of causation between the money supply and the price level. It would take time before it was widely accepted that changes in M lead to changes in P and seldom in the other direction. In a related area, a novel theory on how to measure equilibrium exchange rates—the absence of over- or undervaluation of currencies—was developed. Inspired by the post-war efforts to stabilize floating exchange rates, the Swedish economist Gustav Cassel, introduced the notion of purchasing power parity to measure appropriate levels of exchange rates. The basic notion was that changes in the exchange rates of currencies should equal the difference in inflation between countries (Cassel 1930). While this was an important theoretical advance, its practical use suffered from the lack of reliable domestic price indices at the time. Moreover, there was a problem with the choice of a base year as it could make a significant difference in a period of high and variable inflation. Nevertheless, estimates of purchasing power parity (PPP) have remained useful in measuring the relative prosperity of nations, and are also sometimes used—more controversially—in attempting to adjust the size of countries' share in global output. For instance, in the case of modern China there is a considerable difference between converting the country's output in dollar terms at the current exchange rate and using the higher PPP rate.

Regarding the role of gold in the monetary system, the main focus was on how to measure the adequacy of reserves within the gold standard. As such there were few challenges from academics to the penchant of policymakers in the 1920s to cling to the traditional monetary arrangements. Two important exceptions should be mentioned: as early as in 1920 Gustav Cassel warned that reinstating the gold standard posed a serious risk of deflation (Cassel 1930, 212). While three years later John Maynard Keynes wrote that he did not believe that readopting the gold standard would bring the stability that it used to give (Keynes 1923, 176). These insights would resonate forcefully after Britain left the gold standard in 1931.

The Great Depression

Following a relatively prosperous period during most of the 1920s, the ten-year span between 1929 and 1939 was chaotic and dramatic, starting with the crash of the New York stock market, followed by the Great Depression, the demise of the gold standard and extreme turbulence on currency markets. Coincidentally, monetary and general economic theory made great strides, contributing to a major breakthrough in the thinking of professional economists and many policymakers. The so-called Keynesian revolution would become the basis for shaping economic theory and practice in a large part of the world. But before important needed monetary and economic reforms could take place, the Second World War halted all progress in its tracks.

The strong economic performance of the late 1920s led to great optimism and talk of 'endless prosperity.' Investors translated such optimism into driving up stock prices, often fueled by speculation financed—especially in the United States—by short-term borrowing. When in late 1928 and during the course of 1929 market frenzy continued apace, the Fed's response to the overheating economy was confused. After having failed to get the banks to cut back their lending to stock market investors through moral suasion, officials at the New York Fed wanted to raise the discount rate to calm the markets, but were rebuffed on several occasions by the Board of Governors who had the right to exercise a veto. And when the discount rate finally was raised to 6 percent in August 1929, the economy was already showing signs of slowing down while speculation continued unabated. Given an increased interdependence of national money markets, higher interest rates in the United States had in the course of 1929 led European central banks to raise their own rates. The Bank of England increased its rate from 4.5 percent in early 1929 to 6.5 percent in September, concerned as it was about a drain of its modest gold reserves. The British action did not succeed to stem capital flowing to New York, but did have an undesirable dampening effect on the economy. In the meantime sentiment was turning on the US stock market, with share prices moving downward in September and early October. The market's reaction was mostly sanguine at first, the fall interpreted as a market correction which in time would reverse itself. Great was the surprise when the market collapsed on 24 October 1929 and continued its slide, resulting in a fall in the Dow Jones Index of 25 percent in four days. When the stock market finally reached its bottom in July 1932, the index had fallen by 90 percent. Still relatively inexperienced in setting monetary policy, the Fed had concentrated too much on mitigating stock market speculation, overlooking that a rise in interest rates affects the whole economy and not just a particular sector. As we will see, attempts by central banks to control credit to only one part of the economy (known as selective credit control) has a low success rate.

As a result of the stock market crash, banks were withdrawing their loans to brokers, dealers and other banks, instead investing their funds in safe assets such as government securities and commercial paper. At first the Fed Board ignored the rapid withdrawal of call loans. The New York Fed, better attuned to market realities, opened its discount window and initiated open market transactions. After proposing to lower its discount rate to 5 percent, the Board agreed but on the condition that New York would suspend open market purchases. Its Governor, George Harrison, later acknowledged that in 1928–29 his bank should have raised the discount rate earlier and by a larger amount, the idea being that such action would have slowed the market and the too buoyant economy in a timely fashion, enabling it to lower the rate again when activity on the stock market had cooled down. He also blamed the 'bootleg banking system' through which companies and private persons lent to brokers and dealers outside the regular banking system (Meltzer 2003, 251).

Besides an inadequate response by the Fed to the slowing of the economy, the developing recession was exacerbated by an economic downturn developing in Europe. A main cause of the slowdown on the other side of the Atlantic was the pursuit of deflationary monetary policies by central banks that wanted to protect their gold reserves and in doing so were more or less faithfully following the gold standard rules of the game. The resulting fall in output spilled over to the United States and elsewhere. The stage was now set for a period of unprecedented shrinking of the world economy in peacetime.

Studies conducted decades later, such as by Milton Friedman and Anna Schwartz (1963), placed most of the blame squarely on the policies of central banks in the run-up to the Great Depression. Much earlier a contemporary observer of the role played by central banks in the demise of the gold standard and the economic contraction that followed in large parts of the world, the British economist and senior official at the UK Treasury, Ralph Hawtrey, had reached a similar conclusion. He observed that central banks had, after the return to gold in the 1920s, reverted to the rules of the game of the classical gold standard which caused them to mechanistically restrain domestic credit expansion whenever their gold stocks were falling significantly. This, Hawtrey argued, 'was an objective which made no demands on the reasoning faculty; it could be treated as an article of faith.' While following the rules of the game worked well enough in the nineteenth century, in face of the severe economic vagaries of the years following the First World War, 'faith was no longer enough' (Hawtrey, fifth edition 1947, 140, 41). Hawtrey (a Treasury man) did not, however, mention the rigid balanced budget philosophy which prevailed at the time as a contributing factor to the steep economic decline that occurred.

Europe Catches the Disease

While the American banking crisis was building up steam, conditions in Europe were also deteriorating rapidly. Having recovered from the hyperinflation of 1923, the German economy had performed relatively well in the remaining years of the 1920s. To a large extent external factors pushed Germany into depression. When the Bank of England raised its discount rate in late 1929 and early 1930, the *Reichsbank* not only had to match the hike but go beyond it in view of the precarious level of its reserves. In the post-war period the German central bank continuously had to cope with a modest gold stock, partly due to the large war reparation payments imposed at Versailles. Germany's financial system was vulnerable, being highly dependent on foreign money; at its peak, around 40 percent of deposits held with German banks were owned by foreigners. Large scale withdrawals of these deposits would be disastrous. Concerned about the possibility of a German collapse, financial support from the Bank of England and New York commercial banks provided a temporary stopgap. While sustained foreign capital flight was avoided, the third largest German bank folded when its clients lost confidence as a result of negative publicity. A worse fate befell Austria, also very much dependent on foreign deposits. Despite Austria receiving some foreign loans, confidence in its solvency swiftly evaporated, resulting in a full-fledged collapse following the demise of the country's largest bank, the *Credit Anstalt*. Attempts to save the bank through a combination of public and private lenders were insufficient to compensate for a massive flight of capital. Having just been established as a vehicle for managing German reparations transactions, the Bank of International Settlements (BIS) in Basel, Switzerland, was involved in arranging the (modest) loan syndicate. This action foreshadowed the significant role the BIS would play in the future in providing such services to its member central banks (the Fed unwisely did not participate in the BIS, but instead two New York commercial banks did), which developed into an important forum for cooperation between central banks.

The financial woes of Germany and Austria rapidly spread to Eastern European countries and beyond. Sovereign defaults became commonplace as heavy borrowing by governments, especially in Latin America, came to an abrupt halt in the early 1930s. Falling commodity prices and misguided economic policies were largely to blame. By contrast the French economy continued to grow, aided by its large gold reserves which provided room for flexibility in its monetary policy. Not so in Britain where the overvalued exchange rate hampered its exports and stimulated imports. Moreover, the political landscape was radically changing on the British Isles, labor unions and the Labour Party, making great strides and successfully pressing for social reforms. However, the mindset of politicians and the central bank regarding economic policy had hardly changed. Even when the Labour Party was in power it aimed at balancing the budget, the ideas of John Maynard Keynes not having been fully formulated yet.

Lacking stimulus from government policies and with monetary policy still focused primarily on the exchange rate, production dwindled and unemployment soared, eventually reaching 15 percent. Worries that the British Government might suspend the export of gold (the gold reserves were a perennial concern) or devalue the pound led to capital outflows which in turn prompted the Bank of England to seek international loans. Even though some foreign money was forthcoming, the British Government in secrecy prepared to leave the gold standard. While the central bank was more or less autonomous in setting money market rates, the decision to 'go off gold' was not made by the Bank of England. The choice of an exchange rate regime, and the desired level of the country's currency, is one of the few areas in the monetary domain where the role of modern central banks is limited to that of advisor and not co-decider.

Leaving the Gold Standard

Even though anxiety existed about the future of the pound sterling, the British Government's announcement on 21 September 1931, that it was 'suspending' its adherence to the gold standard after a mere six years was received with panic, the exchange rate of the pound immediately falling by 20 percent against the dollar. As a result of the large devaluation, the gold exchange standard countries which suffered severe losses on their pound deposits, especially Belgium, France and the Netherlands, were highly upset. (Germany was not part of this group as it had abandoned the gold standard a few months before Britain did so.) Not only did the British decision spell the end of the gold exchange standard, but it delivered a mortal blow to the gold standard in general, an institution that had been in place for almost two centuries. A host of countries soon left the fixed rate regime, but a small gold bloc continued clinging to the old system for five more years (Belgium left in 1935). France, Italy, the Netherlands, Switzerland and Poland had to pay a heavy price for staying faithful to gold, their weakened competitive position (the now floating currencies depreciated against the fixed rates of the gold bloc) hurting their economies. The United States did not follow Britain, but devalued the dollar in 1933 and returned to gold in 1934 with its competitive position restored.

The new world of floating exchange rates, with its uncertainty of the outcome of international transactions, raised fears of harming cross border trade and international capital transactions. Recognizing the raised level of risk of losing competitiveness, several governments established funds to enable them to stabilize their exchange rates. Shortly after abandoning gold, the British Government put in place an *Exchange Equalization Account* at its Treasury. It took over the Bank of England's gold, providing the Account with ammunition to intervene in the foreign exchange market and thus regulate the rate of the pound. Although not mentioned at its establishment, the Account was seen not only as a means of countering speculation against the pound but also as a way to insulate domestic credit policy. For the Bank of England this development severely curtailed its freedom of action. To this day the UK Treasury is in charge of the country's international reserves. The Bank of England's role in managing the exchange rate is in principle a technical one. But since exchange rates and monetary conditions are closely related, the actual influence of the Bank on the exchange rate is larger than it may appear.

In 1934 the United States, fearing competitive devaluation by European countries outside the gold bloc, followed the British example. Although President Roosevelt had suspended the gold standard in America in 1933, he reinstated it the following year setting the new official price of gold at \$35 per ounce, up from \$20.67, constituting a devaluation of the dollar of 60 percent. However, the United States' renewed adherence to the gold standard represented a modified version; banknotes were no longer convertible in gold and the public had to relinquish all its gold, receiving coins and notes in return under the *Gold Reserve Act*. Gold was to be used only for international settlements. At the same time the US Government established an *Exchange Stabilization Fund* and provided it with $2 billion derived from the profits of the devaluation. Other countries, including Germany, the Netherlands and Belgium, equally wishing to protect their exchange rate against competitive depreciation, established similar funds. Hand in hand with the race to the bottom in currency values, protectionism, including higher tariffs, quotas and bilateral trade agreements, spread across the globe. These damaging *beggar-thy-neighbor* policies confirmed the conviction of supporters of the gold standard that letting exchange rates find their own way would lead to chaos. And rapid movements of short-term capital (known as *hot money*) proved to be highly disruptive, causing the severe fluctuations in exchange rates which followed the abandonment of gold. Intervention in foreign exchange markets by stabilization funds did not help much as they tended to push down national currencies in tandem, failing to achieve the desired advantage. To bring a halt to this race to the bottom, and after all countries had left the gold standard in 1936, a tripartite agreement was reached between the United States, Britain and France, soon joined by the smaller gold bloc countries, aimed at stabilizing exchange rates. Since the participants could withdraw from the pact after 24 hours' notice, its contribution to restoring confidence was modest.

The American Banking Crisis

In the meantime, as the banking crisis in the United States continued, causing a near paralysis of the financial system, the New York Fed became more amenable to acting as the lender of last resort. In addition the Federal Reserve System, under pressure from Congress, embarked on a program of open market purchases in early 1932. But since America's gold reserves happened to be falling temporarily, the net effect of monetary policy was quite limited. Unwisely the open market program was allowed to peter out after a few months. Revival of the banking system took off only after the *Emergency Banking Act* of March 1933 promulgated a closure of all banks for several days, during which seemingly insolvent banks could be weeded out. The act also provided the President the permanent power to liquidate, close and reopen banks. To provide confidence to deposit holders, the Federal Deposit Insurance Corporation (FDIC), an agency tasked with guaranteeing small- and medium-sized bank deposits, was established. In another reaction to the banking crisis, the *Glass-Steagall Act* introduced a division between regular commercial banking and investment banking in order to prohibit market speculation by commercial banks. (This division was to last 63 years.) These drastic institutional reforms succeeded in restoring confidence, the bulk of the remaining commercial banks reopening soon afterward. A gaping hole remained, however, the Fed failing to pursue an expansionary monetary policy, as it continued to misinterpret developments, such as still failing to distinguish between nominal and real interest rates and a lack of understanding of the importance of a continuing decrease of the money supply, amounting to one-third since October 1929. But the tide was turning under the Roosevelt Administration and its New Deal, which made elevating the price level one of its primary goals. And after the United States abandoned the classical gold standard in January 1934, adopting a much modified version, it in effect created a new monetary order. The ramifications for the American central bank were highly significant, as the role of gold was relegated to a subordinate element in monetary policy and the Treasury and its Exchange Equalization Fund were taking the decisions on intervention in the foreign exchange markets and were regularly interfering with monetary policy in general. The upshot was that monetary policy had almost entirely lost its international role and become focused on the domestic economy.

Losing Central Bank Independence

The *Great Depression* touched the vast majority of countries and in most cases was only partially overcome after 1933, lingering up to the outbreak of the Second World War. There were two striking exceptions: Japan and Germany which by abandoning the gold standard at an early stage (1931) and through a massive build-up of their military resources, succeeded in bringing down unemployment faster than other developed countries. But the cost to the population in terms of scarcity of food and other essentials was substantial. In Britain, while damaging, the depression was not as deep as in the United States. With real interest rates coming down from 9 percent in 1930 to slightly negative in 1933, house building activity led the way to recovery, later strengthened by government deficit spending. The main reasons for Britain's relatively good performance were its early departure from the gold standard and the absence of a banking crisis. While the Bank of England could take some credit for the relative health of the banking system, its monetary role was a limited one during and after the depression, having to play second fiddle to the UK Treasury whose cheap money policy philosophy prevailed. In the United States, which among the large countries suffered the most, a quarter of the working population was out of work in 1932. By 1940 unemployment still stood at 14 percent. Except for a hiatus in 1937, the administration's fiscal policy was appropriate. Despite having made a balanced budget a pillar of his election platform, President Roosevelt accepted that his large work creation projects and social reforms were leading to budget deficits. In contrast to most monetary 'experts' and commercial bankers, Fed Chairman Mariner Eccles, who had never heard of the work of John Maynard Keynes, was in favor of even more government spending and larger deficits (Kettl 1986, 54, 55). Around the same time a major breakthrough occurred in economic thinking led by Keynes, who recommended the use of fiscal policy as an anti-deflationary instrument. And in the monetary sphere, the demise of the gold standard heralded a new approach to monetary policy in which an expansionary stance to combat domestic deflationary forces came to the fore. However, monetary policy had slipped out of the hands of many central banks, in part because of their lack of success in fighting the depression, but also because governments were taking a larger role in economic policy. This was especially true of the Federal Reserve System, who became engaged in regular disputes with the Treasury, which usually prevailed.

On the surface, the Banking Act of 1935, which enabled a reorganization of the structure of the Fed, did not reflect the new reality. Power within the System shifted to the Board of Governors, the regional banks losing their semiautonomous status which had allowed them to keep their own portfolio of assets. The Federal Open Market Committee (FOMC) was institutionalized and the Secretary of the Treasury would no longer attend its meetings. The act also provided the Fed with a new tool. Henceforth it could impose margin requirements on the banks so as to dampen stock market speculation. Nonetheless, at the time the Fed played a subsidiary role to the Treasury which decided on international gold transactions and whether to sterilize them or not, as well as the exchange rate and banking legislation. In fact the Treasury often did not inform the Fed Board of its decisions. Meltzer (2003, 415) describes the situation as the Fed 'sitting in the backseat.' The central bank did try to regain some of its former position, leading to considerable tension with the Treasury whose priority was to keep interest rates quite low so that it could finance the government's budget deficits cheaply. Arguments between the Fed and the US Treasury often focused on the right level of 'excess' reserves of the banks, the level of liquid assets held at the Fed that exceeds the minimum requirements. An increase in this excess was considered by the Fed as indicating more room for monetary expansion than it felt was warranted. And in an attempt to counteract its diminished independence, the Fed raised the minimum reserve requirements three times in the second half of the 1930s, but with little actual impact.

European central banks also lost considerable influence in the aftermath of the depression, the most important monetary and financial decisions falling to their treasuries, the more so when foreign exchange controls became widespread in the late 1930s. This state of affairs would last until the end of the Second World War and sometimes beyond. Like the experience of the Federal Reserve, the Bank of England underwent an erosion of its independence. And although its governor, Montagu Norman, was a respected figure, the UK Treasury was fully in command after Britain had left the gold standard. No longer encumbered by the rules of the game of the abandoned exchange rate regime and unimpressed by some lingering sentiment for a return to gold at the central bank, the Treasury actively pursued a 'cheap money policy.' This was favorable both for the recovery of the economy and the cost of financing budget deficits. For the French central bank, which had never been given more than a trace of independence, not much changed, but in Germany developments were very different. In the 1920s the central bank had been formally granted independence from the state and although in practice this freedom of action was limited, the central bank established itself as an important guardian of a stable currency in the wake of the hyperinflation of 1923. In successfully overcoming inflation, the German central bank's strict governor, Hjalmar Schacht, became something of a celebrity, also enjoying international respect. During his first stint as head of the central bank (from 1924 to 1930), Schacht proved to be a fierce defender of the bank's independence and its remit of ensuring a stable currency. Upon his return as governor of the *Reichsbank* in 1933, shortly after the Nazi party assumed power, Schacht expressed his full support of Hitler and his rearmament strategy and was rewarded by being also made economics minister. At the same time, he continued to stress the need for monetary discipline. However, after a number of years, Schacht had a few run-ins with the dictator who promulgated a new banking law in 1937 that ended the German central bank's legal independence, the government formally taking full charge (Marsh 1992). Disenchanted with the direction of the economy, characterized by minimal international reserves, ineffective wage and price policies and out-of-control government finances, the *Reichbank's* Directorate reported to Hitler in early 1939 that wage and price controls had to be tightened and that spending restraint by the government was urgent. Hitler summarily dismissed these recommendations and fired almost all members of the directorate, including Schacht.

Lessons from the Great Depression

The Great Depression has been extensively analyzed by central bankers and academic economists. Over the years a consensus has emerged as to its causes, as well as the lessons to be learned from that catastrophic period. Ben Bernanke, former Chairman of the Board of Governors of the Fed, extensively studied the Great Depression during his academic years and his conclusions provide an excellent insight in the subject (Bernanke 2000). Bernanke's examination of the evidence led him to conclude, like Milton Friedman, that the main cause of the shrinking world economy was a severe contraction of the money supply, particularly in the United States. The result was a drastic fall in both output and prices, in turn leading to record levels of unemployment. The United States was the epicenter of the downward spiral of the world economy which was transmitted to Europe and elsewhere through the flawed system of the gold standard. Bernanke showed that the worldwide contraction of the money supply in the early 1930s was mainly the result of several reinforcing factors. Many monetary institutions, including the Federal Reserve, had been designed with serious shortcomings and—though unintended—were conducting misinformed policies. Unfavorable political and economic pre-conditions contributed to the monetary collapse. There were also non-monetary factors at work, foremost the banking crises that spread when the depression was already well underway. Debt deflation, leading to sometimes large increases in real terms of the principal of loans extended to corporate and household borrowers, not only contributed to a fall in investment and consumption but exacerbated the problems of commercial banks as the demand for credit shrank. A further important conclusion was that a strong correlation between money (M) and prices (P) had existed, the causation running from the contraction of M to the decline in P (as foretold by the quantity theory of money) but also to the fall in output. Delving deeper into the components of the severe monetary contraction,

Bernanke identified the following main elements: declines in the holdings of real cash balances, a notion developed by the Cambridge School (as mentioned previously), sharp declines in money multipliers (in fractional reserve banking expressed as the ratio of the money supply to base money) and a skewed distribution of the world's monetary gold stock.

However, in the immediate aftermath of the depression, insight in the causes and the propagation of the American economic downturn remained limited. Many policymakers and academics still clung to obsolete and discredited explanations. The central role of the shrinkage of the money supply and the Fed's misguided reaction to the unfolding depression were not yet generally recognized. The gold standard was still seen by many as the preferred central guide for monetary and fiscal policy, who therefore advocated a return to that flawed system, not recognizing that playing by the rules of the gold standard could readily cause a conflict between countries' external objectives (fixed exchange rates and balance of payments equilibrium) and its domestic objectives (full employment and price stability). Part of the reason was that the notion of according primacy to domestic goals was still alien to a host of policymakers and politicians. But change was in the air as the influence of John Maynard Keynes and his message of running budget deficits as the way out of the depression and to lower unemployment was spreading. The Keynesian revolution led to discrediting the balanced budget doctrine and to replacing it with the concept of functional finance. It also led to a lesser focus on monetary policy, its role subordinated to supporting expansive fiscal policies.

The lesson that an adequate money supply was crucial to combat depressions and recessions, as emphasized by Bernanke, and Milton Friedman before him, was initially not fully absorbed. Central bankers such as Mariner Eccles, Chairman of the Federal Reserve Board from 1934 to 1948, argued that simply pumping up the money supply was like pushing on a string (later called the liquidity trap). Although there was considerable truth in this view when dealing with a depression—if there was no demand for it, it was unlikely that bank credit would increase. But jump-starting the economy through fiscal stimulus could soon trigger a revival of bank credit and an increase in the demand for money. The lesson that central banks should not attempt to counteract 'speculative excesses' with across-the-board monetary instruments, as the Fed did in 1929, was better understood. Providing the Fed with the authority to regulate margin credit was a better way to deal with the issue of booming stock markets fueled by readily available credit. Another lesson drawn from the depression experience was that central banks needed to improve their data collection and professionalize their staff. This would enable them to better understand where the economy was heading and to judge the impact of their actions. Perhaps the most important lesson was that clinging to a gold coin or bullion standard—as several central banks were in favor of—was the road to economic instability in a changed world. Also working against the independence of central banks was the (correct) perception that the Fed and its sister organizations in Europe did not perform well during the depression. This loss of independence, while understandable under the prevailing circumstances, would hamper central banks in their operations under the changed economic environment during and in the first years after the Second World War.

A prime example is the fate of the British central bank. John Maynard Keynes, whose sympathies lay with the UK Treasury, was elected as a member of the Court of Directors of the Bank of England in 1941. 'It was a richly symbolic moment,' Keynes remarking: 'I do not know if it is I or the Old Lady who has been made an honest woman of' (Kynaston 2017, 382). Keynes regularly attended the weekly lunches at the Bank which he said he found enjoyable, but confided to a fellow director, that he found the Governor, Montagu Norman, 'always absolutely charming, always absolutely wrong!' (Moggeridge 1992, 629–34). Norman himself 'reluctantly, but more or less uncomplainingly accepted that the war tipped the scales of power away from the Bank and towards the Treasury' (Kynaston, 383).

Wartime Economics

In the run-up to the second global conflagration of the twentieth century, economic policy was increasingly subordinated to the requirements of the military build-up. The future Axis powers, Germany and Japan, were embarking on constructing an unprecedented war machine. They were also striving for a maximum degree of autarky, reverting to import substitution and bilateral trade deals, which out of necessity would sometimes be of a barter nature. Foreign exchange controls proliferated, restricting exports to those not labeled as strategic and halting outflows of capital and gold. Under these conditions the central banks of the future aggressors were fully directed to support their government's efforts by providing cheap loans and administering the strict exchange controls which served to preserve their modest gold and foreign exchange reserves. The

Reichsbank and the Bank of Japan played no role in containing inflation, instead strict price and wage controls were introduced by their governments to repress the increase in prices that would normally follow when government spending shot up and higher taxes lagged behind. The same process, but at a later stage, took place in Continental Europe. Meanwhile, central banks in these countries, fearing an attack by Germany, started to increasingly transfer their gold holdings to safe havens, such as London and New York, in the late 1930s. The classic war chest motive to hoard gold came into full play, creating a scarcity of the yellow metal, which was especially troubling for Germany whose gold reserve was small. The policy of transferring gold abroad for safekeeping proved its worth at the start of the German invasion, the occupying force able to capture only a part of the sizable stocks of the precious metal owned by the countries overrun by the *Blitzkrieg*. But the gold that was left at home in the occupied countries was soon carted off to Berlin and from there to salt mines in Southern Germany toward the end of the war. Only part of the looted gold was recovered after 1945.

The occupied countries suffered further losses because of outright plunder of machinery, commodities and other valuable assets, including art, or receiving increasingly depreciating *Reichsmark* for the purchase of goods often at 'fire sale' prices. Soldiers were also able to buy goods in occupied areas with special 'travel money' at favorable exchange rates. Management of the central banks in occupied countries was soon replaced by local Nazis or collaborators who were doing their part to enrich Germany by accepting huge amounts of *Reichsmark* Treasury bills which sat on their books and for which they had no use. Within Germany, the government financed its ballooning military expenditure through the central bank which obtained the necessary funding through systematically tapping the commercial banks' liquid funds, a practice known as 'noiseless financing.' The Treasury bills issued to the banks were then placed with the central bank. This inflationary form of financing to which the German banks did not dare to refuse, contrasted with the placement of long-term bonds ('war bonds') issued by the governments of the United States and Britain.

When Britain entered the war in 1939, its build-up of military equipment was still modest, forcing it to step up the production of its war machine rapidly to try to catch up with Germany. This effort, resulting in budget deficits, was financed by higher taxes, special government bond issues and sales of treasury bills at low interest rates. The Bank of England had no choice but to acquiesce in the UK Treasury's policy of cheap money, allowing the cost of borrowing to be artificially low. Skirmishes at the beginning of the war between the central bank and the Treasury over matters like exchange controls and open market transactions were soon settled in favor of the latter. As a result, the Bank of England spent the rest of the war mainly as an administrative arm of the government. It also played a subsidiary role in the war-time international discussions on establishing a new monetary order after the war. At a remarkably early stage of the war (starting in 1941), both Britain and the United States were drawing up plans for a reformed system, informed by the traumatic experiences of the 1930s. A blend of these plans, designed by Keynes on behalf of the British Government and Harry Dexter White from the US Treasury, was adopted at the international monetary conference at Bretton Woods in 1944. While the British central bank had some input in its country's position, it played a marginal role from there on. The same was true in the case of the United States, the US Treasury sometimes not even informing the Fed of its ideas.

America Takes Charge

The United States, before entering the war in December 1941, still had not fully recovered from the depression, spare industrial capacity and lingering joblessness, causing concern among politicians and economists. One of these, Alvin Hansen, a Harvard professor and strong supporter of Keynes' ideas, put forward the notion of 'secular stagnation' in 1938. His argument, which received considerable attention, was that technological advances had reached a high level leading to a decline in investment opportunities, and that the US economy had become mature (Hansen 1938). The secular stagnation argument for explaining low growth was revived by Larry Summers (2018). The remedy was sought in increasing government spending and financing budget deficits with cheap money. Keeping interest rates low was precisely what the Fed did throughout the war, declaring early on that it was ready to discount US Treasury bills at 0.375 percent gradually increasing for longer maturities with a maximum of 2.5 percent for 25-year Treasury bonds. These rates prevailed throughout the war. For the rest the American Central Bank, together with the US Treasury, tinkered in the markets to maintain orderly conditions. Wanting to do something as a token of its willingness to contribute to the war effort, besides ensuring low interest rates, the Fed introduced credit controls on the consumption of durable goods. The idea behind this measure was to restrict demand so as to free up resources for military production. But as selective controls do not affect overall demand as long as other credit channels remain open, the measure had only cosmetic value, while also proving difficult to administer. Price and wage controls were introduced by the government at a later stage, outwardly keeping inflation in hand but repressing demand which was to explode once the controls were lifted after the war. All in all, the Second World War was a frustrating period for the Fed, not being able to perform the main task it was set up to do. It feared that by keeping interest rates artificially low it had been turned into an 'engine of inflation' (Meltzer 2003, 581), for which it could later be blamed, but was powerless to throw off the US Treasury yoke. It would take until 1951 before the relationship between the central bank and the treasury was normalized.

Monetary Theory in the 1930s

Some of the most important changes in the history of monetary theory emerged in the 1930s. These theoretical innovations had far-reaching consequences for monetary policymaking. In sum, they relegated monetary policy to a subsidiary role, fiscal policy becoming the main policy instrument. In 1936 John Maynard Keynes' *The General Theory of Employment, Interest and Money*, brought about a radical new way of thinking about economic issues and established macroeconomics as the basis for modern economic policymaking. Keynes rejected the classical liberal theory, in particular Say's law and the quantity theory of money. He showed that the tenet that all production creates its own demand and delivers full employment via the price mechanism and the automatic adjustment of wages is not credible. Keynes pointed out that since wages do not instantly adjust to new economic circumstances no such mechanism can automatically deliver full employment. And as total demand (consumption plus investment) can fall short of supply, unemployment is the result. The emphasis on effective demand and the existence of shortfalls in consumption and investment were central to the development of the doctrine of government deficit spending as a remedy for unemployment. As to the quantity theory of money, to which Keynes still adhered to with some caveats, only a few years before he produced his famous theory (Keynes 1930), he challenged the notion that the velocity of the circulation of money (the V in MV = PY) was fixed and therefore that the money supply (M) solely determined the price level (P). Since classical economics consisted of various not always integrated elements, Keynes saw the need to erect a comprehensive theoretical body encompassing unemployment (the predominant issue of the 1930s), national income, consumption, fixed investment and interest rates. He emphasized that existing theory was static and that his theory was a dynamic one, centered on *expectations*, a concept which would be reinvented in a different context, many years later.

As to the interest rate, Keynes also presented a novel approach. In classical economic theory the interest rate is determined by savings and investment alone, while the quantity theory of money postulates that changes in M do not affect the interest rate but only P. He concluded that the interest rate was thus not satisfactorily determined, but that his theory of *liquidity preference* contained the solution. In Keynes' thinking, the demand for money is based on the liquidity preference of economic agents. While not negating the theory of time preference of interest rates (the longer the economic agents 'park' their money the higher the interest rate they demand), Keynes linked the degree of liquidity that economic agents seek to the level of interest rates. Considering financial assets, such as savings deposits and bonds, as close substitutes for money (cash or checking accounts), economic agents will opt for holding such less liquid assets instead of money (a process which he called dishoarding), causing interest rates to fall, whereas they would increase if liquidity preference was high and hoarding was widespread. Keynes distinguished three motives for holding money, the transaction motive (readily available for immediate payments), the precautionary motive (to allow for adverse situations) and the speculative motive (to be able to react swiftly to investment opportunities). The upshot of the substitutability between money and financial assets is that an increase in M, for instance through monetary easing by the central bank, will lead to households adjusting their portfolios, thereby shifting unwanted M into financial assets. The consequence is that any change in M brings about changes in interest rates on financial assets and since in 'pure' Keynesian thinking interest rates have hardly any influence on expenditure, the role of monetary policy should be limited to influencing interest rates, not output.

Reactions to the *General Theory* soon appeared, including interpretations of the sizable number of difficult passages and criticisms of its contents. One much-repeated criticism was the short-term nature of Keynes' approach, to which he famously answered that 'in the long run we are all dead.' Another criticism, which became prominent only after the Second

World War, was that the *General Theory* (Keynes 1936) neglected to deal effectively with the determination of the price level, in other words it did not adequately explain inflation (or deflation). But in general, Keynes' *magnum opus* was hailed as a major theoretical breakthrough and would largely inform economic policy in decades to come. In short, C+I trumped MV: analyzing economies in terms of expenditure (consumption and investment) instead of the money supply.

In attempting to increase the accessibility of the Keynesian model, the British academic John Hicks developed an approach in which he combined Keynes' ideas with some of the tenets of classical economics in his article 'Mr. Keynes and the Classics: a Suggested Interpretation'(Hicks 1937). He presented his synthesis in the famous IS-LM diagram which became an important tool in teaching macroeconomics and as the basis for an alternative to 'pure' Keynesian theory (Fig. 5.2).

In simplified terms, the diagram expresses the relationship between the interest rate (r) and national income, or real output (Y), as well as the money market. The intersection of the IS curve (the savings and investment equilibrium) and the LM curve (the liquidity preference, or demand

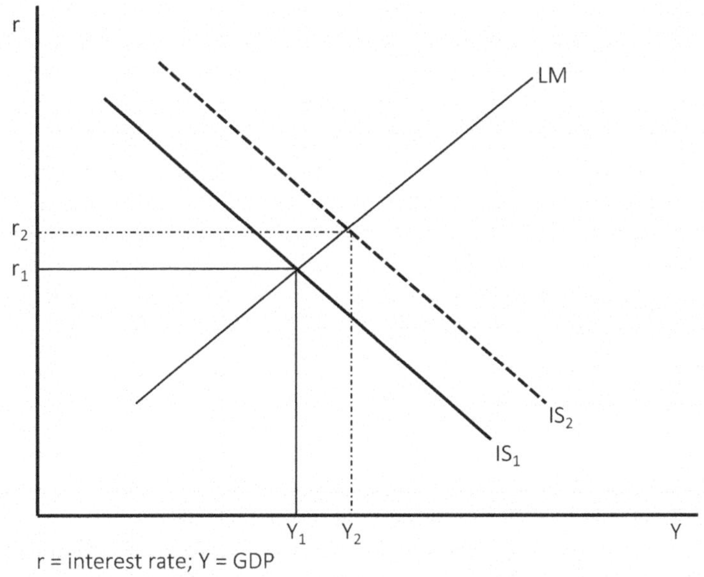

Fig. 5.2 IS and LM Equilibrium

for money, and the money supply equilibrium) depicts the general equilibrium in the economy. In other words, the real economy and the monetary sector are in equilibrium. Regarding the IS curve, the interest rate is the independent variable and national income the dependent variable. The reverse holds for the LM curve. The IS curve, the locus of points of equilibrium in the real and monetary (financial) economy, is downward sloping or slanted to the right. This reflects that national income is higher when interest rates are lower. For the LM curve, national income (Y) is the independent variable and the interest rate (r) the dependent variable. LM depicts the combination of national income and interest rates for which the money market is in equilibrium (money demand equals money supply). The LM curve is upward sloping or slanted to the right since a higher Y implies a lower r. The equilibrium level of IS and LM is known as *aggregate demand.* A shift of the IS curve to the right, reflecting an increase in aggregate demand, raises both national income and the interest rate. And such a shift can be brought about by increasing government spending.

The policy implication is that running a government budget deficit has the same effect as a higher level of fixed investment or a lower savings rate and therefore that deficit financing can remedy a shortfall in demand and hence prevent or mitigate a recession or depression. Fiscal policy is therefore the primary instrument for stabilizing the economy. As regards the implication of LM for monetary policy, an increase in the money supply (M) leads to a downward shift of the LM curve resulting in a lower interest rate and raising the equilibrium level of national income.

Hick's innovative model is not an operational tool for economic policy, the main reason being that it assumes that the price level is fixed (no inflation or deflation). But more elaborate later models, some developed at central banks, were inspired by Hick's pioneering work and became a standard input, besides statistical and qualitative evidence, for the formulation of monetary policy. Nonetheless, the IS/LM curves have remained an important teaching tool.

References

Adams Brown, William: *The International Gold Standard Reinterpreted 1914–1934*, National Bureau of Economic Research, 1940.

Ahamed, Licquat, *Lords of Finance: The Bankers that Broke the World*, Penguin Books, New York, 2009.

Bernanke, Ben: *Essays on the Great Depression.* Princeton University Press, Princeton NJ, 2000.

Cassel, Gustav: *Money and Foreign Exchange after 1914*, Macmillan, London, 1930.

Crabbe, Leland: "The International Gold Standard and U.S. Monetary Policy from World War 1 to the New Deal", Federal Reserve *Bulletin*, June, 1989.

Friedman, Milton and Anna Schwartz: *A Monetary History of the United States 1867–1960*, National Bureau of Economic Research, Princeton University Press, Princeton NJ, 1963.

Hansen, Alvin: *Full Recovery or Stagnation?* W.W. Norton, New York, 1938.

Hawtrey, Ralph: *The Gold Standard in Theory and Practice*, Longman, Green & Co, London, fifth edition, 1947.

Hicks, John: "Mr. Keynes and the Classics: A Suggested Interpretation" *Econometrica* 5, 1937.

Keynes, John Maynard: *A Tract on Monetary Reform*, Macmillan, London, 1923.

Keynes, John Maynard: *A Treatise on Money*, Macmillan, London, 1930.

Keynes, John Maynard: *The General Theory of Employment, Interest and Money*, Macmillan, London, 1936.

Kettl, Donald: *Leadership at the Fed'* Yale University press, New Haven and London, 1986.

Kynaston, David: *Till Times Last Stand: A History of the Bank of England 1694–2013*, Bloomsbury, London, 2017.

Marsh, David: *The Most Powerful Bank: Inside Germany's Bundesbank*, Times Books, New York, 1992.

Meltzer, Alan: *A History of the Federal Reserve 1913–1951, Volume 1,* Chicago University Press, 2003.

Moggeridge, D.E.: *Maynard Keynes: An Economists' Biography*, Routledge, London, 1992.

Summers, Lawrence: "The Threat of Secular Stagnation has not Gone Away", *Financial Times*, 6 May, 2018.

CHAPTER 6

Post-War Progress: 1946–1960

The post-war years were characterized by rapid recovery and sustained economic growth, low unemployment and a tussle for independence by central banks. These years can be usefully divided in the period immediately after the war up to the return of the Federal Reserve as a relatively independent institution in 1951 and the years from 1952 to 1960 during which the successor to the temporary German Central Bank started to flex its muscles, as well as the appearance of the first cracks in the system of fixed but adjustable exchange rates (the Bretton Woods system). As we have seen, the role of central banks was significantly diminished during the 1930s and the Second World War. After the War the main preoccupation of governments was the maintenance of full employment, as illustrated by the passage of the *Employment Act* in the United States in 1946. As a result, the Federal Reserve became committed to fostering maximum employment and purchasing power. Although these concepts were not defined, the American Central Bank at the time accorded considerably more weight to the level of unemployment than to that of inflation.

The Federal Reserve and the Bank of England continued to play a subordinate role to their treasuries in the early post-war years, their main activity being keeping interest rates low to facilitate government borrowing. And to explicitly codify its dominant position, the British Government nationalized the Bank of England in 1946. Nationalization also took place in the late 1940s in Austria, Australia, Argentina, China, India and the Netherlands, as shown in Table 2.1. Most of the European and Latin

O. de Beaufort Wijnholds, *The Money Masters*,
https://doi.org/10.1007/978-3-030-40041-5_6

American Central Banks were government owned by 1951. In West Germany, under the tutelage of the occupying authorities, an interim central bank was established, and given far-reaching powers to combat inflation. Central bank independence was greatest during the 1950s (and remained so until the 1990s) in Germany, Switzerland, the United States (after a hard struggle) and the Netherlands which despite having been nationalized allowed its central bank considerable leeway in conducting monetary policy. Macroeconomic analysis at central banks and by academics was becoming strongly influenced by Keynesian economics, strengthening the view, for instance entertained by the Board of the Fed, that monetary policy was secondary to fiscal policy and hardly an instrument usable for countercyclical action. The main purpose of managing money was seen as ensuring orderly financial markets and keeping interest rates low. A different philosophy held sway in Germany and other relatively independent European Central Banks in which the money supply came to play an important role in their monetary analyses and policy decisions.

Breakthrough

In the United States, before 1951, the Federal Reserve's policy was predominantly based on the objective of keeping interest rates low in support of the governments' debt management policies. Besides a modest attempt to limit credit to the stock market, the central bank frequently moved minimum reserve requirements up and down with little effect. Under pressure from the Treasury, the Fed also—with great reluctance—reimposed controls on consumer credit. Together with price and wage controls, which were prolonged for a while after the war, the recovering American economy was burdened by a host of restrictions, requiring a large administration. Staffers at the Fed, as well as astute outside observers, recognized that the resulting pent up demand was creating a strong potential for inflation. However, the Treasury insisted on the Fed's cooperation to maintain a ceiling of 2.5 percent interest on Treasury bonds. When Fed Chair Mariner Eccles appealed to President Truman, who was much in favor of a cheap money policy, to allow a slight raise in the bond rate, he was rebuffed. 'Eccles's inflation campaign so aggravated Truman that the president decided to not reappoint him as chairman when his third term expired in early 1948' (Kettl 1986, 63). But change was in the air and when the Korean War broke out in June 1950, the Fed stood ready to regain some meaningful role regarding monetary policy. With the US economy already picking up steam, fear of a return of war-time scarcity and rationing led the public to sharply increase its purchases of durable goods. And following the lifting of price and wage controls, inflation shot up at an alarming rate in the second half of 1950, reaching 14 percent on an annual basis at its peak.

The Fed now saw an opportunity to step up its quest for more independence. '[T]he Fed had in thirty-five years gone from an era when the president respected its independence as he did that of the Supreme Court's to a time when the agency had little if any independence' (Kettl 1986, 65). A fierce struggle followed, the treasury insisting that the central bank continue a cheap money policy. The warring parties presented their respective cases several times to President Truman, who preferred controls to address the surge in inflation and was reluctant to act as arbiter. But apparently the argument that the higher cost of government financing would be more than offset by the lower cost of military procurement at a modest level of inflation made an impression on him. When not long after a final inconclusive meeting with the president the feud became public, influential members of Congress and the financial press siding with the Fed. Eventually a compromise was hammered out in the spring of 1951 to which the President gave his blessing. The announcement mentioned that the US Treasury and the Federal Reserve System had reached full accord with respect to debt management and monetary policy (soon known as the *Accord*). In practice it meant that the treasury could accept smaller purchases of government bonds by the central bank, as long as this raised the bond rate no higher than 2.75 percent, but that it would allow short-term rates to rise without interference. The principle that the Fed could now conduct monetary policy without seeking approval from the treasury had important ramifications. It could again concentrate on dampening inflation (in which it largely succeeded in the second half of the 1950s and in most of the 1960s) without political interference, as its founders had envisaged in 1913.

Around that time it became common practice to refer to the Fed's position as 'independent *within* the government.' Although this concept has never been fully spelled out, its purport can be formulated as follows. Being independent within the government is different from being independent *from* the government. It recognizes that the ultimate decision-making powers rest with Congress which can amend or introduce new legislation concerning the Federal Reserve System. But attempts to change the laws governing the Fed in order to make it more dependent on the treasury or Congress could be expected to cause fierce opposition from various quarters. As we shall see, frequent attempts to clip the Fed's wings or even to abolish it have been made since 1951, but have so far failed to garner sufficient support. And as long as the Fed's independence within the government remains undiminished, it enjoys full freedom to conduct monetary policy without approval from the treasury and without bowing to political pressure. Nevertheless, members of Congress, as well as presidents, have with some regularity exerted pressure on the Fed, especially to loosen monetary policy (see also Chap. 14). The politicians were also quick to blame the central bank for economic conditions they considered to be responsible for losing an election, as President Nixon did when he lost the presidential race in 1960. Over time American central bank governors have reacted in different ways to pressures and criticisms, the most pliable arguably being Arthur Burns in the 1970s, and the most independent, Paul Volcker in the 1980s.

Nationalization

Before the War the Bank of England was not formally subjected to government oversight, except that its charter had to be renewed from time to time. But the establishment of the Exchange Equalization Account in 1932 had removed an important segment of the central bank's activities. And in line with the move toward greater government involvement in the economy, the Labour Party led by Prime Minister Clement Attlee (Churchill had lost the first post-war election), as part of its program of nationalization, decided in 1946 to formally take full ownership of the central bank. Although on the surface not much changed, the Bank of England Act of 1946 empowered the UK Treasury to give directions to the Bank if that was deemed to be in the public's interest. At the same time, the central bank was authorized to give directions to commercial banks if deemed in the interest of the public. It is noteworthy that the Bank had not asked for a formal supervisory role regarding the banking system, arguing that its informal contacts with financial institutions—the so-called nods and winks—had proved to be sufficient. But the British Government, wishing to have some control over the business of banking, insisted that the Bank's good reputation made it well suited for taking on this task. And since the central bank would have to request authorization from the treasury before issuing a directive, the government remained the ultimate decider on monetary policy actions.

While central banks are usually subject to pursuing certain goals, such as ensuring price stability and fostering economic growth, the Bank of England Act did not mention what the central banks' wider purposes should be. This surprising omission in theory allowed the Bank to operate with considerable freedom in conducting monetary policy. Yet in view of the prevailing sentiment for keeping interest rates low, so that the UK Treasury could borrow cheaply, the central bank, like its American sister organization, generally remained passive during the first post-war years. It was only involved administratively when Britain lifted its exchange controls on current account transactions, restoring convertibility of the pound in 1947, a premature measure which had to be reversed after six weeks following an attack on the pound. And the Bank of England (whose governor was against the adjustment) was not involved directly when the pound was devalued by 30 percent in 1949 under the par value system agreed at Bretton Woods, in order to restore Britain's competitiveness. During the 1950s little changed in the respective roles of the British Treasury and the Bank of England, by contrast to the increased degree of independence obtained by the Federal Reserve Board in the United States. The prevailing view in Britain was clearly spelled out in 1959 in a report by experts commissioned by the UK Treasury and chaired by Lord Radcliffe. Stating that there was 'no single objective by which all monetary policy can be conditioned,' the committee concluded that management of the government's debt was the only fundamental task of the Bank of England, adding that the Bank 'must …consciously exercise a positive policy about interest rates,' meaning that it should follow a cheap money policy (Report of the Committee on the Working of the Monetary System, London, 1959, 337). This attitude would prevail into the 1970s. Moreover, as regards external relations, the Bank was in the post-war years still in favor of restoring the sterling area, an idea that was backward looking and futile.

Germany: A Different Route

A very different development took place in Germany. At first misery and chaos reigned after the Nazi regime had capitulated. Initially governed in inevitable makeshift mode by the military authorities of the United States, Britain and France, the occupying forces soon recognized the need for institution building. As the German economy would not be able to function without a degree of monetary and financial stability—the *Reichsmark* had become virtually worthless—the Allies set up an embryonic central bank staffed by German nationals. The model for this institution was not to be the *Reichsbank*, which was too closely identified with the old regime and therefore unacceptable to the United States which proposed creating a central bank along the lines of the Federal Reserve. While adding elements of the Bank of England and some of the *Reichsbank's* practices, the successor central bank was to have a decentralized structure, as reflected in its name *Bank deutscher Laender* (BdL). It opened its doors in March 1948 as a body representing the various German Laender (states) in a federal structure. The new Bank was granted independence by the Allies from the government, partly because there was no central government yet (this came only in 1949). The BdL was first of all a coordinating body meant to forge decision-making on monetary policy. But the principle underlying this task was to strengthen the currency and the monetary and credit systems in the common interest. Here we see an early example of the philosophy of *monetary stability* that would be embedded later in the German Bundesbank mandate. But while the BdL was 'not to be subject to the instruction of any political body' (Marsh 1992, 125), it was in the beginning supervised by the Allied Bank Commission. Yet this constraint did not prevent the BdL from becoming progressively assertive in its policymaking and earning a reputation for solidity. (The Commission was terminated in 1951.) Practically in tandem with the creation of the BdL, a complete monetary reform took place, encompassing invalidation of all old currency and by blocking bank deposits. A new currency called the *Deutsche Mark* (D mark) was introduced, new banknotes and coins were distributed and bank accounts gradually freed. The *modus operandi* was similar to the successful monetary reform of the Netherlands in 1946.

The BdL took its task and independence very seriously and under the strong leadership of Wilhelm Vocke did not take kindly to government pressure. It followed a stability oriented policy, using its newly acquired authority to adjust minimum reserve requirements in order to strengthen the impact of changes in its discount rate. A serious conflict with the government took place when the central bank was bent on sharply pushing up interest rates as it anticipated a surge in inflation following the outbreak of the Korean War. Chancellor Konrad Adenauer, concerned about unemployment (still 11 percent at the time), expressed strong displeasure with the central banks' intentions. He backed down, however, as his influential economics minister, Ludwig Erhard, who would later be hailed as the architect of the German 'economic miracle,' argued that a hike in the discount rate would lower Germany's burgeoning trade surplus which was itself a potential source of inflation. Such clashes, this time ending in a victory for the central bank, would become a regular feature of the conduct of German monetary policy. Another tradition initiated by Vocke was to warn the government to follow a stability oriented fiscal policy, in the conviction that substantial budget deficits could swell the money supply and so add to inflation. In later years the German Central Bank would routinely express its views on fiscal policy, usually to the displeasure of the government. There have been few other countries where the central bank has felt free to explicitly and in public take its government to task about its budgetary stance.

Birth of the Bundesbank

After long-drawn out discussions the *Bank deutscher Laender* became the *Deutsche Bundesbank* in 1957, established in Frankfurt. It essentially remained the same institution, enjoying a high degree of independence from the government. Its mission remained ensuring the stability of the currency, both domestically (price stability) and externally (the exchange rate, in practice against the dollar). The Bundesbank Law guaranteed the central bank's almost unlimited independence on matters of monetary policy. Supervision of the banking system remained outside its remit to avoid undue influence by monetary policymakers and supervisory authorities on each other. (The question of whether a central bank should not only conduct monetary policy but also be responsible for the health of the banking system has been debated intensively without reaching a clear consensus. However, in recent years the tendency has been to combine both tasks under one roof.) The members of the Directorate of the Bundesbank (BuBa) displayed an almost fanatical belief in their independence during its 43-year existence. Aided by the strong personalities of its presidents, the Bundesbank became a symbol of stability and solidity, playing a pivotal role in Germany's consensus economy. Importantly, it enjoyed a great deal of support from the public which saw it as the guarantor of price stability in a country with a traumatic history of hyperinflation. (Jacques Delors—a prominent French and European politician—once remarked that not all Germans believe in God, but all believe in the Bundesbank.) So strong was the position of the Bundesbank that it was sometimes referred to as a 'state within a state – an economic policy counterweight to the government' (Marsh, 145). Based on its independence and high level of competence, the BuBa also became a respected member of the international central banking fraternity, although its strong convictions caused discomfort from time to time.

Whereas the Bundesbank could shrug off political pressure regarding its monetary policy, it did not have the final say on the exchange rate. But since the rate of the D mark mattered to monetary policy, it used its advisory role to the hilt. In the first test of wills on whether to revalue the national currency, the government did not accept the central bank's position. The conflict was some time in the making and centered on what policy would be best to choke off inflation. The German economy not only enjoyed a spectacular recovery in the 1950s but was also running increasingly large trade surpluses as its competitive strength powered its exports. Under the prevailing regime of fixed but adjustable exchange rates, the central bank had to absorb the excess of exports over imports by buying dollars (the global reserve currency) in the market. And instead of the shortage of dollars during the first years after the War, Germany's international reserves were accumulating at a steady pace in the late 1950s. Like other European countries who were running surpluses against the United States, the German central bank started to convert part of its dollar holdings into gold.

In the beginning demands for converting dollars into gold did not bother the United States as its gold reserves were ample, but the picture changed around 1960 when the US dollar came under pressure for the first time. As the flow of dollars into Germany continued, the Bundesbank grew concerned about the increase in the money supply resulting from its purchases of dollars needed to keep the D mark within the narrow band of ¾ percent—on both sides of parity—required under the Bretton Woods system. A discussion with the government ensued on how to deal with the conflict between internal (the domestic economy) and external equilibrium (the exchange rate). Nipping inflation in the bud by raising the discount rate would lead to greater inflows of capital and end up in the already burgeoning reserves, while on the other hand, lowering the discount rate in an attempt to hold on to an undervalued exchange rate would do nothing to weaken inflation. The President of the Bundesbank took the position—despite some internal opposition from his staff—that the exchange rate parity was sacrosanct, preferring to lower the discount rate and reduce the minimum reserve requirements. This time the German Government prevailed, deciding in March 1961 to revalue the D mark by 5 percent (the Netherlands did the same), on the grounds that the resulting lower import prices were the best remedy against inflation in the prevailing economic circumstances, including the United States' unwillingness to devalue the dollar. And a dearer D mark would also bring down the external surplus. This rare defeat of the Bundesbank temporarily damaged its credibility. What made this incident special was that it pitted a government that saw the danger of inflation as the greater threat and a central bank wedded to a fixed exchange rate. The monetary policy versus exchange rate dilemma would return in Germany several times in the following decades.

Elsewhere

In Japan, the central bank remained subordinated to the government which steered monetary policy through its so-called *window guidance*, a euphemism for a system of credit restriction. As regards setting the level of the yen, within the margins of the par value system, the Bank of Japan simply followed orders from the Japanese Treasury. No fundamental changes in the constrained status of the central banks of France, Italy and Belgium occurred during the post-war period, cheap money policies orchestrated by their treasuries being the norm. While the same regime prevailed in Sweden, the central bank did protest against its inability to conduct a more independent monetary policy, leading to the resignation of its Governors in 1948 and 1957 (Fregert 2018, 127–128), but the effort bore some fruit in later years. During the decolonization of the 1950 and 1960s, a sizable number of new central banks were established. Technical assistance provided by established central banks and the International Monetary Fund provided important input in shaping the new entities. But while a degree of independence was sometimes written into new monetary laws, in practice it was the government that was in charge in these countries. And in the Eastern European countries where Communists had taken over the government after the Second World War, as well as in China where the Communist Party came into power in 1949, the old central banks were either disbanded or turned into state banks which had no monetary task other than issuing bank notes. And such issuance was totally dependent on the parameters of central planning, following the model of the Soviet Union.

In essence the Dutch monetary school, as it came to be known, sought to identify the sources of money creation. Such an analysis of the *counterparts* of increases (or decreases) in the money supply would allow the central bank to concentrate its policies on the cause(s) of any monetary disequilibrium. It was assumed that money should only be created by the private sector (the banking sector) and that the public sector needed to refrain from contributing to inflationary impulses. The government should therefore have to finance any deficit by issuing long-term bonds

Box 6.1 Monetary Theory and Analysis

Keynesian theory was dominant for many years after the War. Refinements were made, but the essential body of work of the British economist remained intact. Most academics and other economists focused on the role of fiscal policy as *the* instrument to influence the economy. Monetary policy as a tool to counter inflation or to stimulate the economy was paid scant attention. There were exceptions, however, in countries where growth of the money supply was considered to be of considerable importance. These were the countries where monetary stability was accorded a high priority against the background of low unemployment and early instances of inflation (especially at the time of the Korean War). In Germany expansion of the money supply was seen as an important indicator of the state of the economy and the desired level of interest rates, but was not based on rigorous monetary analysis. In the Netherlands, however, the central bank followed an analytical approach based on the notion of monetary equilibrium (also known as neutral money), a state in which the money supply does not exert an inflationary or deflationary influence on the economy. This was not a new concept, having been initially developed by Knut Wicksell, a Swedish economist from the early twentieth century (Wicksell 1936), but it was the first time an attempt was made to make it operational. The Netherlands Bank's analysis would inform its monetary policy for a long time, starting in the early 1950s and continuing to the mid-1960s, as reflected in its *Annual Reports*. In those days it was considered an important innovative approach, but was eclipsed in later years by the monetarist tenets of the Chicago economist Milton Friedman (addressed in Chap. 7).

(monetary neutral) and not by issuing short-term treasury bills (monetary financing). But for a country like the Netherlands, with its very open economy, concentrating only on domestic causes of money creation would ignore what happened to the balance of payments. Hence, the central bank had to extend its analysis to include the external sector's contribution to the growth of the money supply. And at a time that the Dutch economy—like the German one—was running large balance of payments surpluses, inflationary impulses from abroad (imported inflation) had to be reckoned with. The ideal situation, however, would be for the external sector to be in equilibrium, implying that it was not contributing to overall money creation. In such a situation the central bank needed to concentrate only on credit creation by the commercial banks. This was generally done by concluding so-called gentlemen's agreements between the central bank and the commercial banks. In practical terms this approach was a form of direct credit control. Part of the reason for applying direct controls was Keynesian skepticism concerning the effectiveness of changes in interest rates on private sector spending, but also the recognition that higher interest rates would encourage capital imports, complicating the imperative of maintaining a fixed exchange rate under the par value system.

In order to ascertain whether the money supply was growing too fast, the Netherlands Bank monitored what it called the ***national liquidity ratio*** which measured the money supply as a percentage of nominal national income (M/Y). When the liquidity ratio exceeded 40 percent—deemed the equilibrium level on the basis of past experience—the growth of M was considered to be inflationary. In other words, if the growth of the money supply in a given period (say 6 percent) exceeded the growth of the nominal national income (say 4 percent), it was desirable to bring down the liquidity ratio by 0.8 percent. Two other elements of this approach completed the Netherlands Bank's monetary analysis. While the money supply was generally measured as the sum of currency held by the public and the demand deposits held at commercial banks (later to be named M1), so-called ***secondary liquidities***, that is financial assets that could be converted into money at short notice with no or minimal loss, were included in the numerator of the liquidity ratio, as they were considered to be relevant for the spending potential of the private sector. These assets, also called quasi money, consisted of time deposits and foreign currency deposits of residents, as well as a fraction of savings deposits held by residents with Dutch banks. Essentially this is the definition of M2, which became an important indicator of monetary policy across many countries in the 1970s and 1980s.

One of the main problems with the liquidity ratio approach was the implicit assumption that the velocity of circulation of money was more or less constant, as in the classical quantity theory of money. But interpreting a downward trend in the liquidity ratio starting in the latter half of the 1960s, to which an increase in velocity on account of more efficient methods of payments had contributed, became quite challenging. In Chap. 7, in which the widespread revival of a sophisticated version of the quantity theory is discussed, the way is described in which the velocity issue was dealt with in later years. Another factor rendering the liquidity ratio as an indicator of monetary tightness questionable was the significant increase in Dutch interest rates in the course of the 1960s, which in all likelihood diminished the demand for money as higher yields were obtainable on capital market assets.

A related theory, known as the *monetary approach to the balance of payments* (MAB), proved to be more durable. While starting from a different perspective, namely the external sector instead of the domestic monetary configuration, it applies some of the same basic relationships between the main sectors of the economy. The MAB was developed in the 1950s by Jacques Polak and his research staff at the International Monetary Fund (IMF) and like the Netherlands Bank's approach, it was inspired by the search for solving a practical problem (Polak 1957). As the IMF was established mainly to temporarily cover financing needs of countries which were running unsustainable balance of payments deficits, it needed tools to 'stop the bleeding' and require countries borrowing from it to return to a sustainable external position, after which they could repay the Fund. Inserting monetary elements into a general Keynesian framework, Polak and his staff emphasized the relationship between domestic credit creation and the balance of payments. As excessive credit expansion leads to a monetary leak, or spillover, resulting in a balance of payment deficit, it is domestic credit that should be restrained to achieve the required adjustment. In due course ceilings on domestic credit expansion were incorporated in the IMF's loan agreements and have continued to be applied over the decades. How this approach was applied in Britain's programs with the IMF in the 1970s is described in Chap. 7.

The Phillips Curve

While not an element of mainstream monetary theory, the macroeconomic model developed in the late 1950s by A.W. Phillips, a professor at the London School of Economics, had such an impact that central banks had to take its tenets into account. Based on an examination of British data from 1861 to 1957, Phillips found a strong inverse correlation between wage inflation and unemployment (Phillips 1958). In later versions, prices rather than wages were plotted against unemployment in a curve that represented a trade-off between the two. The relevance for governments and central banks was that with higher inflation, unemployment would come down, whereas when the price level was constrained, for instance by tight monetary policy, unemployment would rise. For central banks of the Keynesian persuasion the message was that allowing more inflation would stimulate the economy and bring down unemployment permanently. Studies for the United States seemed to confirm the existence of such a trade-off. However, the validity of the Phillips curve model was challenged in the late 1960s by professors Edmund Phelps (1968) and Milton Friedman (1968) on theoretical grounds. They argued that in modern wage bargaining, it is real wages that parties focus on and that increases in nominal wages would therefore incorporate expectations of inflation. Implying that the Phillips curve could shift meant that there was no permanent trade-off and that in the long run inflation and unemployment developed independently of each other. In other words, the long-run Phillips curve's shape was vertical. But monetary policy does not tend to be concerned with the long run (the policy horizon usually does not reach beyond a few years) so that the existence of a short-term trade-off between inflation on the one hand and economic growth and unemployment on the other continued to inform central bank policies. But, as mentioned in Chap. 7, the notion of a short-term trade-off would come to be challenged on theoretical grounds in the 1970s (Fig. 6.1).

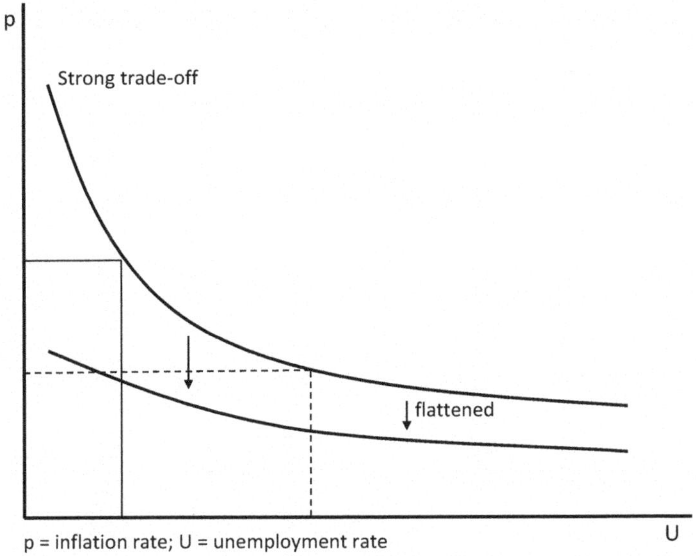

Fig. 6.1 The simple Phillips curve

References

Fregert, Kas: "Sveriges Riksbank: 350 years in the Making" in Rodney Edvinsson et al, *Sveriges Riksbank and the History of Central Banking*, Cambridge University Press, 2018, 90, 142.

Friedman, Milton: "The Role of Monetary Policy", presidential *Address*, American Economic Association, 1968.

Kettl, Donald: *Leadership at the Fed*, Yale University Press, New Haven and London, 1986.

Marsh, David: *The Most Powerful Bank; Inside Germany's Bundesbank*, Time books, New York, 1992.

Netherlands Bank, *Annual Reports*, 1950–1966.

Phelps, Edmund: "Money- Wage Dynamics and Labor Marker Equilibrium", *Journal of Political Economy*, vol 67, no 4, 1968, 678–711.

Phillips, A.W.: "The Relation between Unemployment and the Rate of Change of Money Wage Rates in the United kingdom 1861–1957", *Economica*, vol. 25, issue 100, 1958, 283–299.

Polak, Jacques:" Monetary Analysis of Income Formation and Payments", *International Monetary Fund Staff Papers,* 1957, 1–50.

Radcliffe Committee, *Report on the Working of the Monetary System*, United Kingdom Treasury, London, 1959.

Wicksell, Knut: *Interest and prices: A Study of the Causes Regulating the Value of Money,* Stockholm, 1898, translated from the German, Macmillan, London, 1936.

CHAPTER 7

Growth and Stability: 1961–1971

To an important degree modern central banking had been established in the United States and Germany as well as in some smaller European countries by the early 1960s. Not only had these institutions become (more) independent from their governments, honed their analytical capacity, as well as increased their arsenal of policy instruments, they had often become important players in national debates on economic policy. Moreover, central bank cooperation had also been reestablished and was becoming institutionalized, including regular meetings at the Bank for International Settlements. While the Bank of England continued to function at a high level of competence, its influence was somewhat diminished by virtue of its limited independence and the fact that New York had taken over London's position as the main financial center in the world. In other large countries, including France and Italy, while having been modernized in several ways, their rather weak monetary institutions carried comparatively little weight in international monetary debates of that period. The 1960s saw some increase in the role of central banks in shaping their countries' economies, but did not lead to greater independence in policymaking. At the same time, the German Bundesbank and its sister organizations in smaller European countries consolidated their distance from government interference and political pressure.

O. de Beaufort Wijnholds, *The Money Masters*,
https://doi.org/10.1007/978-3-030-40041-5_7

The Fed Struggles

Following the Accord with the US Treasury, the Federal Reserve was freer to move short-term interest rates, but did so mainly with the purpose to smooth conditions in the money market. The American Central Bank, under the leadership of its long-serving Chairman, William McChesney Martin, became more forceful in warning against inflation and opining on the economy in the early 1960s. Martin was a pragmatist and often deftly slalomed between the positions of the Fed and the Treasury where he had been a senior official. But although the Fed claimed it had become equal (in power) to the Treasury, in reality it remained something of a junior partner to that agency. In instances when it attempted to assert itself by means of tightening monetary conditions, it not only experienced push back from the White House, especially under President Lyndon Johnson, but also from Congress. As a result of such political pressure, monetary policy mostly only consisted of modest adjustments in the discount rate, open market transactions and small changes in the minimum reserve requirements.

Explaining how the Fed conducted monetary policy, Martin stated: 'Our purpose is to lean against the winds of deflation and inflation, whichever they are blowing' (Kettl 1986, 83). And the central bank implemented monetary policy in a discretionary manner, its Chairman not particularly interested in the growth of the money supply (M). (The full debate between monetary rules and discretion was still in its early stages.) Attesting to his compromising nature, Martin felt compelled to—at least partially—finance budget deficits voted by Congress. He also cooperated with the US Treasury by refraining to take any policy measures at those times the Treasury was conducting borrowing operations, known as a policy of 'even keel' which could lead to a delay in necessary monetary adjustments. And the Fed went along with an attempt to keep long-term interest rates low by means of 'operation twist' which entailed purchases by the central bank of long-term Treasury bonds and simultaneous sales of short-term Treasury paper. The results of the operation were disappointing, however. Nonetheless, during much of the 1960s the Fed did not encounter serious policy challenges. The economy was growing at an unusually fast clip (4.4 percent on average), while inflation remained gratifyingly low at an annual average of 2.5 percent during the period 1960 to 1969. Unemployment had also come down, falling to a historical low level of 3.4 percent.

President Kennedy, who entered office in 1961, appointed a team of Keynesian economists as his advisors who believed strongly in the—then rather novel—Phillips curve trade-off. Their main objective was to achieve the lowest possible unemployment rate and in the process accepting a higher rate of inflation. At the same time, a growing number of the members of the Fed's Board of Governors embraced such a stance. The consequence was that the Fed under Martin, although he was in the habit of expressing his concern about burgeoning inflation, was co-opted in an exercise in coordination between the Fed and the Government, with active involvement from time to time by the White House. The process of coordination proved to be detrimental to the Fed's independence as Martin tended to buckle in meetings of the so-named Quadriad which comprised the heads of the Treasury, the Chairman of the President's Council of Economic Advisors, the Fed and sometimes the President himself. In theory, coordination encompassed a 'policy mix' of fiscal and monetary policies; fiscal policy would be directed at the domestic economy and the central bank would deal with the growing American balance of payments deficit. In practice, priority was overwhelmingly accorded to bringing down unemployment and scant attention was paid to the balance of payments. The US policy toward its external sector was dubbed 'benign neglect' to the chagrin of European countries who complained that the outflow of dollars, resulting from a string of balance of payments deficits, led to imported inflation in their countries. In response the surplus countries stepped up their demands for receiving gold for what they considered their excessive US dollars holdings. In time the continuing drain of gold would endanger the stability of the international monetary system.

The thought that the Fed could, with some modest adjustment of short-term interest rates, have a significant effect on the balance of payments was not justified, as the Kennedy administration soon realized. The upshot was that other stronger measures were needed to support the US dollar which had come under pressure as markets began to fear a devaluation of the American currency. In order to stem capital flowing from the United States to Europe, the government resorted to direct controls. It introduced an interest equalization tax of 1 percent on foreign borrowing to make the American capital market more expensive for non-residents and followed up with a 'voluntary restraint program' on bank loans. Since the German authorities on their part had also introduced capital controls (a 30 percent reserve requirement on foreign deposits with German banks and a 25 percent tax on interest payments by German banks to non-residents), capital leaving the United States was reduced for a limited time. However, such actions were blunted when the Bank of England raised its discount rate from 5 to 7 percent to defend the pound in November 1964. The Fed countered with an increase of merely 0.5 percent of the federal funds rate—which it had started to target—but this raise proved to be insufficient to impress markets. Year after year, money continued to flow from the United States to Europe, partly as a result of an interest rate ceiling on deposits held with American commercial banks known as regulation Q, a rule stemming from the Glass-Steagall Act of 1933. Controlling credit creation in such a crude way had become hopelessly outdated, creating distortions in financial markets and contributing to the rapid growth of the Eurodollar market. This market, consisting of US dollar deposits held at European banks by private entities, operated outside the control of central banks, grew rapidly from the 1960s onward. Because of the Fed's regulation Q, American banks with branches or subsidiaries in Europe could pay higher rates on deposits than prevailing in the United States. It would take a long time for Congress to abolish interest rate ceilings on account of misdirected political considerations. At the time, the Fed considered measures to constrain the rapid growth of this offshore market (around 25 percent a year), but could not arrive at a satisfactory solution. Moreover, positions differed on whether the Eurodollar market created (broad) money outside the control of central banks and whether the US balance of payments deficit contributed to this market's growth.

Independence Challenged

The Fed was actively involved with defending its independence in the 1960s. Both Congress and the White House complained from time to time about the level of interest rates and President Johnson veered from suspicion of the Fed and gave Martin the famous 'Johnson treatment' (inviting Martin for a walk or to his ranch to massage the Fed chairman to follow an easier monetary policy) to bouts of conciliation. How much the treatment worked has not been revealed. But Martin was obviously a 'survivor' and would serve 19 years as Fed Chairman. His approach to monetary policy was pragmatic. He had little use for the growth of the money supply in the formulation of monetary policy, although M started to figure as a secondary indicator in the late 1960s, with free reserves of the banks and nominal interest rates serving as the primary tools to gauge the degree of tightness of monetary policy. Increasingly, outsiders and some economists within the Fed criticized the lack of a clear monetary framework guiding the central bank, while the theories of Milton Friedman were gaining in influence. Friedman's emphasis on the importance of the money supply and the need to develop a fixed monetary target while letting the exchange rate float was, however, still considered somewhat outlandish at the Fed. Keynesian economics and policies remained the contemporary approach. Unemployment was above all the primary concern of policymakers and 4 percent was considered to be the desired level. It turned out later that this number was too low from the point of view of keeping inflation from accelerating. Subsequently when the Nixon Administration took over in 1969, unemployment had fallen to 3.4 percent, in itself a harbinger of the persistent inflation to follow in the 1970s.

Disagreement About the Balance of Payments

The US balance of payments troubles mounted during the 1960s, but little was done to address the problem, except for imposition of a number of direct controls that were often circumvented. The Kennedy Administration expressed concern about the situation and worked with the main European countries plus Japan and Canada in the so-called Group of Ten to reform the strained international monetary system. However, the willingness of the Johnson Administration to sacrifice domestic policy objectives to redress the American external imbalance was minimal. The Fed was much more concerned than the US Treasury about the mounting American balance of payments deficit and the increasing expectations of a devaluation of the dollar, but could only delay the problem with a number of piecemeal measures. Charles Coombs, the Fed's point man on markets, regularly badgered the Treasury to allow it to intervene in the foreign exchange market for more than modest amounts (Coombs 1976). But the central bank did make good use of its bilateral swap agreements with other central banks. Such swaps in which a purchase of, say, German currency against dollars is combined with a forward transaction which reverses the German mark purchase in, say, three months have proved to be an effective way of dealing with short-term foreign exchange crises. But if they are indefinitely extended—which no central bank wants to do—can the central bank swaps contribute to longer-term solutions? Crucially, the Fed felt constrained in using its interest rate policy to support the dollar. The result was large conversion of dollars into gold by foreign central banks, leading to an increasing mismatch of the American gold stock and its official dollar liabilities.

A Monetary Awakening

As for the Bank of England, it continued to focus on maintaining orderly markets, mainly by means of open market operations. It also viewed the position of the banking system through the prism of their liquidity ratio (liquid assets as a fraction of total liabilities), traditionally kept at 30 percent as a minimum, on a voluntary basis. These practices were in line with the conclusions of the report of the Radcliffe Committee whose neglect of a clearly articulated monetary policy was to linger well into the 1970s. Essentially the Bank was treading water as the economy received excessive fiscal stimulus and the balance of payments moved increasingly into negative territory. Throughout the 1960s the British economy was hampered by an overvaluation of its currency and the government's inability to address the problem as long as it maintained a fixed exchange rate. At the Bank of England, devaluation of the pound was ruled out because it was considered a breach of the rules under the par value system and floating the pound a leap into the unknown, with possible dire consequences. Moreover, lowering the value of the pound was seen as a loss of prestige and detrimental to the position of London as an international financial center. It would also spell the demise of the sterling area which had been quite beneficial for Britain. And when the Labour Party under Harold Wilson came into power in 1964, it ruled out devaluation as it did not want to be seen as the party of devaluation (the devaluations of 1931 and 1949 had both occurred under a Labour government). Wilson's stance implied that there was no basic disagreement on the need to defend the currency, but the Bank felt that the government was not doing enough to remedy the situation. It considered the government's fiscal policy too much focused on keeping unemployment low (it remained in the range of 1.5 to 2 percent for a long time), yet it had to be careful with making its views public as markets were likely to react by selling pound sterling.

Britain Calls on the IMF

The Bank did what it could to keep markets orderly, which meant frequent large-scale interventions (selling dollars) to keep the pound within the band allowed under the IMF rules. In addition to intervening in the spot market, the central bank was very active in the foreign exchange forward market as a tactic to delay the loss of reserves. Deploying foreign exchange controls and increases in the Bank rate at times of crisis provided only temporary relief. And its use of market psychology was overdone. To some it seemed that 'the Bank was addicted to psychological warfare' (Capie 2010, 1940). The result was that Britain's dollar reserves were generally too small for sustained support of the currency, forcing the central bank to rely regularly on international cooperation to finance recurring balance of payments deficits. The first line of defense consisted of procuring loans from a consortium of other central banks, often arranged through the Bank for International Settlements. Such rescue operations were structured as loans of a limited duration, making it inevitable for Britain to approach the IMF for medium-term financial support.

Domestic Credit Expansion

Working with the IMF on large scale financial support proved to have an important by-product. In its discussions with the British authorities, the Fund, applying the monetary approach to the balance of payments, asked for monetary data. But those numbers were quite scarce given the lack of interest in Britain in developing a comprehensive monetary analysis. Since the IMF wanted to include a condition on monetary policy (besides on fiscal policy) in its loan agreement, the Bank was now forced to delve into monetary theory and develop a statistical basis for tracking money aggregates. It did so successfully with the help of a few bright young macroeconomists. (Up to that point the central bank employed very few trained economists, in contrast to several other sister organizations.) The monetary condition (or performance criterion) agreed upon with the IMF was the rate of domestic credit expansion (DCE), a breakthrough in the annals of the Bank of England. Recognizing that in an open economy such as in the British case, a too rapid extension of credit by the banking system would spill over and produce balance of payments deficits that would eventually become too large to finance, the British authorities developed a modern framework for monetary stability. Since sizable budget deficits (or public sector borrowing requirement in the more precise British definition) were equally responsible for excess demand, the Fund also required strong measures to keep fiscal gaps in check, much to the satisfaction of the central bank which had frequently pointed to the need for restraining government spending. All in all, it took the IMF and the growing influence of Milton Friedman's monetarist views (to be described under monetary theory) to develop a modern approach to monetary policy in Britain.

The System Comes Under Strain

The 1960s was a period of rapid growth and low unemployment for most European countries, still part of a catching-up process after the Second World War. There was therefore little need for an active monetary policy for domestic reasons. As a corollary, monetary instruments were largely the same as before, except that changes in the discount rate had become more of a signaling device. But it was not a tranquil period for central banks in view of the increasing strains in the international monetary system. Hence the obligation to maintain fixed exchange rates against the dollar had again become their main preoccupation. In contrast to the United States and its policy of benign neglect in dealing with its unsustainable balance of payments deficit, the Europeans remained fully committed to the par value system. As it required them to amass large amounts of dollars through market intervention which they could not fully sterilize, they were concerned about the inflationary impact of the dollar glut. The main complaint was that the United States was responsible for imported inflation in their countries, causing a conflict between the internal and external objectives of their policies. In Germany the Bundesbank, supported by its government, wanted to 'discipline' the United States, because it was not prepared to revalue the D mark again, following the experience of 1961. Instead it chose to demand settlement in gold by the United States, as did France, Italy, the Benelux countries and Switzerland (Japan stayed on the sideline), hoping to force the United States to adjust its policies in favor of external adjustment. The Fed and the US Treasury responded by trying to persuade European central banks to stop demanding gold against their surplus dollars. Germany obliged in 1967, but others, particularly France under its gold-obsessed leader Charles de Gaulle—mainly for political reasons—did not fall in line. Toward the end of the 1960s the ratio of American gold to dollars held by foreign central banks had become so lopsided that fears of a dollar devaluation were widespread.

Box 7.1 A Monetary Counterrevolution

Monetary theory was undergoing a radical transformation in the 1960s, Milton Friedman laying the foundation of what came to be known as the *Monetary Counterrevolution*. The name was coined as Friedman's resurrection of the quantity theory of money, in an adjusted form, ran counter to Keynesian economics and its subordination of the role of money. The Chicago professor had already developed the main tenets of his theory in the 1950s, but it was not until the 1960s that his line of thinking gained considerable support. Friedman rejected Keynesian macroeconomic analysis, placing the role of money at the center of his economic analysis. His book *A Monetary History of the United States, 1867–1960*, co-written with Anna Schwartz (Friedman and Schwartz 1963), as well as Friedman's 1967 American Economic Association lecture on monetary policy (Friedman 1968) became highly influential. On the basis of his analysis of economic history, Friedman claimed that the main cause of the Great Depression was a defective application of monetary policy by the Federal Reserve in the 1930s, especially by allowing the money supply to contract at a time a rapid expansion was needed. This widely accepted conclusion triggered a defining debate on the role and nature of monetary policy and interest rates in mature economies. On the one side, the Keynesian camp remained convinced that fiscal policy was the main tool to ensure adequate demand and sustained economic growth. On the other side, the Friedman camp emphasized the dominant importance of money in the functioning of an economy. The latter approach, known as *monetarism*, not only counted many adherents among academics, but it also brought about important changes in the conduct of monetary policy at various central banks in the 1970s, as described in Chap. 9.

Monetarism constituted a resurrection of the quantity theory of money adjusted to modern conditions. Monetarists consider the Phillips curve to be (largely) irrelevant, focusing mostly on the long run in which any disturbance in the economy would ultimately be neutralized, whereas Keynesian analysis is mainly concerned with the short run. Monetarists' central tenet is the need for neutral money, a state of equilibrium when the money supply has neither a deflationary

(*continued*)

Box 7.1 (continued)

nor an inflationary effect on the economy. They postulate that output, or real GDP, is mainly determined by the growth of the money supply in the short run and by changes in the level of prices in the long run (a period not explicitly defined). Changes in the growth rate of M do not affect prices in the short run since wages and prices tend to be rigid, or 'sticky,' reacting to a tightening or easing of monetary policy with a lag (mostly between 9 and 12 months). Therefore monetary neutrality exists only in the long run, whereas in the short run changes in the money supply affect real output and employment temporarily and are therefore non-neutral. An important element of monetarist analysis is that the velocity of circulation of money (V) is assumed to be stable and predictable. A stable V does not mean that it is a constant, but as long as velocity is predictable it can be incorporated in the determination of the optimal change in the money supply. Also, but often not mentioned explicitly, monetarism is largely predicated on the existence of flexible exchange rates which render monetary policy free to pursue domestic objectives.

The main policy recommendation that follows from the monetarist approach is the introduction of a target for the growth of the money supply. Decisions regarding a monetary target are generally based on a number for an annual increase of the money supply corresponding with an increase in (expected) real output and an acceptable rate of inflation, for instance an annual increase in real GDP of 3 percent and of 2 percent inflation, making for a target for M of 5 percent annual growth. Initially most monetarists assumed that a zero rate of inflation was optimal, but this position was later abandoned as it would on average entail changes in M too close to bringing about price deflation (the question of an appropriate inflation target is discussed in Chap. 9).

Another element in setting the target for M is to take into account possible changes in velocity over the medium-term when V shows a trend-like development, but in practice this was seldom made explicit. Assuming that V was not an issue, in Friedman's view central banks should rigidly stick to their money supply target, to be set at an annual or monthly horizon. Such an approach implies that monetary policy is placed on auto pilot with central banks unable to

(*continued*)

Box 7.1 (continued)
make discretionary decisions based on changing circumstances. To maintain the fixed growth path of M, short-term interest rates have to be frequently adjusted to ensure compliance with the rule. The implication for central banks under such a strict regime is a significant loss of independence. With this side effect in mind, a lively debate was triggered between a rules based monetary policy and one based on discretion. Over time both approaches were reflected in policies pursued by monetary authorities.

Box 7.2 The Monetary Trilemma
Experience with conflicting policy objectives led to the insight that it is not possible to simultaneously achieve three monetary objectives: a flexible exchange rate, an autonomous monetary policy and the free movement of capital across borders (Fig. 7.1). The incompatibility of these three strands of policy, generally known as the *monetary trilemma* or the *impossible trinity*, was demonstrated by the Canadian economist and future winner of the Nobel Prize in economics, Robert Mundell (1963), and Marcus Fleming (1962), a British national, when both were working at the Research Department

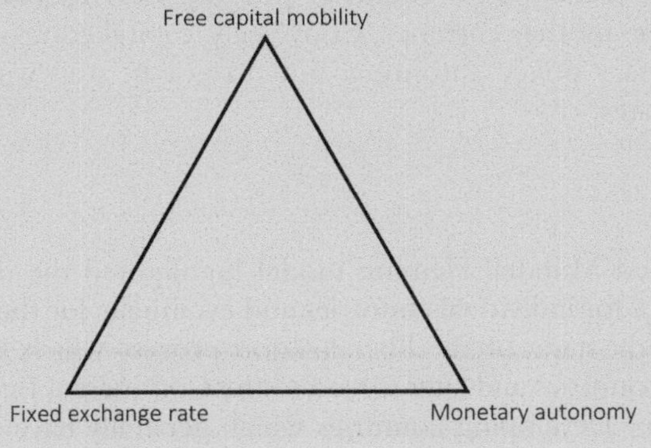

Fig. 7.1 The monetary trilemma

(*continued*)

Box 7.2 (continued)

of the International Monetary Fund in the early 1960s. Central banks and treasuries had in the heyday of the gold standard already grasped the existence of a conflict between a fixed exchange rate and monetary policy directed predominantly at domestic objectives. As explained in Chap. 3, this tension was a major cause of the breakdown of the gold standard in the 1930s. But since capital controls were extensively applied in the early days of the Bretton Woods system of fixed but adjustable exchange rates, they did not play a significant role in the choice of monetary regimes. And the Articles of Agreement of the IMF, which emphasized the need to abandon trade and payments restrictions, did not mention the liberalization of capital movements among its objectives. However, based on the premise that similar to the long-held principle that freedom of international trade contributes to a better allocation of resources and higher economic growth, freeing up capital movements would contribute to a better distribution of investible resources in the world economy. Hence, capital account liberalization among developed countries became a priority objective from the late 1950s onward. It would also lead to full convertibility among national currencies as was the case under the pre-war gold standard. As the momentum of greater capital mobility increased, capital control measures were more often taken into account when deciding on monetary regimes. Lifting capital flows can be compatible with floating exchange rates, but poses a challenge for countries pegging their exchange rate to the dollar or another currency. Conversely, capital controls can support monetary policy autonomy but do not fit well with floating exchange rates.

The so-called Mundell-Fleming model highlighted the importance of capital mobility for individual countries and eventually for the global economy, at an early stage of the liberalization process which started in the Anglo Saxon countries and later spread to the Continental European countries and Japan. Developing countries which generally have 'thin' foreign exchange markets in which they sometimes intervene heavily were less inclined to open up their economies in the financial sphere. While policymakers and academics found (and still find) the monetary trilemma a useful analytical tool, it is seldom found in its purest form, many countries adding a third—theoretically incompatible—element to its policy arsenal. For instance, the authorities of an economy with a floating currency and monetary policy autonomy may sometimes adopt capital controls, especially with respect to short-term assets, when their country is prone to sudden, large in- or outflows of capital. Such a 'mixed' system has been frequently applied in Asian and Latin American countries.

References

Capie, Forrest: *The Bank of England 1950s to 1979*, Cambridge University Press, 2010.

Coombs, Charles: *The Arena of International Finance*, John Wiley and Sons, New York, 1976.

Fleming, Marcus: "Domestic Financial Policies under fixed and Flexible Exchange Rates", International Monetary Fund, *Staff Papers*, no 9, 1962, 363–399.

Friedman, Milton and Anna Jacobson Schwartz: *A Monetary History of the United States 1867-1960*, National Bureau of Economic Research, Princeton University Press, Princeton NJ, 1963.

Friedman, Milton: "The Role of Monetary Policy", presidential *Address*, American Economic Association, January, 1968.

Kettl, Donald: *Leadership at the Fed*, Yale University Press, New Haven and New York, 1986.

Mundell, Robert: "Capital Mobility and Stabilization Policy", *Canadian Journal of Economic Policy Series*, 29, 1963, 475–485.

CHAPTER 8

Overcoming the Great Inflation: 1970–1983

The international monetary system based on fixed but adjustable exchange rates lasted for a period of 25 years, coming to an end in 1971. As the world economy was changing, following the initial post-war period during which the system worked well, fault lines began to appear in the 1960s. The de facto gold/dollar standard came under increasing pressure as the US balance of payments swung from a surplus to a deficit while Europe and Japan ran ever larger surpluses, accumulating sizable dollar reserves in the process. The surplus countries complained that the United States, which could finance its external deficit with its own currency, was flooding the world with dollars, thereby causing 'imported' inflation elsewhere. When the United States halted the conversion of dollars into gold in August 1971, a whole new monetary order came into being after futile attempts to restore the Bretton Woods system ceased in 1974. The world monetary landscape had now by default morphed into a system of floating exchange rates with little oversight and therefore often was dubbed a 'non-system.'

But all was not chaos and two major and one minor currency blocs emerged, the by far largest being the US dollar zone. At the same time Western European countries, which had been striving for greater integration of their economies and concerned about the damage that could be done to their internal trade by large exchange rate fluctuations, decided to erect a European currency bloc with fixed rates among its members. A third, much smaller, bloc was represented by the sterling area which would

O. de Beaufort Wijnholds, *The Money Masters*,
https://doi.org/10.1007/978-3-030-40041-5_8

in the course of the 1970s be greatly reduced. Japan allowed the yen to float on its own, closely monitoring the course of the dollar. And Canada, after a period of pegging to the US dollar, also opted to float on its own. The Soviet Union and (mainland) China, which had remained outside the Bretton Woods system, continued to strictly control their currencies, while many smaller countries closely tracked or monitored the dollar and intervened regularly in the foreign exchange market, not prepared to have their exchange rates fluctuate wildly.

As a result of this major break with the past, many central banks experienced a new and high degree of freedom in the 1970s to conduct monetary policy focused on domestic objectives. And since economic growth had generally been strong in the 1960s and inflation recognized as a growing problem, their focus shifted toward dampening increases in the price level. The inflation threat was amplified when energy prices quadrupled following bold action by the oil exporters' cartel (OPEC) in late 1973. But since the new inflation shock was the result of cost push rather than demand pull factors, policymakers differed in their approach to the new challenge. Some central banks, while recognizing that the steep rise in oil prices was akin to a tax increase, felt duty bound to face inflation head-on, also in view of the risk of second-round effects in the guise of increased wage demands, in turn followed by a further jump in inflation. The German Bundesbank unapologetically followed this course. Other central banks, especially those whose independence from their governments was limited, preferred to react at a more measured pace, wishing to avoid a deep recession—the United Kingdom and Italy being prime examples. But the slow adjusters allowed inflation to get out of hand, paying the price in lower growth and exchange rate crises.

Germany: Pragmatic Monetarism

Restoring the importance of money in formulating economic policies in the 1960s was foremost an academic movement led by Milton Friedman. Central banks were at the time, as described in Chap. 7, paying increasing attention to the money supply as an indicator of economic conditions, but had not advanced to the stage where targets for the growth of the money supply became the lodestar of monetary policy. The German Bundesbank, which had always shown a strong conviction that economic conditions benefitted greatly from a stable monetary environment, was first in adopting a regime of money targeting. Having chafed against the exchange rate constraint and reluctant to revalue the D mark under the Bretton Woods system, the German Central Bank was free after 1973 to forcefully pursue its anti-inflation stance. Convinced that the quantity theory of money formed the best theoretical foundation, it chose to aim at controlling the money supply and keep its growth within announced limits. Though inspired by the work of Friedman and others, the Bundesbank's monetary framework introduced in 1975 differed from the theoretical model in that it was not intended as a rigid single number rule, but a relatively flexible guide aimed at anchoring inflation through expectations. It rested on two pillars: control of the money supply and managing expectations of the social partners and the public by means of clearly announcing its numerical targets. The latter introduced an important element in the conduct of monetary policy and focused mainly on influencing wage negotiations so as to avoid a spiral of wage and price increases. By announcing numerical monetary targets, the Bundesbank signaled to labor unions and employers' associations what they could expect with respect to inflation and economic growth in the medium term so as to supply a basis for their wage negotiations, which in Germany were mostly a collective undertaking.

Adopting a Target

In 1973, in a preliminary step, the German central bank adopted (but did not announce) the central bank money stock as its main policy indicator, and when it announced the new formal framework in December 1974, expressed its target using the same concept, which it was to maintain unaltered until 1988. Acknowledging that M1 (currency in circulation and demand deposits) alone represented an insufficient measure of liquidity available on more or less short notice and without loss in nominal value, the central bank money stock also included time deposits with a maturity up to four years as well as savings deposits and savings bonds with a maturity of less than four years. (In order to reflect their lesser degree of liquidity, time and savings deposits were weighted on the basis of their respective reserve requirement ratios.) In 1988 the definition was altered by dropping the weighting and calling the slightly revised concept M3. The inclusion of such secondary liquidities, or near money, was reminiscent of the definition of money applied by the Netherlands Bank in earlier decades.

In picking a target number for annual increases in the money supply, the Bundesbank went back to the Irving Fisher equation, taking as its point of departure that the sum of an increase in real output and of the price level equals the sum of growth of the money supply and of money velocity. In practical terms the central bank arrived at a number for the monetary target by an estimation of the long-run potential output growth plus the inflation rate it considered unavoidable. And any estimated structural increases in velocity (usually small) were subtracted from that number, but were largely ignored by the financial sector and wage negotiators. In its first announcement of a target for the growth of central bank money—8 percent for 1975 as a whole—the Bundesbank stated that the number chosen reflected the requisite scope for the desired rate of economic growth while attempting to avoid renewed inflationary pressures (following the oil price shock of 1973) on account of monetary developments. To add to the acceptance of the new approach, it mentioned that the Federal Government was in full agreement with the central bank's initiative.

Medium-Term Orientation

It was considered of great importance that in deriving the target number, estimated *potential* output growth figured in the calculation instead of expected real output growth based on forecasts for the next year, underlining the Bundesbank's philosophy of refraining from stimulating the economy in the short run. In that vein the level of unemployment did not figure under this approach. What counted was a medium-term orientation suitable for anchoring inflation expectations. Over time the concept of 'unavoidable' price increases caused some confusion, and from 1984 onward, the Bundesbank simply assumed a medium-term level of inflation of 2 percent, a number to be widely adopted by other central banks in future decades. Testifying to its flexible stance on monetary policy, the central bank did not attempt to redress previous overshooting of the monetary target, but simply started a new annual exercise at the level of money supply at the end of the year. After expressing the target as a point number until 1978, it moved to a target zone allowing some leeway for temporary influences on the economy. The results of this policy of *pragmatic monetarism* were impressive, even though the money supply target was missed with some frequency. During the first four years, with the target set at 8 percent each time and despite some overshooting every year, inflation came down from almost 6 percent to 2.7 percent. Between 1979 and 1985, annual targets were lowered from a range of 6 to 9 percent to 3 to 5 percent and were met each time. But the inflation scorecard was mixed, reaching a peak of 6.3 percent in 1981, then falling to 2 percent (in accordance with the rate of 'unavoidable' price increases) in 1985. In the remainder of the 1980s, although the target (with a midpoint of 5 percent) was missed thrice and met only once, anchoring of expectations had clearly been established with inflation fluctuating between zero and 2.8 percent This performance was superior to that of other advanced countries, while German economic growth remained satisfactory, except for the recessions of 1974–75 and 1981–82 (following the second oil crisis.) Over the years the German approach to monetary policy remained remarkably consistent and was maintained until 1998 when the Bundesbank was subsumed under the European Central Bank.

Having studied the Bundesbank experience thoroughly, Adam Posen, an academic who has served as a member of the Monetary Policy Committee of the Bank of England, drew an important lesson from the relative success of the BuBa's policy. He concluded that 'transparency in the form of communication about a publicly defined numerical goal is the key to anchoring expectations. And when it comes to communication more is more.' By regularly explaining its policy to the public at large and not only to market participants, the German Central Bank cemented its credibility (Posen 1997). The importance of clear and frequent communication is nowadays widely recognized, as related in Chaps. 12 and 14.

American Price Explosion

After the Second World War, on account of its vast economy and deep financial markets, the United States was the only country that could finance its balance of payments deficits using its own currency, US dollar claims being the only monetary asset that foreign central banks were prepared to hold besides gold. This special position—which had developed spontaneously—allowed the United States to pay scant attention to its external position most of the time. Its stance toward the string of balance of payments deficits it incurred was to give it a low priority, dubbing it a policy of 'benign neglect.' As Paul Volcker wrote years later, 'Presidents – certainly not Johnson and Nixon – did not want to hear that their options were limited because of the weakness of the dollar' (Volcker and Gyohten 1992). And when the pressure on its gold stock became too severe, the United States broke the link of the dollar to gold in 1971. The American currency was officially devalued in the same year and again in 1973, while surplus countries (Germany and Japan and smaller countries like the Netherlands) agreed to revalue their currencies. But these actions were too little and too late to save the par value system. With the dollar freely floating against other currencies, the Federal Reserve, which was not involved in the decision-making on the exchange rate regime anyway, could now direct its attention fully to its domestic objectives. With inflation starting to pick up around the turn of the 1960s, this would seem to hold down the increase of the general price level. However, at best the central bank's efforts to do so were halfhearted. As Meltzer (2009, 843) observed: 'The years 1973 to 1979 were the least successful period for postwar Federal Reserve policy.'

After Arthur Burns took over as Chairman of the Fed, he demonstrated a limited belief in the efficacy of monetary policy. In his view wage and price controls were a better option to call inflation to a halt. President Nixon was dead against imposing such controls, but was intent on having accommodative monetary policy pave the way to his reelection. As Burns wrote in his diary: 'The president will do anything to get reelected' (Burns 2010). In practice, Burns followed an eclectic approach, implicitly paying heed to the short-term trade-off between unemployment and inflation. And despite his frequent warnings about the dangers of inflation, his policy decisions fell short of what was required to dampen inflation. As a result of political pressure, including from Congress, faulty economics, and the oil price shock of 1973, inflation accelerated from an annual rate of 3.6 percent in early 1973 to a shocking 10.7 percent in mid-1979. Burns was unlucky in the sense that higher energy prices acted as a large tax increase pushing up both the price level and the rate of unemployment as a steep recession materialized in 1974. The unusual combination of higher inflation and joblessness became known as *stagflation*, a new phenomenon that could not be explained in terms of the Phillips curve. While not wishing to implement monetary tightening during a developing recession was understandable, the Fed was too willing to ignore the evidence that accelerating inflation was already underway and becoming ingrained in the expectations of the public.

Price and Wage Controls

Burns suggested implementing price and wage controls as a means of dampening rising prices, an interventionist idea that went against the grain of mainstream economics and the philosophy of the administration. The attraction for Burns was that controls would enable the Fed to refrain from raising interest rates, never popular with politicians and the public. Eventually Nixon, who felt that something had to be done to lower inflation, as public dissatisfaction with soaring prices, particularly for food and energy was growing fast, made a U-turn, going along with direct controls. The decision turned out to be hugely mistaken as inflationary pressures were building up

Table 8.1 Consumer price inflation (%)

	1977–80	*1979*	*1980*
United States	9.9	12.5	11.7
Japan	5.1	5.5	6.8
Germany	4.1	5.2	5.3
Netherlands	5.0	4.7	6.5
Canada	9.3	9.3	10.6
France	10.5	11.2	12.8
Italy	15.2	17.2	19.4
United Kingdom	12.4	15.9	14.1

Source: International Monetary Fund

while controls were in force, and once lifted, pent-up demand pushed up prices dramatically. By then an inflation psychology had taken hold among the public which had become convinced that the authorities were unable and unwilling to do much about rising prices. The Great Inflation was underway in the United States but would also hold sway in many other countries in the world as illustrated in Table 8.1. Only in Germany, the Netherlands and Japan inflation did not reach double digits between 1977 and 1980. It would take severe disinflationary measures in other countries during the 1980s to tame what was becoming runaway inflation.

There were periods when the Fed did increase interest rates to bring down growth of the money supply within non-binding targets, but unlike in Germany, these spells of tightening generally lasted only briefly as monetary policy reacted to short-term developments. While the Fed had started to take a stronger interest in changes in the money supply in the early 1970s, it was opposed to announcing money supply targets. While it formally adopted targets for liquid reserves of the banks, it did so in a narrow band of short-term interest rates. Like his predecessor, McChesney Martin, Burns took the view that he had to finance the governments' budget deficits as they resulted from congressional action. Despite regularly warning against inflation, he went along with the political priority of keeping unemployment low, even if it led to higher inflation. And as it turned out, the end result was that both prices and joblessness increased, in contrast to what the Phillips curve would predict. By going along with the president's wishes the Fed allowed inflation to become entrenched, so that when, after Nixon had resigned, the central bank took more forceful action, it was too late to halt the Great Inflation.

The Fed Chairman had an easier time under the Ford administration, but after a brief spell of trying to slow inflation, monetary policy was eased when the recession of 1974 and 1975 struck. During the economic malaise which characterized the term of President Jimmy Carter, rising unemployment and high inflation continued unabated. Under these conditions the Fed kept a low profile, caught in the dilemma of unattractive policy choices. At this stage America's poor economic performance, as well as the European perception that US Treasury Secretary Blumenthal was 'talking down the dollar,' (Solomon 1982, 345) eroded confidence in the world's largest economy. When the dollar exchange rate went into a nosedive in 1977, a strong support package was put together which included a sizable increase in the swap arrangements that the Federal Reserve had concluded with other central banks and which helped to temporarily restore a degree of confidence. At that juncture the Fed faced an agonizing problem. It had for many years advocated stronger medicine to defend the dollar, especially much larger purchases of its own currency with its foreign exchange holdings. But since the treasury determined exchange rate policy, the central bank's exhortations had little impact.

Independence Challenged Again

A significant increase in congressional attempts to reduce the Fed's independence occurred during the 1970s. Chairman Burns had to testify regularly before a critical House and Senate who were not impressed by his track record. After several years of discussion and a raft of proposed legislation, the Full Employment and Balanced Growth Act, better known as the *Humphrey-Hawkins Act* was signed into law by President Carter in 1978. A law inspired by Keynesian economics, it emphasized the importance of full employment in making economic policy, going further than the Employment Act of 1946. Its implications for the Federal Reserve's policies were of great importance. Contrary to the Act of 1913 establishing the Fed, the central bank's mandate was spelled out, requiring it 'to establish a monetary policy that maintains long-term growth, minimizes inflation, and promotes price stability.' The Fed had now been given a dual mandate to guide its policies. Most other central banks had a single mandate, namely price stability, with no mention of economic growth or unemployment (the general question of central bank mandates is discussed in Chap. 9). Furthermore, the central bank was to present a written report on its monetary policy to Congress twice a year and required the Chairman of the Fed to connect its monetary policy with the Presidential economic policy. And to add to the overreach, the Act specified a goal for unemployment of 3 percent for adults and not higher than 4 percent for inflation, which also had to be brought down to zero per cent by 1989. However, these objectives were not set in stone and could be revised by Congress over time. Quite a few insiders and academics doubted that the promulgated goals were compatible. It was also clear to many observers that a level of 3 percent unemployment was lower than what could be considered a natural rate (a level of joblessness at which inflation was low and not accelerating) at the time. It certainly was a stretch to push inflation down to zero which also would not seem desirable. It would take another 36 years before the Fed announced that its inflation target was 2 percent, although the number was not a surprise.

The United States: Reluctant Monetarism

Having been relieved of the exchange rate constraint after 1973, the American central bank did not embrace monetarism as its guiding principle, although it did monitor growth of the money supply as one among a number of indicators. It focused mainly on short-term interest rates which it steered through open market interventions. At meetings of the FOMC, decisions on the desirable level of the federal funds rate tended to result in small adjustments, usually a quarter or an eighth of a per cent during the first half of the 1970s. Monetary policy in the United States lacked a clear framework and a longer term vision. It also remained beholden to the traditional Phillips curve analysis and tended to be more concerned about the level of unemployment than of inflation.

Skeptical about monetarism à la Friedman, it took congressional action to get the Fed to pay more attention to monetary developments. At first the Fed refused to inform Congress about the central bank's views concerning the expected growth of the money supply, arguing that M1 was not a good indicator because velocity was not stable. But soon Chairman Burns reversed course, publicly announcing targets for M1 for 1975–76. This practice became embedded when Congress passed the *Federal Reserve Reform Act* of 1977. It required the central bank to report on its planned rate of money growth. The Fed responded by announcing targets for annual growth of M1, M2 and M3 as well as for the bank credit proxy (total deposits) and revised the numbers every quarter. Publishing so many targets and revising them frequently was often viewed as an intentional smokescreen. And since new targets started from the level of the actual outcomes, irrespective of overshooting or undershooting, the ensuing base drift further complicated the interpretation of the numbers. The upshot was that Congress, which had earlier passed the *Government in Sunshine Act*, had achieved greater transparency at the central bank but not much actual clarity. Moreover, confidence in the Federal Reserve was seriously eroded when price increases did not slow down during the second half of the 1970s, the great inflation continuing unabated. Short-termism and a reluctance to allow substantial fluctuations in interest rates, as well as a preoccupation with the stubbornly high level of unemployment, doomed the first five years of the monetarist experiment from the start. Monetary targeting by the Fed was maintained until 1984, but only applied with conviction during Paul Volcker's tenure as Chairman of the central bank from 1979 on.

Britain on the Brink

In parallel with the dismal performance of the American economy in the 1970s, it was 'the worst decade of the century in British monetary, financial and macroeconomic history' (Capie 2010, 483). The problems were manifold: excessive monetary expansion, especially in the early 1970s; the energy crisis of 1973–74; frequent strikes followed by unsustainable wage increases; fiscal laxity; a severe currency crisis in 1976 and rampant inflation at a rate exceeding that of most other advanced economies. The Bank of England faced a very difficult situation, its influence on these various factors being quite limited. While its monetary policy ought to have been stricter, the central bank was hamstrung by insufficient independence from the government. The Bank also struggled with the development of a more relevant monetary framework in line with the agnostic legacy of the Radcliffe Committee. But change was in the air and while monetarism was eyed with suspicion by the monetary authorities, outside pressure facilitated a move toward monetary targeting.

While targeting the money supply at the American central bank lacked the commitment and medium-term orientation necessary to influence expectations as practiced by the German Bundesbank, the same reluctance with respect to adopting rules for the growth of the money supply prevailed at the Bank of England. Having come somewhat late to the view that money does indeed matter, the British central bank—whose ranks had been strengthened with highly qualified young economists—gave serious thought to a framework for monetary policy. The process of conversion to a more monetarist stance was enhanced by contacts with the IMF staff who were interested in reliable monetary statistics, similar to the Fund's insistence on data on domestic credit expansion in Britain in the mid-1960s.

Choosing a Target

The Bank of England, while still following the agnostic approach to the relevance of the money supply during the 1960s, started to examine the usefulness of monetary aggregates in setting monetary policy in 1970 in what Capie has described as a 'watershed' in thinking at the Bank of England (Capie 2010, 444). Charles Goodhart, a former academic, wrote an influential article in the Bank's *Quarterly Bulletin* titled 'The Importance of Money' (Goodhart 1970). Subsequently a wide-ranging discussion within the Bank of England and with the UK Treasury was set in motion. It encompassed the usefulness of monetary targets, their modalities, definitions of money, operational techniques, effects on interest rates, the market for government securities and the influence of government deficits on money creation. Given the many factors to be taken into consideration, progress was slow in reaching some kind of consensus on how to proceed. Monetary aggregates were developed but did not play a central role in setting policy until October 1976 when a goal for monetary growth of 9 to 13 percent for 1976–77 was announced. When soon afterward Britain suffered another severe attack on the pound, the IMF was again called in and the emphasis shifted to domestic credit expansion as the central monetary variable. A ballooning balance of payments deficit made it necessary to curb lending by banks. The IMF also insisted on cutting government spending, much to the satisfaction of the Bank which had on several occasions warned the government that a large public sector borrowing requirement (PSBR) swelled the money supply. This position flowed from the counterpart analysis of money growth which highlighted the role of budget deficits not financed in the capital market as a cause of money creation.

Monetary targets were initially, after much deliberation, set as a range of the rate of growth of M3, after having also experimented with Mo (base money), M1 and sterling M3 as the relevant measure to target. Changing definitions was the result of perceived shifts in the demand for money equations. In other countries practicing monetary targeting, such as Switzerland, the chosen monetary variable was usually adjusted less frequently (Table 8.2).

Besides discussions on monetary targets, a comprehensive effort was made within the Bank of England to develop effective operational tools to control money and credit. An incomes policy (price and wage controls), introduced by the government in an attempt to dampen inflation, was not a success. It was therefore up to the central bank to find ways to control credit expansion and thereby lower growth of M and ultimately inflation.

Table 8.2 Definitions of money

Mo	Base money, comprising currency (notes and coins) in circulation plus commercial banks' deposits with central banks.
M1	Narrow money, comprising currency in circulation plus demand deposits held at banks.
M2	Broad money, comprising M1 plus time deposits (certificates of deposits) held at banks plus non-bank foreign currency demand deposits held at domestic banks.
M3	Broad money plus, comprising M2 plus money market deposits plus longer term time deposits plus savings accounts.
Sterling M3	(UK only) Comprising M3 minus non-bank foreign currency deposits with domestic banks.
M4	Very broad money, comprising M3 plus various semi liquid money market instruments.
Divisia M4	Comprises 'regular' M4 with components weighted according to their degree of liquidity.

Concluding that the long applied reserve to assets ratio of the banks of 12.5 percent had been ineffective, various other approaches were tried. Although some initial success was achieved, special deposits required from banks when credit was seen as expanding too quickly proved to be insufficiently effective. To strengthen the impact of such deposits, the Bank from time to time called for supplementary deposits (SSD), popularly referred as the *corset*. But by 1979 the central bank decided that the corset was not all that good a fit and abandoned it. Another innovation aimed at making interest rates more flexible was establishing a Bank of England minimum lending rate (MLR) derived from market rates, while maintaining Bank rate which was adjusted less frequently. The main attraction of MLR was that it could be adjusted without formal approval of the Chancellor (minister of finance), unlike changes in the Bank rate. A few years later, following pressure from the UK Treasury, MLR was 'administrated,' that is no longer set by the Bank on its own. It was abandoned in 1979. In the end open market transactions came to be relied on again as the preferred operational tool.

The Great Inflation Ended

The turning point in the inflationary process coincided with two major events in 1979: the appointment of Paul Volcker as Chairman of the Fed and the coming into power of Margaret Thatcher in the United Kingdom in the same year. In the United States, President Carter was at his wits' end on how to deal with runaway inflation—prices were rising at an annual rate of 13 percent—and how to restore confidence in the American economy and the dollar. He picked Volcker, then President of the Federal Reserve Bank of New York, known as a forceful and decisive person who was committed to controlling inflation, to head the central bank. Volcker realized that drastic action was needed to fulfil the task at hand. Huddling with his advisors he hatched a plan to make monetary policy effective, resulting in a new approach to monetary control which he unveiled on October 1979. The conservative new British Prime Minister was equally determined to rid her country of increases in prices averaging around 15 percent in the late 1970s. But unlike in the United States, Mrs. Thatcher did not rely on her central bank, which she was not prepared to grant more independence, to take the actual monetary policy measures to bring down inflation drastically. Instead she relied on her economic advisor, Alan Walters, an academic and ardent monetarist who clashed regularly with the Chancellor, Nigel Lawson. But Lawson nevertheless wrote in an obituary that: 'For all his faults, Walters had the great strength that he was prepared to argue with Ms. Thatcher on issues when he was convinced that she was mistaken' (Lawson 2009).

Volcker Takes Charge

As Chairman of the Fed, Volcker, a pragmatist devoid of ideological adherence to a particular economic philosophy and with a deep knowledge of financial markets, introduced a form of shock therapy (although he did not call it that) to break the prevalent inflationary psychology. And in order to change expectations, interest rates would have to be raised to very high levels which would lead to recession and hence encounter strong political and public resistance. Factually this approach implied the existence in the short run of the Phillips curve, despite the chairman's denial, although he did emphasize that a stricter control of the money supply would bring down both inflation and unemployment in the longer run. But how to make much higher interest rates palatable? Volcker addressed the problem by emphasizing the importance of control of the money supply by means of strictly adhering to monetary targets and not continuing the previous half-hearted approach to targeting.

To achieve better monetary results a change in the central banks' operational procedures was introduced. Instead of relying on changes in interest rates, it shifted its focus to changes in the level of reserves held by the commercial banks with the Fed. More precisely, the Fed would henceforth conduct its monetary operations by controlling the *non-borrowed* part of the banks' reserves held at the central bank. Volcker announced that larger fluctuations in the federal funds rate could therefore be expected, explaining that in order to meet their official minimum reserve requirements, the banks had to borrow from the Fed through the discount window for which it applied a surcharge of 3 percent for large banks. In addition, Congress passed the *Monetary Control Act* in March 1980, providing additional powers to the central bank by making non-member banks and non-bank financial institutions subject to reserve requirements of the System. The full import of these changes was often not fully understood and met with considerable skepticism.

The most positive reaction came from Europe which welcomed higher rates as they would raise the severely depreciated dollar exchange rate. As a result of squeezing bank reserves, the Fed allowed nominal short-term interest rates to rise to unheard of heights, peaking at 21 percent and with ten-year government bonds reaching a yield of 14 percent. Despite the uproar such high rates (which were considerably lower in real terms) caused, the Fed defended its policy with reference to its operational procedures, stuck to its guns, bringing down the federal funds rate only when signs of disinflation started to appear in the course of 1981. Two years later, the battle against inflation in the United States was won as prices rose only 4 percent in 1983. Not fully understood at the time, Volcker's 1979 'reform' of monetary policy by cleverly shifting the focus from interest rates to monetary targets had strong political overtones as changes in interest rates could be presented as the unfortunate but necessary by-product of keeping the money supply in check. Alan Greenspan, who succeeded Volcker as Fed Chairman in 1987, described Volcker's policy maneuver as 'arguably the most important change in economic policy in fifty years,' by urging the FOMC to 'no longer try to fine-tune the economy by focusing on short-term interest rates,' but to 'clamp down on the amount of money available to the economy.' And that it 'took exceptional courage' for him to push America into the brutal recession of the early 1980s' (Greenspan 2007, 85).

British Disinflation

In Britain a similar process of disinflation accompanied by recession took place in the early 1980s. The incoming Conservative Government led by Margaret Thatcher presented an ambitious program of deep-seated economic reform aimed at achieving financial stability by bringing down both inflation and the fiscal deficit. This *Medium Term Financial Strategy* was to last four years during which important progress in structural reform was to be made. Ancillary aims were privatization of state-owned enterprises, deregulation and reducing the power of the trade unions. As to the monetary pillar of the strategy, the Bank of England engineered a liquidity squeeze which pushed up interest rates to high levels, wringing out inflation at the cost of recession. But this was a price the Thatcher Government was prepared to pay, despite severe labor unrest, in the interest of a fundamental improvement in the performance of the British economy. It succeeded breaking the back of inflation, which had ranged between 10 percent and 25 percent in the 1970s, reducing it to 5 percent in 1983. Economic growth returned after 1982 to higher levels than during most of the post-war era, ending Great Britain's lagging behind in the European context. Contrary to the experience in Germany and the United States, whose central banks took the initiative to tighten monetary policy and sustain modest growth of the targeted monetary aggregates, the Bank of England followed instructions of the UK Treasury, functioning as its executive arm. It did, however, not only play a purely operational role, but also advised the UK Treasury on the modalities of monetary policies such as the choice of monetary targets. But having to play a subordinate role with respect to the formulation of what is generally considered to be the main task of a central bank was a source of disaffection to those within the Bank of England who felt that their skills were superior to those of their counterparts at the treasury. It would take until 1997 before the independence of the Bank of England was greatly strengthened.

Other Advanced Economies

The Great Inflation also came to an end in other advanced economies, the most successful being Japan which succeeded in reducing inflation from above 20 percent in the early 1970s to a mere 2 percent in 1983. Strong guidance by the government in bank lending was a major factor in achieving this result, the Bank of Japan also acting mainly as an executive agency of the treasury. It took considerably longer in France and Italy to achieve lower levels of price increases and these remained above those of other industrial countries. By contrast, smaller European countries such as the Netherlands and Switzerland, whose central banks enjoyed a high degree of independence, were able to achieve inflation rates by and large as low as those in Germany. Good performances were also achieved in Australia,

Canada and New Zealand among others. The way was now open for a large part of the world economy to operate in an environment of low inflation accompanied by satisfactory growth rates. Thus began the period now known as the Great Moderation which would last for a quarter of a century.

Box 8.1 Monetary Theory: Keynesians Versus Monetarists

The Great Inflation of the late 1960s and the 1970s spawned a lively academic debate between Keynesians and Monetarists. As described in Chap. 7, Milton Friedman initiated a monetary counterrevolution which enjoyed widespread support in the 1970s. Chicago University Professor Robert Lucas became the most prominent opponent of Keynesian macroeconomics and its subordination of the role of money. He emphasized the importance of the microeconomic foundations of macroeconomics and posited that relationships that were generally believed to hold in an economy, such as between inflation and unemployment, could unravel in response to changes in economic policies. In what came to be known as the influential *Lucas critique*, he also argued that Keynesian economic models neglected the role of expectations in the decision-making of economic agents. Moreover, what was relevant was not just adaptive expectations, based on past observations of variables such as inflation, but *rational expectations* which were based on all available information. While economic agents could misjudge future inflation they would not do so systematically, but learn from their mistakes and on average draw the right conclusions over time. The main implication is that in reaching decisions on such central variables as real wages, negotiations between workers and firms are largely based on rational expectations concerning future inflation (Lucas 1972). Lucas' contribution to monetary theory is widely regarded as representing a neo-classical approach. In other contributions, Lucas averred that not only was there no Phillips curve trade-off in the long run, but that such a trade-off did not exist in the short run either, a view that was to be refuted in later years. It was also shown to be a faulty proposition, as reflected in the real world short-term effect on unemployment of the anti-inflation policies in the United States and Britain of around 1980.

(*continued*)

Box 8.1 (continued)

The debate continued in the mode of *rules* versus *discretion*, with monetarists arguing in favor of the superiority of monetary rules or targets over the (Keynesian) approach which allows central banks considerable flexibility to decide on the stance of monetary policy. According to the monetarist school such discretion in policymaking tends to lead to 'fine tuning,' reflecting a bias on the part of the authorities in favor of keeping unemployment low as against containing inflation. In a seminal contribution entitled 'Rules Rather than Discretion: The Inconsistency of Optimal Plans' (1977) Fin Kydland, a Norwegian economist, and an American academic, Edward Prescott, built on Lucas' criticism of flexibility in macroeconomic policy. They introduced the concept of *time inconsistency*, which holds that when a central authority announces a plan for an optimal outcome of a certain policy action, it can change its mind at a later stage, thereby eroding confidence in its actions. For a central bank the implication is that if it announces that it will bring down inflation, but repeatedly fails to deliver on its promise, it will lose the confidence of economic agents. Such time inconsistency will undermine the credibility of the central bank as economic agents will assume that price increases will continue as before. Since expectations of continuing high inflation will not change agents' behavior (in this case leading to lower spending and reduced demands for wage increases), they will produce continuing high inflation. (This is exactly what happened during Chairman Burns' tenure at the Federal Reserve. His stern warnings against inflation were in most instances not followed up by monetary tightening.) Kydland and Prescott concluded therefore that rules for monetary policy would produce better results than discretionary decisions. Their views resonated with many academics and central banks. It should be mentioned, however, that some central banks, in particular the German Bundesbank, had introduced monetary targets a few years before the future Nobel Prize winners had published their work.

The case for discretion was made again in a modified form in the 1980s by Kenneth Rogoff. Arguing that a degree of discretion in monetary policymaking would provide better results than following rules or rigid targets, he advocated that central banks should be

(*continued*)

Box 8.1 (continued)
allowed to run monetary policy independently from governments. As a further safeguard against loss of credibility he proposed that central bank governors should have a stronger aversion to inflation than the public in general (Rogoff 1985).The Harvard Professor is often credited with fostering central bank independence which, as we will see, became a worldwide movement in the late 1980s and beyond. (Six years before Rogoff made his suggestion, Paul Volcker, a known inflation fighter, had been appointed Chairman of the Fed.)

References

Burns, Arthur, *Inside the Nixon Administration: The Secret Diary of Arthur Burns*, ed Robert Ferrell, University Press of Kansas, Lawrence KS, 2010.

Capie, Forrest: *The Bank of England 1950s to 1979*, Cambridge University Press, Cambridge, 2010.

Goodhart, Charles: "The Importance of Money", Bank of England *Quarterly Bulletin,* June 1970.

Greenspan, Alan: *The Age of Turbulence: Adventures in a New World*, Penguin Press, New York, 2007.

Kydland, Fin and Edward Prescott: "Rules rather than Discretion: The Inconsistency of Optimal Plans", *The Journal of Political Economy*, June 1977.

Lawson, Nigel: Obituary Sir Alan Walters, *The Guardian*, 5 January, 2009.

Lucas, Robert: "Expectations and the Neutrality of Money", *Journal of Economic Theory,* 1972, 103–24.

Meltzer, Alan: *A History of the Federal Reserve 1970-1986*, Volume 2, book 2, Chicago University Press, 2009.

Posen, Adam: "Lessons from the Bundesbank on the Occasion of its 40th (and Second to Last) Birtday", *Institute for International Economics*, Working Paper No 97–4, Washington DC, 1997.

Rogoff, Kenneth: "The Optimal Degree of Commitment to an Intermediate Monetary Target", *Quarterly Journal of Economics,* November 1985, 169–189.

Solomon, Robert: *The International Monetary System 1945-1981*, Harper & Row, New York, 1982.

Volcker, Paul and Toyoo Gyohten, *Changing Fortunes: The World's Money and the Threat to American Leadership*, Time Books, New York, 1992

CHAPTER 9

Central Banking and the Great Moderation

After ridding their economies of stubborn inflation, central bankers and governments were keen to find new remedies for taming future inflationary tendencies. They were greatly aided in this pursuit by work done by academics. Their collective efforts contributed substantially to the creation of an extended period of satisfactory economic outcomes. Known as The *Great Moderation,* the years following the early 1980s represent a period of relative calm for central banks, which lasted for a quarter of a century, but came to an abrupt end with the Global Financial Crisis of 2007–09. The consensus view is that 25 years of 'relaxed' central banking lulled the monetary authorities into a degree of complacency, as is explained in Chap. 11. However, the focus of this chapter is on the crucial changes made in the early 1990s that laid the foundation for a long period of low inflation and modest unemployment in the advanced countries. The main causes of such relative tranquility reside in the world-wide adoption of central bank independence and the movement toward direct inflation targeting.

Although the 1980s represented a period of good macroeconomic performance in the global economy, not all was well in some other parts of the world and remedial action was required. These were the Latin America debt crisis, the first domestic banking troubles in the United States since the 1930s, as well as upheaval in foreign exchange markets as the dollar underwent strong gyrations. Coming as a surprise, Mexico in August 1982 announced that it needed large foreign financing to avoid defaulting

O. de Beaufort Wijnholds, *The Money Masters*,
https://doi.org/10.1007/978-3-030-40041-5_9

on its external debt. In due course other Latin American countries who had also borrowed imprudently, mainly from American banks, experienced difficulties in servicing their foreign debt. Although such financial bail-outs are basically the responsibility of governments, central banks can be drawn into the process as advisors and facilitators. This was the case with the Latin American debt crisis where the Fed played an important role as provider of emergency financing together with other central banks assembled through the Bank for International Settlements, in the period pending a large loan (bridge financing) from the IMF. Chairman Volcker played a leading role, also because of his contacts with the big American banks and recognition of the danger to their liquidity and eventually solvency if Mexico and other countries were to default. The American money center banks remained fragile for a number of years until at the end of the 1980s when US Treasury Secretary, Nicholas Brady, launched a scheme which required the banks to negotiate in good faith with their Latin borrowers to reduce their debt, while the IMF and World Bank set aside funds to help debt-ridden countries to buy back their bank debt at a discount. The international institutions also provided additional support to collateralize a portion for interest payments, allowing troubled countries to issue bonds that incorporated lower interest rates and longer maturities.

Lender of Last Resort Operations

Such major financial stability issues were few and far between during the post-war years and were resolved successfully. When the secondary, or 'fringe,' banks in Britain came under severe strain in 1974, following financial deregulation which made the bigger banks more competitive, the Bank of England organized a rescue operation dubbed the 'lifeboat.' It entailed the large banks joining the central bank in pooling funds to bail out fringe banks that were judged to be solvent (a number of them were allowed to go under) to contain the risk of hurting London's reputation as a major financial center. It took quite some diplomatic efforts by the Bank of England to line up the private sector, but after the success of the 'lifeboat' it was rewarded with enhanced prestige (Capie 2010, 538–41, 578–568).

In the United States, where no large bank had failed since the Great Depression (the collapse of smaller banks was routinely resolved without much drama by the regulators), Continental Illinois Bank, the seventh largest in the United States, had to be rescued in 1984. Conti, as it was known, had not only made large loans to Latin America but also to Penn Square, a small bank specialized in lending to domestic energy producers who were hit hard when oil prices fell in 1982. Soon after Penn Square was declared bankrupt, Conti started losing access to the interbank market. The Chicago Fed stepped in as lender of last resort, providing a loan of $3.6 billion, the largest amount ever lent by the System. In addition the FDIC assumed $3.5 billion in debt. Determined not to let the bank go under, regulators provided permanent capital to the troubled institution while removing its management. In an unprecedented move, the FDIC guaranteed all deposits, included those that were not insured, an early example of 'too big to fail.' In line with Bagehot's rule, Conti had to pay 1 percent above the discount rate for its borrowing. While Conti survived under the shortened name Continental Bank, its shareholders were largely wiped out, leaving the government with 80 percent of its shares which was gradually reduced until Bank of America took over full ownership.

The Fed was not as deeply involved in the crisis of the American savings and loan industry in 1985–86. These institutions followed a business model of attracting savings deposits and lending these funds at (much) longer maturities, mainly as mortgage credits. Financial deregulation, including the termination of the interest rate ceilings on savings deposits (regulation Q), affected the competitiveness of savings and loan institutions, in a similar fashion as the secondary banks in Britain a decade earlier. To stave off contagion the Fed provided advances to many of the troubled institutions and—unlike in the case of Conti—at a standard rate. In many instances the insolvent savings banks were sold off or merged. The eventual cost to tax payers reached a staggering $150 billion. And since several instances of fraudulent behavior were detected and the distinction between the roles of the regulatory agencies blurred, Congress took an interest in the debacle. After long deliberations, legislation was passed to prevent similar mishaps in the future. The Federal Deposit Insurance Corporation Improvement Act (FDICIA) of 1991 called for action by regulators before waiting for institutions to fold, such as ending dividend payments or the closure of institutions. Unfortunately the often confusing patchwork of regulatory agencies in the United States was left in place and remains almost unchanged to this day, to the detriment of the regulatory independence of the Fed.

Dollar Dilemma

Another major monetary event in the 1980s was the result of large gyrations of the dollar exchange rate. The restoration of confidence in the American economy combined with high interest rates, led to a very large appreciation of the dollar from 1982 onward. Frequent interventions in foreign exchange markets initially failed to slow down the process. Part of the reason was that a large part of the interventions were sterilized by central banks and therefore did not affect domestic monetary conditions. The rise of the dollar reached its peak in February 1985 when one US dollar bought 3.30 D mark compared with 1.75 in July 1980. Concerned American exporters lobbied hard for measures to reverse the course of the dollar. Together with falling exports, imports surged, leading to very large balance of payments deficits, raising the specter of protectionism to which many members of the American Congress were not averse. US Treasury Secretary James Baker, wishing to bring down the trade imbalance, called for a meeting of the ministers of finance of the five largest economies to discuss coordinated action to engineer an orderly depreciation of the dollar. Following deliberations at the Plaza Hotel in New York in September 1985, the participants reached an agreement, known as the *Plaza Accord*. Apart from not very specific pledges about the policies each of them would follow, they announced their intention to coordinate interventions in currency markets so as to move rates toward their fundamental levels.

While central banks are not normally part of the final decision-making on exchange rates—a prerogative of ministers of finance, as mentioned earlier—they expressed concerns about the agreement. Monetary policy can have an important impact on exchange rates and having to steer domestic monetary conditions to help reach exchange rate objectives was especially problematic for the Fed and the German Bundesbank. Fed Chairman Volcker was unhappy with the pressure from the US Treasury to bring down interest rates at a faster pace, as he felt that inflation expectations were not fully adjusted yet. And the Bundesbank, headed by Karl Otto Poehl, wanted to give priority to its monetary policy objectives rather than taking part in large-scale interventions. But despite misgivings the central banks showed some flexibility, even though this meant a small dent in their independence.

Unexpectedly the dollar depreciated so steeply that a mere year and a half after the Plaza Accord, the five countries came together again to try to halt what had become an undershooting of the dollar exchange rate.

Heavy interventions, mainly conducted by the German Central Bank (to the tune of $20 billion), had not brought about the hoped for reduction in the American trade balance, prompting Secretary Baker, who after Plaza had unsuccessfully badgered the Fed and the Bundesbank to lower interest rates, to try a new round of coordinated action. The result was a new agreement, known as the *Louvre Accord* after the site of the deliberations, the Group of Five announcing that shifts in currency rates since the Plaza Accord had substantially contributed to reducing external imbalances. And as (then) current rates had moved within range of their fundamental positions, the participating countries pledged to cooperate closely to keep exchange rates where they were. The Accord initially succeeded in calming the markets, but this effect gradually withered away, demonstrating the difficulties of coordinated policy actions among countries. It also meant that large central banks felt free again to pursue their objective of price stability without paying (much) heed to the value of their currencies. For smaller countries tracking the currencies of a large trading partner (such as the Netherlands, Belgium and Austria) such freedom did not exist, the more so as European monetary integration moved forward.

The Rise of Eclecticism

After its first successes in bringing down inflation, the Federal Reserve moved away swiftly from monetarism. It now deemphasized the importance of monetary aggregates and quietly dropped non-borrowed reserves as its operational tool, returning its focus to short-term interest rates. At the same time the central bank continued to pursue an anti-inflationary stance, except when showing a degree of flexibility during the currency upheavals of the mid-1980s. Inflation expectations take time to adjust, especially after a prolonged period of rapid price increases and it took until 1986 before this stage was reached in the United States. By then an eclectic approach to monetary policy had evolved, the FOMC increasingly taking into account developments in the real economy, such as changes in productivity, wage growth and employment. Monetary targets evolved into guidelines, reflecting the shift to more data-driven analyses. Although this development reflected a move back to discretion, Chairman Volcker and his successor Alan Greenspan did not embrace the Phillips curve analysis which their staff regularly included in their forecasting models. And both Chairmen were skeptical about the usefulness of econometric models in general.

During most of the 1980s and 1990s growth and inflation in the United States were satisfactory, the Great Moderation having taken hold in a climate of steady expectations. The Fed's eclectic approach served it well during this period, as well as in the early 2000s, to which period we turn later. The smooth sailing during these years was interrupted by two main events, one a matter of general confidence, the other communications and transparency. On 19 October 1987, a mere two months into Alan Greenspan's first term as Fed Chairman, panic swept across world stock markets, starting in Hong Kong and reaching Japan and Europe in a matter of hours before it hit the New York Stock Exchange. Equity prices fell by 23 percent as confidence disappeared, wiping out large earlier gains which in retrospect were seen as an overvaluation of the stock market. So-called program trading, a new phenomenon by which large swathes of transactions were computer driven, was also identified as a cause. The Fed immediately sprang into action, lending liberally to the increasingly illiquid financial markets, thereby succeeding in averting a full-blown crisis.

By contrast to this well executed lender of last resort role, the Fed, which like practically all central banks at the time, was reluctant to provide information of its inner workings, surprised the markets in February 1994 by unexpectedly announcing a tightening of monetary policy. The central bank had not changed its benchmark interest rate of 3 percent for three years and while the economy was coming out of a recession, it gave no hints about its concerns of an uptick of inflation, catching financial market parties off guard. Further increases in the federal funds rate to 6 percent followed later, leading to large losses, especially in bond markets. This incident elicited calls for more openness by the central bank and better communication of its actions and intentions. It would, however, take quite some time before important changes were made on this front. The matter of communications is treated more fully in Chap. 12.

The impact of the stock market crisis of October 1987 was similar in Britain to that in the United States: a drop in stock prices of 26 percent. The Bank of England too was quick to lend freely to the market, thereby restoring calm. However, unlike the Fed, the British central bank did not unwind its liquidity support in a timely fashion, resulting in a period of high inflation. Prices and wages remained under control in Germany, the independent Bundesbank continuing to ensure a measured pace in the growth of the money supply. The German Central Bank, following a medium-term policy strategy, did not abandon its pragmatic application of monetarism until it was absorbed into the European Central Bank in

1998. It did, however, face an important challenge after the fall of the Berlin Wall in November 1989, dealing with the question how best to integrate the weak East German economy into the highly competitive West German one. Central to the problem was the rate at which the East German currency would be converted into the strong Deutsche mark. Despite the Bundesbank's position that a one to one ratio made no economic sense, it was overruled by Chancellor Kohl for political reasons. Choosing parity was a sympathetic gesture toward the East German population, but seriously retarded the recovery of its industry.

Central Bank Independence

The degree to which central banks can make policy decisions without political constraints has for the most part of their history been a defining factor in the way they function. When still conducting regular banking activities in their early years, their commercial business was free of government rules and regulations. And if endowed with a monopoly of issuing bank notes they could pretty much operate as a profit maximizing entity. But as limits were placed on their bank note issue by the government, such as the Peel Act of 1844 in Britain, central banks in democratically ruled countries (under dictatorial regimes central banks perform as mere technical government agencies) lost some of their independence. This development was an important step in the evolution of the Bank of England, and of some embryonic European central banks, toward a configuration of checks and balances, increasingly embedded in legislation.

An interesting example is that of the German *Reichsbank*, established in the early 1870s with minimal autonomy, but whose successor, the Bundesbank, would become one of the most independent central banks in the world. As for the Bank of England, its history is one that goes in a different direction, in the course of the twentieth century losing its capacity to independently conduct monetary policy. It took until 1997 before the Bank was largely relieved of government interference. And as we have seen, the independence of the Federal Reserve System, which was considerable in the 1920s, suffered as a result of its poor performance during the Great Depression and was only partially restored in 1951. Moreover, the American central bank's independence was compromised under the Nixon administration, contributing to an acceleration of an already worrisome rate of inflation. Since the Great Inflation of the 1970s and early 1980s was a global event, it proved to be a catalyst for providing greater independence to central banks worldwide.

Both academics and policymakers became convinced in the course of the 1980s that the greater the central bank autonomy in a country, the lower its rate of inflation. This finding was backed up by empirical research, such as that performed by Alesina and Summers (1993) which showed a clear inverse relation between an index of central bank independence and inflation. During the 1990s a substantial number of countries saw their rates of inflation coming down after their central banks had been granted more independence. New Zealand led the way in this process at the end of the 1980s, by drastically strengthening the position of the NZ Reserve Bank. As to whether a higher degree of independence, suggesting a relatively tight monetary policy, would be detrimental to economic growth, most studies showed no significant correlation.

While much of the literature confirmed the link between central bank independence (CBI) and inflation, a note of caution was injected into the debate concerning the measurement of CBI. The relationship between the two variables is not straightforward, the concept of CBI encompassing several elements, some of which are non-quantifiable and therefore difficult to interpret. Academics such as Cuckierman (1992) and Eijffinger and De Haan (1996) emphasized the need to look at these elements separately and weigh them to arrive at a justifiable estimate of CBI per central bank. Such an exercise should contain an evaluation of their legal status, monetary policy independence (which can be split into goal independence and instrument independence), personal independence and financial independence. Also relevant but not directly related to autonomy are central banks' role in supervision of the financial system, their degree of accountability and their informal interactions with the government, including types of policy coordination.

Legal Provisions

Central bank laws are universal, but fairly different in content and clarity. Most legal statutes describe the objectives to be pursued, but in a few cases, the most notable that of the Bank of England before 1997, the relevant legislation did not explicitly mention a monetary policy goal. The most common proscribed objective is that of price stability, but it is usually left to the central bank what definition of price stability to apply. In other instances the goal of maintaining price stability is combined with that of maintaining exchange rate stability, or similar formulations. Some central bank laws mention stability in general terms. Much less common is providing a central bank with a dual mandate, as in the case of the Fed, where the combination of price stability and maximal employment was introduced in the late 1970s. This blend is sometimes criticized as combining two potentially conflicting objectives which in theory renders the central bank less independent. Another approach is a combination of a primary goal and a secondary one, usually price stability and supporting general economic policies when price stability has been achieved, the prime example being the European Central Bank statute. But references to a secondary objective are almost never made in public debates. In theory a stand-alone objective of maintaining price stability is likely to provide more independence than other formulations. In practice, however, central banks will tend to avoid single mindedly pursuing low or zero inflation when faced with a severe recession.

Central bank laws, besides laying down the objective(s) to be pursued, occasionally contain a provision prohibiting political interference with the central banks' policies, constituting an important defense against government pressure and considered a hallmark of independence. Here too, the European Central Bank is *the* example of far-reaching protection. By contrast, several central bank statutes contain an explicit right for the government to give directives to its monetary institution. Examples are the Bank of England (until 1997) and the Netherlands Bank (until 2000). A directive being the 'nuclear' option, governments are reluctant to take that route, especially when the central bank defends itself in parliament with the possibility that the minister of finance is overruled and forced to resign. Although the law provided for the possibility of the Netherlands Bank receiving a government directive, this never happened with the Dutch central bank enjoying a great deal of autonomy in practice. The foregoing illustrates that legal provisions regarding central banks are not always a good indicator of the actual degree of CBI. Much depends on the enforcement of such provisions, as well as the stature and inclinations of the governor of the monetary institution. A significant gap between de jure and de facto autonomy has in the past existed in a number of instances, for example in some Asian and Latin American countries.

Monetary Policy Independence

Central bank independence is arguably more evident in the leeway allowed in the conduct of monetary policy. Policy independence can be divided into *goal* independence and *instrument* or *operational* independence. While the ultimate goal of monetary policy is in most cases price stability, or more precisely low inflation, it can be left to the central bank's own judgment what this means in practice and how to achieve it. Before the move to direct inflation targeting, which will be discussed in the next section, central banks with goal independence could define their own intermediate targets such as growth of the money supply, the ratio of money to national income and domestic credit expansion. The German, Swiss and the Netherlands' central banks enjoyed this freedom, but the Federal Reserve was constrained by congressional oversight. After the introduction of the euro, all its participants became members of the Euro System, consisting of the European Central Bank (ECB) proper and the national central banks, which enjoys complete goal independence.

Instrument independence allows central banks to choose which instruments or combination thereof they wish to apply to achieve their goals. The most common operational methods are adjustments of short-term interest rates, by raising or lowering the central banks' benchmark rate using open market sales and purchases, its discount rate and the rate at which it remunerates banks' deposits (reserves). Some central banks have over time made regular use of minimum reserve requirements, the Federal Reserve being a prime example. While Western central banks have relied less in recent years on this instrument, the Chinese Central Bank nowadays employs it as a major tool of monetary policy. Instrument independence is partial when a central bank lacks full autonomous power to set interest rates in the money market. For instance, when it is obligated to facilitate the governments' borrowing requirement or required to directly finance budget deficits (monetary financing), a central bank can only use its monetary tools within the confines of the government's debt management policies. Another constraint is an obligation to support the exchange rate policy of the government when it conflicts with domestic monetary goals. As we have seen, such instances involving major central banks have occurred in the past in the United States, Britain, France and Italy. In Germany clashes between the Bundesbank and the minister of finance over exchange rate policy were not uncommon, but these tended to be differences among equal partners, the central bank being under no formal obligation to make monetary policy actions dependent on certain goals of the government.

Personal independence exists when the governor and other top officials of the central bank cannot be dismissed at will and egregious or fraudulent behavior is required for their removal. Such protection is not routinely embedded in central banks' statutes, but may be based on long-standing custom. Fixed-term appointments with a relatively long duration, such as five years (the Fed's 14-year terms are an outlier) have become the best practice. Reappointment can have a drawback as the sitting governor might be influenced in his/her decision-making by seeking to stay on. A long fixed term with no allowance for extension, such as a one-time eight-year term for members of the European Central Bank's Executive Board, discourages such behavior. The fact that central bank governors, and usually other top officials as well, are appointed by the government, in principle detracts somewhat from the degree of independence. However, central bank statutes often require that a governor be knowledgeable about monetary and banking matters or such like formulations.

Truly autonomous heads of central banks can be compared to highest court judges, appointed by the government but fully independent in their decision-making. Going a step further, a central bank can be so powerful that it can be de facto considered a fourth independent branch of government alongside the executive, the legislative and judicial branches. The position of the German Bundesbank, sometimes described as 'a state within a state' belonged to this category. The European Central Bank, since its inception recognized as the world's most autonomous monetary institution, is a special case given its status as a supranational entity. Its unique position is discussed in Chap. 10.

Financial independence is reflected by a central banks' obligation to share profits with its government. Although they are not profit maximizing entities, central banks do generate income, the main sources being interest earned on investing its international reserves and lending to the private sector by discounting eligible paper and providing advances. Most central banks manage their countries' reserves, invested since the breakdown of the Bretton Woods system in deposits and short-term securities in foreign currency (mainly US dollars). Many central banks also still hold gold even though the gold standard is long gone, often as a kind of protection against extreme conditions (war chest), but earn no income on their stash. Usually central banks have an agreement with their governments to retain sufficient income to meet their operational expenses and to maintain a certain amount of internal reserves against contingencies. The remainder of the income or profit is credited to the government for which it figures as part of its budgetary revenues. Profit-sharing agreements are mostly a technical matter outside the glare of publicity, but can become contentious when the government uses them as a pressure instrument by severely limiting the part of its income that the central bank can retain, thereby affecting its independence.

Ranking Independence

Ranking the degree of central bank independence is imprecise as the factors determining autonomy cannot be quantified with confidence. Legal independence alone is not a reliable indicator since in some instances, especially in developing countries in the past, central bank statutes did not reflect the actual situation. Personal independence of its governors is also difficult to compare across central banks as much of it is not spelled out in legislation or rules, but based on custom. Attempts to quantify personal independence have been based on the turnover rate of governors as a proxy. It is assumed that the (much) higher turnover rates in a number of Latin American countries than in that of central bank governors in North America, Northern Europe, Japan and the Antipodes indicate less autonomy. Financial independence measurement is even more problematic. The most reliable indicators are those based on policy independence, with central banks enjoying goal and instrument autonomy ranking highest. Putting together these various indicators, academics have developed indices for ranking overall independence. Figure 9.1 provides rankings for 1989 and 2019, illustrating the important changes that took place regarding CBI over a 30-year span. They incorporate the degree of transparency, which correlates significantly with independence. More weight has been given to evidence of actual interference by governments in monetary policy than to legal provisions which are sometimes ignored. (See the case of Turkey described in Chap. 14.)

The most striking development is the disappearance in this ranking of central banks that became part of the European System of Central Banks in 2000. For instance, the *Banque de France* was accorded considerably more independence in 1993. In 1997 the Bank of England was made instrument independent and moved up in the rankings. The Reserve Bank of New Zealand was transformed from a central bank with a low degree of independence to one with a high one. Many central banks of emerging

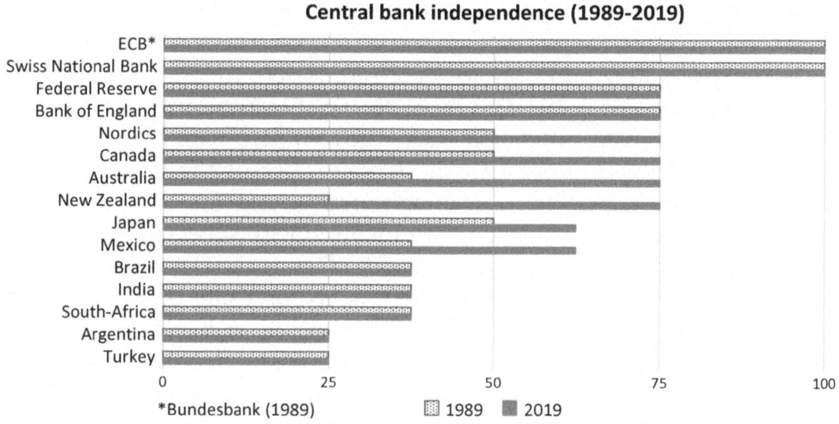

Fig. 9.1 Central Bank Independence 1989 and 2019. (Source: Nergiz Dincer and Barry Eichengreen (2014) and own estimates)

market and developing countries also became (much) more independent, among others those of Chile, Colombia, Korea and Mexico. As an accompaniment of greater independence, central banks generally became more *accountable*. Information was more readily provided by heads of these institutions, regularly appearing before parliament to explain, and if necessary, defend their policies. They were also required to publish periodic reports on monetary developments, such as the *Inflation Report* of the Bank of England, followed by a host of other central banks. Reporting on financial stability has also become widespread. While more accountability might appear to reduce central bank independence, it should rather be seen as protecting the position of the institution against uninformed attacks.

Supervision of the Banking System

During the debates on independence the issue of separating the monetary task of central banks from that of the supervision of banks, or combining the two, also became a subject of deep discourse. No formula or best practice emerged and the number of countries with stand-alone monetary policy and those combined with supervision was about equal. (There is no evidence that there is any significant impact on independence on this score.) The Bank of England, the Australian Reserve Bank, the central banks of the United Kingdom, France, Italy, Japan, the Netherlands, New Zealand, Spain, Brazil and others were responsible for supervising their banking systems and sometimes other financial institutions as well. In a few cases supervision was shared with a government entity. The Federal Reserve shared supervision with the Comptroller of the Currency, the FDIC and state supervisors, a complicated arrangement with serious drawbacks, as we will see later on. Not involved with supervision were the central banks of Austria, Belgium, Canada, Denmark, Germany, Sweden and Switzerland and several others. Arguments for a split between monetary and financial supervision are (1) the concern of banking problems influencing monetary policy, and (2) the notion that leaving supervision to the government is appropriate because it would directly or indirectly pay for rescuing banks. Arguments against separation are (1) the need for monetary policymakers to have detailed insight in developments in the financial system, (2) combining monetary policy and prudential supervision can help avoid systemic problems (Goodhart and Schoenmaker 1993).

Illustrating the difficulty of weighing the various arguments con and pro, the Bank of England was strongly criticized when CCIB, a poorly managed bank, went under and important losses were incurred. The British solution in 1997, when the central bank was accorded instrument independence by the new Blair Government, was to split off supervision from the Bank and create a separate Financial System Authority. But in 2010 the conservative Cameron Government returned the responsibility for supervision to the Bank. In another major development, prudential supervision was transferred in the euro area to the European Central Bank in 2012, significantly reducing the tasks of the national banks which are part of the Euro System. This topic is discussed more fully in Chap. 10.

Inflation Targeting

More or less parallel with the world-wide shift to greater independence, central banks were searching for a better target on which to base their monetary policy decisions. Monetary targeting was found wanting as attempts to find a money aggregate that best reflected the demand for money became increasingly unsuccessful. Goodhart's law, which states that when an observed empirical relationship between two economic variables starts to be relied on for policy purposes it will no longer hold, is often mentioned in this context. (Charles Goodhart is a prominent British economist who early in his career worked at the Bank of England.) Among the major central banks only the German Bundesbank, which focused on money demand in the longer run, continued to practice a pragmatic form of monetarism in the 1990s. Other central banks were relying more and more on an eclectic approach, basing their monetary policy actions on a range of mostly real economic data. But the feeling that eclecticism was neither fish nor fowl, led to a combination of data-driven decisions and rules. The result was *inflation targeting*, choosing a benchmark for price stability to be attained by data-driven monetary policy operations. After New Zealand introduced inflation targeting (IT) in 1989, a mounting number of central banks adopted a similar regime. Like a high degree of independence, targeting a certain level of inflation has remained the standard best practice for most central banks and has been actively promoted by international bodies like the International Monetary Fund and the Bank for International Settlements.

The New Zealand experience is instructive as inflation targeting (IT) was the center of a complete reversal of economic policy in this small open economy. The new approach did away with overregulation and rigidity in the scope of an extensive liberalization. Adopting a free floating exchange rate was part of this makeover. Abandoning the fixed exchange rate required that some other form of anchor for monetary policy was needed. The innovative solution was introducing IT with the immediate aim of bringing down inflation from an uncomfortable level of 5 percent per annum. Cognizant of the need for creating the right kind of structure in which the Reserve Bank of New Zealand could successfully operate an IT strategy, the new central bank law contained a number of major reforms. These included a clear mandate for the central bank to pursue (only) price stability, according it instrument independence, and removing the obligation to finance budget deficits. After a brief transitional period, the government set the target at a rate of price increases of between zero and 2 percent. A few years later the upper limit was increased to 3 percent, mainly for political reasons. The time horizon applied was 6 to 8 quarters. An unusual feature of the New Zealand model is that the central bank governor is solely held responsible for achieving the target and can be dismissed when a special committee concludes that he/she is not diligently striving to meet the assigned target. However, as is customary, the government has the prerogative of choosing between giving monetary policy or other economic policy objectives priority when considered necessary. The New Zealand experiment was a success, as is borne out by the central bank consistently achieving its inflation target. The ultimate success rests on a major shift of expectations from acceptance of the too high rate of inflation to a credible adherence by the central bank to a publicly announced target.

The Kiwi Model

Early adopters of the Kiwi model were Canada, Australia, Sweden and Chile (the first emerging market country to do so). Among the major countries, Britain was the first to move to an IT based monetary policy, but the United States and Japan did not follow suit. European countries which, besides Germany, were potential members of the European Monetary Union, following the Maastricht Treaty of 1992, concentrated on meeting the criteria for membership (including an inflation target) and narrowing their foreign exchange rates toward that of Germany. (This process is described in Chap. 10.) The Canadian IT regime, introduced in 1991, generally followed the same structure as practiced in New Zealand, although the rules on accountability did not include any personal responsibility of the head of the central bank. What stands out with respect to the approach followed by the Bank of Canada (BOC) is its lucid analysis of the monetary transmission mechanism, often described as a 'black box' given its complicated nature (Longworth 2000). A solid understanding of monetary transmission is an important element in the good working of an IT regime. The BOC identified three monetary transmission linkages. The first is from the monetary instrument, in this case the very short-term interest rate, to other financial variables: the term structure of interest rates (yield curve), the rates paid by banks on deposits and charged for loans, as well as the floating exchange rate. The next step plots the linkage between financial variables to total demand (consumption and investment) and the output gap (the gap between the trend rate of potential output and actual output). The third linkage connects the output gap, inflation expectations and the exchange rate with the rate of inflation. Considerable weight has been placed on the effect of changes in monetary conditions to influence inflation via the output gap, although the gap is not measurable but estimated and contains a realistic margin for error. In countries with less sophisticated analytical tools and economic models this can be a weak point in their understanding of the monetary transmission process. Keeping forecasting models simple has therefore been recommended by the IMF.

The first major country to adopt an IT regime, the structure developed in Britain—somewhat different from that in New Zealand—has served as a model for many other central banks. The background for Britain's switch to a rules-based strategy was its exit in September 1992 from the European Rate Mechanism (ERM), a regime which required participants to be keep their exchange rates within certain margins in the run-up to European monetary integration. Abandonment of a fixed pound sterling rate was immediately followed by a depreciation of the pound by 15 percent, elevating inflation expectations from 4.5 percent a year to 6 percent ten years ahead. This episode reflected a significant loss of credibility and galvanized the Bank of England to introduce IT. While relatively successful, some of the preconditions for a durable IT regime were missing. To remedy the situation the British Government announced in May 1997 that the central bank would henceforth be instrument independent and incorporated the change in the *Bank of England Act* of 1998. However, the degree of independence of the British central bank is still constrained to the extent that the Treasury remains entitled to give the Bank directives, but only in extreme economic circumstances and with the consent of parliament. The decision-making structure of the Bank was also changed and placed with a nine-person Monetary Policy Committee (MPC). (Unlike other central banks in major countries, the Bank of England appoints a number foreign citizens as members of the Committee.) To foster accountability and transparency a number of innovations were introduced. Minutes of the MPC's monthly meetings, including votes of individual members have to be published. In the event of a breach of the inflation target of 2.5 percent by more than 1 percentage point in either direction, the Bank of England has to write an open letter to the Chancellor of the Exchequer explaining the reasons for missing the target. And as is common in other countries, representatives of the Bank have to appear before parliament on a regular basis.

A Successful Strategy

Whereas the Bank of England had operated with a target range of 1–4 percent from 1993 to 1995, it chose to move to a point target of 2.5 percent as it worried about 'range bias' which could introduce a tendency to keep actual inflation at the upper band of the range. What also stands out in the British approach to IT is the view that 'an inflation targeting framework is as much a safeguard against deflation as against inflation' (Haldane

1995). With the experience of the Great Inflation still fresh in many central banker's minds, the risk of deflation was hardly ever considered a matter of concern until the end of the Great Moderation in 2007.

In the more technical domain, the Bank of England in its inflation forecasting exercises makes use of a probabilistic approach depicted in a so-called fan chart over a two-year horizon. As time passes the fan becomes wider, reflecting the increasing probability of deviations from the target in both directions. The forecast horizon of two years is based on the estimated length of monetary transmission lags (around one year for output and two years for inflation). Since exchange rate movements under a floating regime tend to affect open economies relatively strongly and therefore can have a substantial influence on the price level via imports, the Bank of England and other central banks from countries with a relatively large external sector need to monitor the nature of currency movements closely. Distinguishing between temporary and permanent movements and those of a monetary or non-monetary nature is important. Whether an exchange rate 'shock' is expected to be permanent rather than temporary or of a non-monetary instead of a monetary nature needs to be taken into account in inflation forecasts. But such distinctions are often difficult to make and cannot be relied upon all that much. All in all, the move to inflation targeting has been a success in Britain—as in many other countries—inflation remaining close to the point target.

Emerging Countries Follow

The first emerging country to introduce inflation targeting, *Chile* paved the way for many other countries at the same stage of development. The Central Bank of Chile was granted instrument independence in 1990 at a time the country was suffering from high inflation caused by excessive expansionary policies. Realizing that bringing down inflation from the then prevailing level of 27 percent to a much lower rate in a short period of time was not possible, the central bank wisely opted for a gradual approach. After ten years of steadily reduced targets, the objective of stationary low inflation was reached and a new target range of between 2 and 4 percent per was announced. The permanence of the targeting framework was strengthened when the government adopted a floating exchange rate, removing the potential constraint of having to support the currency. By following a gradual course under an IT regime, the desired result was achieved without significantly affecting economic growth while maintaining full employment. The Chilean experience demonstrated that IT can also work when inflation is quite high at the outset.

Monetary policy geared toward an inflation target has become a hallmark of modern central banking. It has been adopted by all economically advanced countries with the exception of Denmark which is de facto pegged to the euro. Members of the euro area of course collectively adhere to the inflation target set by the European Central Bank. A majority of emerging market countries (Venezuela being an outsider) and several developing countries now operate similar regimes. The popularity of inflation targeting is reflected by the numbers: after 21 countries adopted such a regime in the 1990s, by 2017 the number was 63 (counting the euro area as one). There is no clear preference for point targets or target ranges, but 2 percent inflation (plus or minus 1 percent) is the most common number for mature economies. Only two central banks—the European Central Bank and the Swiss National Bank—aim for inflation slightly under 2 percent. After many years of discussion the Federal Reserve announced an IT of 2 percent in 2012. One of the reasons for making explicit what was already an implicit goal was the Fed's dual mandate and opposition to having an inflation target without also striving for a quantified goal for unemployment.

Best Practice

The popularity of IT notwithstanding, it has not always and everywhere been a success as, for instance, demonstrated by Turkey in the first years of the 2000s when that country's adoption of IT proved to be premature. It was somewhat more successful in later years. (It later pursued a target of 5 percent, plus or minus 1 percent.) The IMF became an active promoter of IT, especially for countries with less sophisticated economies and financial systems, searching for a suitable anchor. Based on the experience of central banks, moving away from exchange rate or monetary targeting, the international organization spelled out the prerequisites for a credible and durable regime of inflation targeting. It pointed out that a clear objective of monetary policy (preferably price stability) and instrument independence is a sine qua non for starting out on a path of IT and that political interference with monetary policy is undesirable, especially forcing the central bank to engage in financing budget deficits. Furthermore, support from the general public, through communication, transparency and education, is an important ingredient for success. Accountability is also essential and can be achieved through regular press conferences and speeches, the publication of inflation reports, appearances before parliament and explanations of causes and remedies when targets are not met. The British example of an open letter of explanation can be considered a best practice. In its early days, IT was often viewed with skepticism but gradually gained broad acceptance as inflation came down and stayed down. Inflationary expectations became solidly anchored in many countries as their central banks gained credibility as the time inconsistency problem was overcome. Another important feature of a sound IT regime is the availability of an effective operational monetary policy instrument. Ideally this is the lever of short-term interest rates, usually executed by means of open market transactions, but where financial markets are not well developed direct credit controls can be an alternative.

Monetary Transmission

At a more technical level, some understanding of the monetary transmission mechanism is highly desirable. Models such as the Canadian analysis, as described earlier above and a more recent detailed version presented by the European Central Bank are good examples (Fig. 9.2). However, in view of the complicated nature and use of non-observable variables in such models, it is advisable for younger central banks to start off with simple forecasting models.

Whatever the advantages of sophisticated and complex models, they have to be adjusted as the economic and financial environment changes in order to remain relevant.

Measuring Inflation

Much thought has also been given how to best measure increases in prices for purposes of monetary policy. In the end two indices are considered to provide the most relevant information. First, and generally used as the 'official' measure of inflation, is the consumer price index (CPI), also known as *headline* inflation. This index is comprehensive, but not always comparable or all-inclusive as housing costs are sometimes left out or defined differently. Increases in asset prices (shares, real estate) are generally 'ignored' even though they are relevant for general economic conditions and financial stability. (Financial stability is treated in Chap. 13.) Headline inflation is the measure that households follow rather than

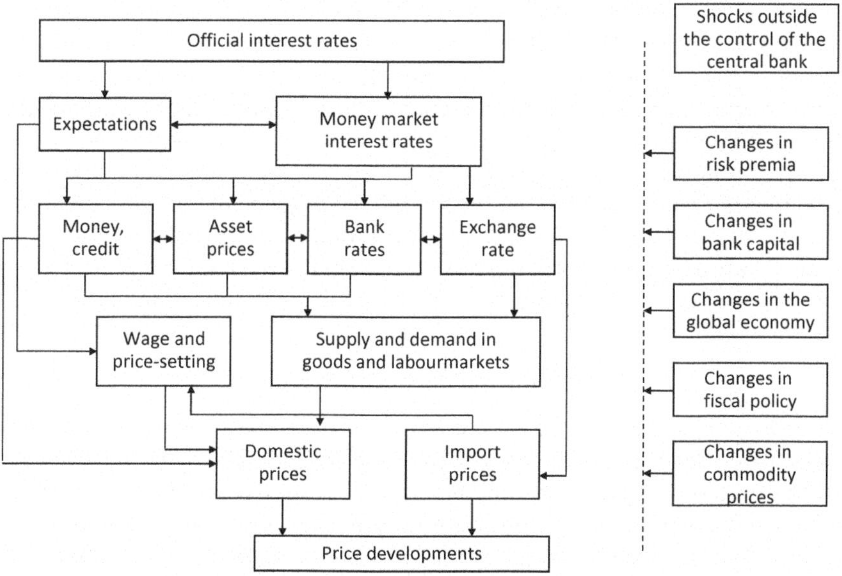

Fig. 9.2 Transmission Mechanism of Monetary Policy. (Source: European Central Bank)

underlying or *core* inflation which excludes the price of food and energy, because they show considerable fluctuations. Although headline inflation determines whether central banks have met their target, they also closely follow core inflation. For instance, in cases of large movements in the price of oil, policymakers tend to 'look through' what is likely to be a temporary factor. Despite differences among central banks in the modalities of their inflation targeting policies, the main features of IT are very similar and have proved to be very durable, as a comprehensive study by John Murray, former Deputy Governor of the Bank of Canada, shows (Murray 2017). IT has now existed for over a quarter of a century and is the most successful of all monetary regimes practiced over time. Stanley Fischer, who produced prestigious academic work before serving in high positions in international organizations, as Governor of the Bank of Israel and Vice-Chairman of the Fed, has described inflation targeting as 'a real case of progress in economics, a result of the interaction of theory and empirical evidence' (Fischer 2003, 168).

Central bankers rightly claim credit for their role in bringing about the Great Moderation. While the monetarist approach applied in a pragmatic German manner initiated the process of disinflation, the movement to world-wide central bank independence and its practical application in the form of inflation targeting ensured the long duration of the moderation. But it should not be overlooked that non-monetary factors also played a role in the process. Greater fiscal discipline of governments and a modicum of structural reform, likewise contributed to this result. In addition, globalization and technological advances have led to more integrated markets and increased competition, thereby keeping consumer prices low.

Emerging Market Crises

The Great Moderation bypassed many emerging countries (ECs) that suffered from deep financial crises between 1994 and 2002. Those affected were situated in Asia, Latin America, as well as Russia and Turkey, in all of which the economic and political consequences were dire. Massive bail-outs and drastic policy changes in the besieged countries ensured that the impact on the real economy of advanced countries was limited. But since foreign commercial banks had lent generously and sometimes foolishly to ECs, they ran the risk of large losses. These lenders, mostly banks from the United States, Europe and Japan, also benefited from the protection provided by the IMF financial bail-outs of the ECs, but were reluctant to share the burden. Hence a considerable effort was made by their central banks by nudging, and in some instances pressuring, their commercial banks not to pull out their money, but to roll over their maturing claims on ECs. Known as private sector involvement (PSI) the effort produced mixed results. The fact that the Federal Reserve was not an active participant in this exercise did not help. Its reluctance stemmed from fear of being sued if American commercial banks were to incur losses that could be attributed to PSI (private sector involvement). In addition, their close contacts with commercial financial institutions, which often were subject to their prudential supervision, European central banks and the Bank of Japan played a major role in advising their governments who took the final decisions on bail-outs and bore the concomitant risks.

Central banks were more directly involved in the crisis countries, but as they generally enjoyed little independence from their governments, monetary policy, often misdirected under pressure from the political authorities, had to be drastically overhauled, usually as part of IMF programs.

Their role in the excessive foreign borrowing of their governments, which in addition bore an exchange rate risk, was at most a technical one. However, regarding their supervisory task, they were seriously remiss in exercising their mandate of keeping the financial sector safe. The situation could be described as an accident waiting to happen. Some central banks were also found to have covered up large drains of their international reserves in an attempt to avoid an erosion of confidence. A good example is Thailand where the management of the national bank continued to report the size of its official reserves at around $30 billion, without mentioning that a roughly similar amount was owed in forward exchange rates contracts and that therefore net reserves were effectively zero. In Korea the central bank had neglected to report that a large share of its reserves was not freely usable, being encumbered by certain liabilities. In such instances top officials and political leaders were replaced (and even sent to jail). In almost all of the ECs that underwent a financial crisis—Korea being an important exception—a major cause of their troubles was maintaining an overvalued exchange rate.

Exchange Rates as Monetary Target

Rather than introducing an inflation target, several governments of emerging countries preferred to manage the exchange rate as a means to combat inflation in the run-up to the financial crisis that engulfed them in the 1990s. By maintaining an overvalued exchange rate, which lowers import prices and feeds through into consumer prices, they found an 'easier' way to deal with rising prices than facing the problem directly through fiscal and monetary policies. Doubts expressed by their central banks were generally brushed away. But after a while investors lost confidence and capital inflows into emerging countries shrank dramatically.

Overvaluation eventually led to unsustainably large balance of payments deficits which in turn stimulated capital outflows. Many of them also ran large budget deficits. Since central banks in ECs did not enjoy the degree of independence of their counterparts in advanced economies, their governments deserved a large share of the blame for this miscalculation. However, 'fear of floating' was usually also deeply embedded within central banks. As East Asian and Latin American countries ran out of reserves they turned to the IMF for support, and as part of an agreement on economic policies with that institution let their exchange rate float. With a return of confidence and limited intervention in their foreign exchange markets, monetary policy was largely freed to focus directly on achieving price stability. Concomitantly, central banks were given more independence. Inflation targeting was introduced on a wide scale, but in view of the 'thinness' of foreign currency markets in ECs, it was recognized that full flexibility of exchange rates was often not an optimal solution. Hence the new regime was dubbed 'inflation targeting rate plus,' allowing for limited intervention.

An extreme case of unwise use of the exchange rate to keep inflation low is Argentina's introduction of a *currency board* in 1991. (Managing a currency board is akin to operating under the gold standard. The central bank has to maintain full convertibility against another currency, in this case the US dollar.) Having gone through regular bouts of hyperinflation, the Argentine Government passed a radical law linking the peso to the US dollar in what was expected to be an irrevocable parity of one to one, in the hope of importing the United States' much lower rate of inflation. In order to maintain parity, the central bank's role was relegated to that of an automatic pilot. Every movement in Argentina's official reserves had to be matched with an equal amount of domestic monetary extraction or expansion, as required by the 'rules' of the currency board. For Argentina's experiment to be successful over a longer period, it needed to keep its domestic costs, especially wages, in line with those of the United States. This proved to be impossible in a country like Argentina with its very strong labor unions and dysfunctional political system. After a number of years of apparently reasonable results (without outside knowledge that unfavorable budget outcomes were hidden), a massive outflow of capital catalyzed by a loss of confidence related to unsustainable balance of payments trends, the government was forced to abandon its discredited scheme. Soon the now floating peso depreciated sharply and domestic prices increased rapidly. A record large debt default by Argentina cut off its access to international capital markets and forced brutal internal adjustment. Unlike other ECs, the Argentine Government, after abandoning the currency board in the early 2000s, hardly strengthened the position of the central bank which remained hobbled by an ineffective regime, resulting in many years of high inflation.

Box 9.1 New Approaches in Monetary Theory

The debate between adhering to rules for monetary policy and the discretionary approach based primarily on judgment never ended, although after the monetarist bent lost ground in the 1980s, the introduction of inflation targeting established something of a middle ground. Alternatives to direct inflation targeting were advanced from time to time, the most influential being the approach suggested by Stanford Professor John Taylor in his influential article 'Discretion versus Policy Rules' (Taylor 1993). What came to be known as the *Taylor Rule* is a formula that relates the short-term interest rate, which central banks steer through open market transactions, to the prevailing economic conditions, as reflected by the degree to which current output deviates from potential output, and the rate of inflation. The formula reads:

$$r = p + .5y + 0.5(p - 2) + 2.$$

Where r is the short-term interest rate, p is the rate of inflation and y is percent deviation of real GDP from a target, better known as the output gap.

In policy terms, Taylor's formula states that the central bank will raise its target interest rate (the federal funds rate in the United States) by 0.5 percent for each percentage point that the rate of inflation surpasses the central bank's inflation target of 2 percent and also by 0.5 percent for each percentage point that output increases relative to its potential. The formula proved to be a good fit for the Fed's monetary policy in the 1980s and 1990s and up to the Great Recession. Since then, depending on the definitions used for p and y, its performance has been less impressive and therefore often considered unfit to serve in a prescriptive role. Nevertheless, Taylor's formula is a valuable analytical tool which, although not used as a fixed rule by central banks, has served as an additional piece of information in support of qualitative judgments on the state of the economy. Those who support a bigger role for the Taylor rule in deciding on monetary policy actions argue that the rule would reduce uncertainty and increase the credibility of future actions of central banks by diminishing the time inconsistency that discretion can create.

(*continued*)

Box 9.1 (continued)

Since Taylor believes that his rule should not only serve as a description of past monetary policy decisions but also as a benchmark for the conduct of current policy, he has been critical of the Federal Reserve's policies on occasion. In his view the American Central Bank kept monetary policy too loose from 2001 until the Great Recession, blaming the Fed for contributing in large measure to the excesses in the financial system that led to the Global Financial Crisis that erupted in 2007. Taylor has argued that the Fed erred strongly on the side of accommodation for fear of a deflation à la Japan, from which that country suffered following an unsustainable financial and real estate boom in the late 1980s and early 1990s. Taylor also pointed out that a similar loosening of monetary policy in Europe, which deviated from his rule, had—like in the United States—caused a house price boom which ended in a deep crash. Others have, however, argued that the Fed's easy policy in the early 2000s is best explained by a concern that a speedy increase in interest rates (as in 1994) would have serious repercussions for the bond market.

The Taylor rule has remained popular with some academics and politicians, sometimes inspired by a desire to reduce the Federal Reserve's independence. Former Fed Chairman, Ben Bernanke, while expressing Taylor's contribution as valuable, has challenged the usefulness of its role as a prescriptive formula for actual policymaking (Bernanke 2015). Bernanke disputes Taylor's claim that his rule should be followed practically constantly and that deviating from it can be very costly, pointing to the unsustainable house price boom of the first half of the 2000s, which he believes was largely caused by too low interest rates. Bernanke also takes issue with Taylor's assertion that the central bank's monetary stance since the end of the Great Financial Crisis has been too loose and that it continued its policy of keeping interest rates very low for too long. When mapping the original Taylor rule against the Fed funds rate, the relationship between the two is quite close up to 2009, but then breaks down, the 'Taylor' rate falling relatively deep into negative territory since 2011, that is after the Great Recession.

References

Alesina, Alberto and Lawrence Summers: "Central Bank Independence and Macroeconomic Performance: Some Comparative Evidence", *Journal of Money, Credit and Banking*, May 1993, 251–62.

Bernanke, Ben: "The Taylor Rule", The Brookings Institution, 2015.

Capie, Forrest: *The Bank of England 1950s to 1979,* Cambridge University Press, 2010.

Cuckierman, Alex: *Central Bank Strategy, Credibility and Independence*, MIT Press, Cambridge MA, 1992.

Dincer, Nergiz and Barry Eichengreen: "Central Bank Transparency and Independence", *International Journal of Central Banking*, March 2014, 189–253.

Eijffinger, Sylvester and Jacob de Haan: *The Political Economy of Central Bank Independence*, Special papers in International Economics no 19, Princeton University, 1996.

Fischer, Stanley: "Modern Central Banking", *Presentation* at the Bank of England, June, 1994, reprinted in Stanley Fischer, *IMF Essays from a Time of Crisis,* MIT Press, Cambridge MA, 2003.

Goodhart, Charles and Dirk Schoenmaker: "Institutional Separation between Supervisory and Monetary Agencies", *Paper presented at the Conference on Prudential Regulation, Supervision and Monetary Policy,* Bocconi University, Milan, 1993.

Haldane, Andrew: "Inflation Target", Bank of England, *Quarterly Bulletin,* August, 1995.

Longworth, Peter: "The Canadian Monetary Transmission System", in Mario Blejer et al (eds), *Inflation Targeting in Practice*, International Monetary Fund, 2000.

Murray, John: "Inflation Targeting after Twenty-Eight Years: What have we Learned?" Norges Bank, *Arbeidsnoted* 217/4, Oslo, 2017.

Taylor, John: "Discretion versus Policy Rules in Practice", *Carnegie-Rochester Series on Public Policy* 39, December 1993, 195–214.

CHAPTER 10

The European Central Bank: A New Power

Jeroen Hessel

Twenty Years of EMU and ECB

With the signing of the Maastricht Treaty in 1992, the Member States of the European Union started an unprecedented monetary experiment. For the very first time, advanced economies in Europe envisaged to give up their monetary sovereignty and form a monetary union. Monetary policy would be conducted in this currency union at the European level by a supranational central bank. Despite substantial skepticism from political and economic perspectives (Jonung and Drea 2009), the Economic and Monetary Union (EMU) was established in 1999. At the time, the new European Central Bank—located in a rented tower in the center of Frankfurt—still had to establish its reputation. As a youngster among central banks, the ECB was standing in the shadow of its illustrious and credible predecessor, the Bundesbank. And there was considerable doubt whether the ECB would manage to keep inflation as low and stable as the Bundesbank had.

Twenty years on, the European Central Bank (ECB) has been transformed into what is generally considered to be the most important and effective institution in the European Union. Located in an impressive new building in the east of Frankfurt, the ECB has played a crucial role in solving the existential crisis that the monetary union experienced in the aftermath of the global financial crisis of 2008. In 2012, the famous 'whatever it takes' speech of ECB President Mario Draghi set in motion events that

O. de Beaufort Wijnholds, *The Money Masters*,
https://doi.org/10.1007/978-3-030-40041-5_10

stabilized financial market turbulence at the height of the euro crisis. Since then, the ECB has implemented several new policies and acquired new responsibilities. In 2014 it also became responsible for banking supervision within the monetary union. Despite these clear successes, the transformation of the ECB has also been accompanied by increased criticism. Concerns that the ECB may have become too powerful, and its policy measures too intrusive, have even led to court cases. German citizens questioned the legitimacy of the ECB's *Outright Monetary Transactions* (OMT) program before the German Constitutional Court, albeit without success.

This chapter describes the development of the ECB and its policies in the 20 years since the start of the euro. It does so against the backdrop of the broader economic and institutional developments in EMU and its Member States, because many of the developments in the responsibilities and policies of the ECB are intimately linked with the wellbeing of the monetary union as a whole. It contains two main messages. First, despite its unique institutional setting, the ECB is quite normal. Many of its policies and the dilemmas it faced are very similar to those of central banks in other advanced economies. These include the need for supplying liquidity support during the 2008 financial crisis, avoiding deflation and the large scale use of unconventional monetary policies.

Second, at the same time, the ECB is special due to the constellation of the monetary union. One the one hand, some of the institutional shortcomings of the monetary union forced the ECB to go further than other central banks did. With the Outright Monetary Transactions (OMT) for example, the ECB made explicit that it would (under circumstances) act as lender of last resort for governments. Many other central banks have not been as explicit concerning this possibility. On the other hand, some of the ECB's policies have been more controversial than of the other central banks. For example, in a monetary union the potential losses related to liquidity support to banks and the purchase of sovereign bonds could lead to politically sensitive redistribution between Member States.

The structure of this chapter is as follows. After a description of the original set-up of the monetary union and the ECB as its centerpiece, the first decade of the project is described. Subsequently, after some initial successes, the growing vulnerabilities, which were exposed during the Global Financial Crisis and the European Sovereign Debt Crisis, are identified. This is followed by an evaluation of the repairs conducted to remedy the design flaws. Finally, the future position and role of the ECB are reflected on.

Establishing the Monetary Union: The Search for Stability

Run-up to the Maastricht Treaty

The idea of a monetary union in the European Union goes back all the way to the Werner report in 1970. Already then, it was clear that exchange rate stability, and eventually a monetary union, was needed to fully reap the benefits of European integration and especially of the internal market. Without a common currency, Member States still had the possibility to devalue their exchange rate to gain competitiveness over other EU countries.

Despite this economic logic, the idea of a monetary union never really gained political momentum for several decades. Instead, the EU opted for several forms of fixed but adjustable exchange rate regimes, starting in 1971. The European Monetary System (EMS) was introduced in 1979, allowing European currencies to fluctuate within a margin of ±2.25 percent of each other. An important drawback of these types of exchange rate arrangements is that they are sensitive to financial market speculation and crises. EU Member States therefore regularly experienced periods of market turbulence and exchange rate realignments. Between 1979 and 1993, the EMS saw as many as 54 realignments of weaker currencies against the D mark. Moreover, these crises became more frequent and more severe when European countries liberalized their capital accounts and capital mobility increased considerably. Subsequently the severe EMS-crises in 1992 and 1993 forced several countries to devalue and Italy and the United Kingdom to even exit from the mechanism. In reaction to these events, EMS fluctuation margins were widened to ±15 percent. With these increasingly severe consequences for Member States and for the functioning of the internal market, the idea of a full monetary union became more attractive on economic grounds.

Meanwhile, political momentum had also increased considerably due to the fall of the Berlin wall in 1989, and the subsequent desire for German reunification. Geopolitically, a monetary union would enable EU countries to embed an enlarged Germany more strongly within Europe. Moreover, it would give other European countries like France more influence over monetary policy in Europe than under a regime of pegging the exchange rate to the D mark. As a result of these rather unique economic and political developments, EU countries decided after all to form a monetary union with a single European currency: the euro.

Macroeconomic Stability

A central goal of the Maastricht Treaty was to ensure that the new common currency would be sufficiently stable. Germany was not willing to give up its D mark without rock-solid guarantees for macroeconomic stability. The aim of the Maastricht Treaty was therefore to prevent the economic policy mistakes that had plagued many European Member States in the 1970s and 1980s: high inflation and large budget deficits and rapidly growing government debt.

In order to ensure a high degree of stability of the common currency, it was agreed that countries would only be able to join the monetary union if they met strict convergence criteria related to monetary and budgetary stability. According to the Maastricht Treaty, Member States would have to meet the following criteria (now article 140 of the Treaty on the Functioning of the European Union—TFEU):

1. A high degree of *price stability*, measured by an inflation rate not higher than 1.5 percent above the average inflation of the three best performing Member States.
2. *Exchange rate stability*: an exchange rate within the ±2.25 percent fluctuation margins for at least two years without severe tensions, in particular without devaluing.
3. *Durable convergence*, measured by long-term interest rates not higher than 2 percent above the average of the three best performing Member States in terms of price stability.
4. *Sound and sustainable public finances*, measured as a budget deficit below 3 percent of GDP and the level of government debt below 60 percent of GDP.

In the run-up to the start of EMU, extensive political discussion took place on how strictly these criteria should be interpreted, the goal being to determine which countries would qualify for the monetary union from the very beginning. Eventually the European Council applied the debt criterion leniently, by stating that countries with debt levels that were declining at a sufficient pace toward the 60 percent threshold would also qualify. This decision was especially welcome for high debt countries like Italy and Belgium. It enabled a broad group of 11 countries to join EMU in 1999, and Greece shortly thereafter.

A second way to ensure macroeconomic stability was declaring that the budgetary convergence criteria (3 percent deficit and 60 percent debt) were to remain valid when participating in EMU. The intention was to prevent countries from letting their public finances to deteriorate again once their place in the monetary union was secured. The Maastricht Treaty therefore contained an excessive deficit procedure (now article 126 TFEU), which requires the Council of Ministers to issue warnings, and ultimately to impose financial sanctions on Member States that continue to breach the deficit criterion. In order to facilitate compliance, the Amsterdam treaty of 1997 contained new budgetary rules under the Stability and Growth Pact (SGP). The SGP prescribed countries to strive for a balanced budget over the business cycle, so that they could withstand normal recessions without breaching the 3 percent deficit threshold. Moreover, the Maastricht Treaty also explicitly stated that the EU and other Member States would not be liable for the debts of individual countries, the so-called 'no bailout clause' (article 125 TFEU). While the Maastricht Treaty thus contained strict and detailed budgetary rules, other aspects of economic policy were largely left to Member States themselves. The only obligation was to regard them as 'a matter of common concern' and to coordinate them within the Council of Ministers (Article 121 TFEU).

Monetary Stability

On the monetary side, the original set-up of the monetary union also contained many safeguards to ensure that inflation would remain low and stable. The European monetary framework was relatively strict, and deviated in important ways from the frameworks in other advanced economies. Several of these deviations were related to the success of the monetary framework of the German Bundesbank. It was hoped that this would help the ECB to establish its credibility. The following features stand out in particular.

First, the primary objective of the ECB is to maintain price stability (article 127 TFEU). Other objectives, like growth, a low unemployment level or the broader objectives of the EU are only relevant as long as the primary objective is met. This strong emphasis on price stability differs from (the few) central banks with a dual mandate, like the US Federal Reserve which has both low inflation and low unemployment as primary objectives. However, the ECB's set-up is broadly consistent with the establishment of 'inflation targeting' frameworks introduced by many central banks in advanced countries at the time.

Second, the Governing Council of the ECB adopted a quantitative definition of the price stability objective in 1998. Price stability was defined as a year-on-year inflation rate below 2 percent. For reasons of flexibility, this objective was to be achieved over the medium term, thought to be around two years. The use of a quantitative inflation goal increases transparency and credibility, and is also a key ingredient of most inflation targeting regimes. However, the ECB's definition of inflation *below* 2 percent raised the question whether this objective was symmetric, that is whether deviations above the target were treated the same as deviations below the target (Blanchard 2019).

Third, to achieve this objective, the ECB opted for a somewhat unusual two-pillar monetary strategy. The first pillar was based on monetary analysis. It compared the growth of broad monetary aggregates to an annual reference value of 4.5 percent that was based on projections for trend growth, changes in the velocity of money and inflation. The second pillar contained the real economic factors that directly affect the inflation outlook, such as economic growth, developments in wages and other costs. The use of the monetary pillar was inspired by the monetary strategy of the Bundesbank, though it was no longer a common practice among central banks at the time. As a result, the ECB strategy deviated from the strategy of direct inflation-targeting of many other central banks.

Fourth, unlike in many other countries, the Maastricht Treaty contains an explicit prohibition of monetary financing of budget deficits (article 123 TFEU). The ECB is prohibited from directly purchasing bonds from governments in Member States, although purchases on the secondary market are allowed. This legal clause is also strongly related to German monetary history. The prohibition of monetary financing is meant to prevent the type of hyperinflation that plagued Germany in the 1920s and after Second World War.

Finally, the ECB was made legally independent and was prohibited from taking instructions from anyone when carrying out its tasks (article 130 TFEU). Such formal central bank independence was partly a legacy of the Bundesbank, but also in line with an international trend as well. Many other central banks were also made legally independent around the time of the Maastricht Treaty (described in Chap. 9). But since the ECB's independence is part of the EU Treaty, and thus can only be changed by unanimity among 28 Member States, it is sometimes referred to as *the most independent central bank in the world.*

First Decade: Success and Underlying Vulnerability

Initial Skepticism

The start of the monetary union was met with skepticism from several sides. One line of criticism focused on political economy factors, reflecting doubts whether the institutional set-up would be sufficiently credible. From the monetary side, many observers expressed 'curiosity' whether the newly established ECB would be able to keep inflation down as well as the illustrious Bundesbank. The ECB's somewhat divergent monetary framework was not seen as a reassurance feature (Blanchard 2019). It was also questioned whether the European budgetary rules had sufficient 'bite' to ensure that Member States kept their public finances within the prescribed boundaries (Buiter et al. 1993). More generally, it was argued that the monetary union would need to be a genuine 'political union' to succeed (Feldstein 1997), although it often remained unclear what exactly such a political union would have to entail.

Another line of criticism was based on the so-called theory of optimum currency areas. Many academics argued that EMU would not fulfill the criteria of such an optimum currency area. Compared to the United States, European Member States had a higher risk of country-specific (or asymmetric) shocks (Bayoumi and Eichengreen 1993). Unlike the United States, they also lacked the adjustment mechanisms to deal with such shocks. Cross-border labor mobility was lower (Décressin and Fatás 1995), flexibility of wages and prices was less and a federal budget was absent (Sala-i-Martin and Sachs 1992). As a result, European countries would, so the argument went, find it much harder than US states to cushion asymmetric shocks after giving up their national monetary policies. And this would hamper the functioning of EMU.

Apparent Success

The monetary union was set in motion despite these criticisms, underscoring that it was partly a political project. And the first decade of EMU was a success in many ways. The most important achievement was that the ECB turned out to be very credible in fighting inflation. The monetary policy decisions from the Governing Council—taken in practice by consensus—were influenced by a variety of economic developments, including movements in oil prices and the exchange rate of the

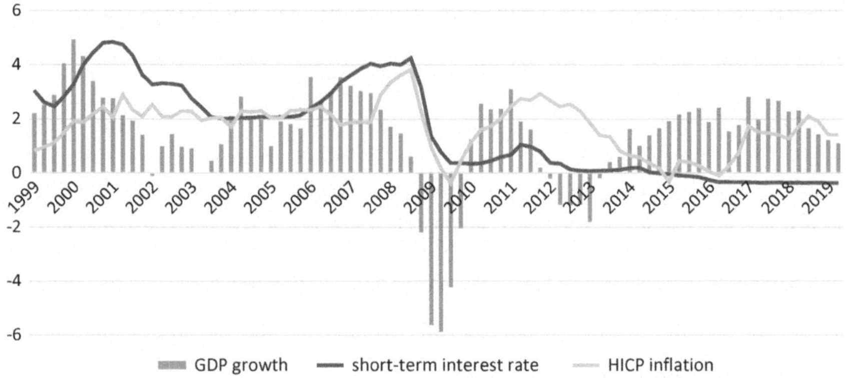

Fig. 10.1 Growth, inflation and short-term interest rate in the euro area

euro. The interest rate decisions in the first years were particularly driven by the economic fluctuations that surrounded the so-called dot-com bubble which burst in 2000 and contributed to a global recession in the years thereafter (Fig. 10.1). In the end, average annual inflation in the euro area amounted to 2.05 percent from 1999 to 2008, almost exactly matching the inflation goal. This favorable outcome may have been partly due to worldwide trends, such as globalization, that helped keeping inflation under control in many countries. But, importantly, inflation expectations in the euro area were just as well anchored as in other advanced economies from the very beginning (Hartmann and Smets 2018). The fears that the ECB would not be sufficiently credible therefore soon proved to be unfounded.

After four years of experience, the ECB conducted a review of its monetary policy strategy (Hartmann and Smets 2018). This resulted in two adjustments. First, the Governing Council clarified that the target for price stability was to maintain inflation rates below, *but close to*, 2 percent over the medium term. The goal was to emphasize that the ECB aimed for a sufficient inflation buffer and hence would also act if inflation was too far below the target. This was relevant because the recession in 2002 and 2003 had led to discussion on possible deflation risks in many advanced economies. The adjustment also aimed to make clear that the inflation target of the ECB was not asymmetric. As a second adjustment, the ECB changed the order of the two pillars of its strategy, which in effect meant that the emphasis on monetary developments would become less important. The first pillar was now the economic analysis that contained the broad assessment of factors relevant for the inflation outlook. In practice, these factors were the most important drivers of the interest rate decisions by the Governing Council. The monetary analysis now became the second pillar, and would act as a cross check on the economic analysis from a more medium to long-run perspective.

Turning to other aspects of the monetary union, economic growth in the euro area was reasonable at 1.5 percent per year. While this was significantly lower than the 2.4 percent average in the previous two decades, the decrease in growth rates was to some extent a global phenomenon—at least in advanced economies (Reichlin 2019). The only area of the monetary union where the track record was more mixed was public finances. The most apparent flaw in the enforcement of the European budgetary rules was breaching the 3 percent of GDP threshold for the budget balance in 2002–2003 by both France and Germany. Unfortunately the Council of Ministers decided not to impose the sanctions that were available under the Treaty when both countries subsequently failed to reduce their deficits below 3 percent within the required timeframe. More generally, the more ambitious budgetary goal of the Stability and Growth Pact, namely to reach a balanced budget over the business cycle, was not achieved by most EMU countries. This meant that while public debt levels declined, they did not do so as fast as when all rules had been fully adhered to.

Despite the fiscal hiccup, there was an exaggerated sense of optimism at the end of the first decade of EMU. In June 2008 the European Commission stated almost euphorically that: 'structural budget deficits are at their lowest levels since the 1970s' (European Commission 2008a) and that 'EMU is a resounding success' (European Commission 2008b). Jonung and Drea (2009) claimed that the initial skepticism based on the theory of optimum currency areas had turned out to be unfounded in the paper entitled 'The euro. It can't happen. It's a bad idea. It won't last.' In retrospect, these optimistic statements were made only a few months before the fall of the American investment bank, Lehman Brothers, triggered the Global Financial Crisis.

Growing Vulnerabilities

In hindsight, the optimism after the first decade was an 'oddly uncritical' attitude (Pisani-Ferry 2018). In due course it became crystal clear that important vulnerabilities were already building in both EMU and its Member States. Yet these imbalances had somehow remained under the radar at the time. A plausible explanation is that many academics and policymakers failed to realize that the economic tectonic plates were shifting. The main cause of these movements was the deregulation of financial sectors and the liberalization of international capital flows since the early 1990s. It turned out that the monetary union was not well-suited to weather this change.

Since the start-up of the common currency, *financial* factors had become much more important in advanced economies than in the 1970s and 1980s. Besides the impact of rapid international financial developments and integration in the euro area, reduced exchange rate risks due to dealing with a single currency instead of a variety of rates, further stimulated cross-country capital flows (Lane 2013; Obstfeld 2013). To illustrate the pervasive nature of the change, the average size of foreign assets and liabilities of euro area countries increased from around 70 percent of GDP in the mid-1990s to almost 300 percent of GDP just before the financial crisis.

These financial developments led to a strong increase of credit, house prices and the size of banking sectors in many EMU countries. But the results differed significantly between Member States. Within the monetary union persistent and long-lasting divergences in the growth of credit and house prices, in relative prices and in current account balances (De Haan et al. 2015, see also Fig. 10.2) emerged. The largest imbalances—credit and housing booms, loss of price competitiveness and current account deficits—built up in Southern Europe for a number of reasons. These countries experienced a strong decline in long-term interest rates due to their EMU membership, and were still going through a process of financial development and economic convergence. Moreover, institutions and policy frameworks may have been more vulnerable in Southern Europe. As a result, countries like Greece, Ireland, Italy, Portugal and Spain (the so-called GIIPS) proved most vulnerable during the crises that followed.

Second Decade: Crises and Design Flaws in the Monetary Union

The Global Financial Crisis that reached a boiling point in September 2008 was driven mainly by turmoil due to a collapse of the US housing market (see Chap. 11).This first phase of the crisis mainly hit the euro area via the large internationally oriented banks in Northern European countries like France, Ireland, Belgium and the Netherlands. These banks had bought large amounts of packages of securitized US (subprime) mortgages that resulted in credit losses and trading losses (as the complexity of these products made them unpredictable and hence illiquid). In Europe, this part of the financial crisis resulted in the drying up of the interbank market, significant losses for banks and the need for public support of banking sectors in several countries.

Southern European banks and Member States were relatively shielded from this initial phase. The situation changed when their domestic imbalances started to unwind after the global change in financial conditions. The Southern countries suffered a much stronger than expected deterioration of public finances, on the back of corrections in current accounts, house prices and household debt levels (Gilbert and Hessel 2014). Triggered by the shock of a strong upward revision in the Greek budget

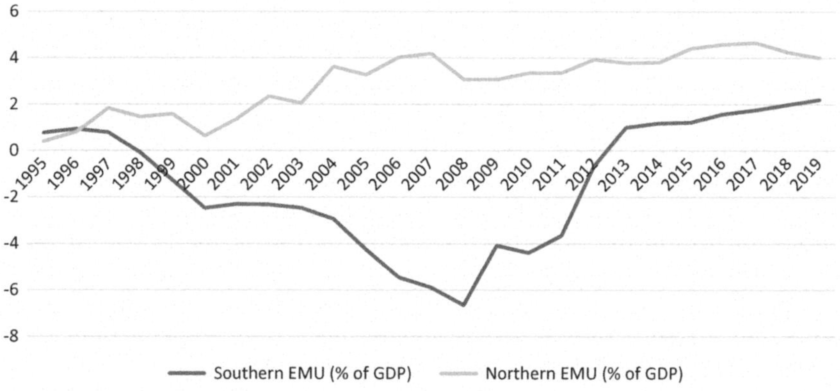

Fig. 10.2 Current account balances in the euro area. (Note: based on data from the original 12 EMU member states only. Southern European Countries are Greece, Italy, Ireland, Portugal and Spain. Northern European Countries are Austria, Belgium, Finland, France, Germany, Luxemburg and the Netherlands)

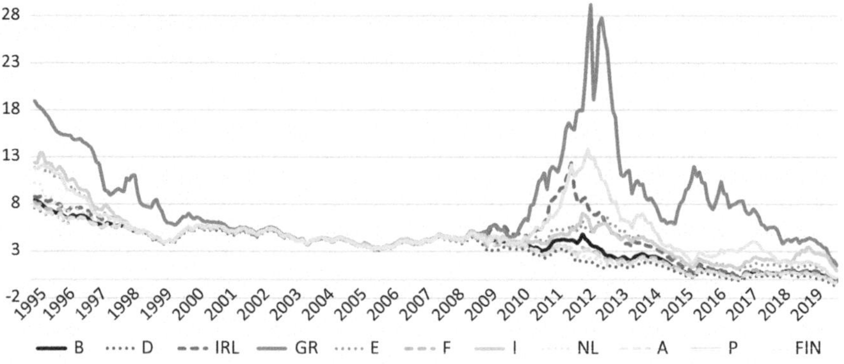

Fig. 10.3 Long-term interest rates in the euro area

deficit, long-term interest rates in Southern European countries increased steeply in 2010. The resulting European sovereign debt crisis unfolded (Fig. 10.3), leading to severe financial fragmentation and funding difficulties for both governments and banks. A wide range of crisis measures were taken by national governments, the European Council and the ECB, to tame financial markets. Yet the tide only started to turn decisively after ECB President, Mario Draghi's famous 'whatever it takes' speech in the summer of 2012.

The European Sovereign Debt Crisis exposed design flaws in the initial set-up of the monetary union, with the growing role of financial factors amplifying existing vulnerabilities. It also exposed new ones that had not been foreseen (Hessel et al. 2017). Four flaws can be identified that by now have been addressed in some way or the other. The monetary union has been strengthened considerably as a result, although further improvements remain necessary. The first flaw is that the safeguards for sound public finances in the Maastricht Treaty proved to be ineffective. In particular, the balanced budget requirement of the Stability and Growth Pact was poorly enforced, so that deficits did not improve enough in good times. As a result, several improvements have been implemented. For example, the decision-making process regarding the budgetary rules was strengthened after the crisis. The European Council of Ministers now needs a qualified, instead of a simple majority to block sanctions proposed by the European Commission. It remains to be seen how much compliance and enforcement have actually improved (Council of State 2017).

Second, EMU's initial structure paid too little attention to other macroeconomic imbalances like current account deficits, housing booms and private debt levels. The new macroeconomic imbalance procedure (MIP) brought economic imbalances into sharper focus. Under this procedure, the Commission analyses the risks of imbalances in Member States and assesses whether an imbalance is excessive. If it is, the Council of Ministers issues policy recommendations, and may impose penalties if a country fails to implement them. In addition, Member States have themselves introduced macroprudential policy frameworks, which enable them to impose higher capital requirements during financial booms (see also Chap. 13).

Third, the financial turmoil was amplified because national governments and financial sectors proved closely interconnected, the so-called sovereign-bank nexus. As European commercial banks hold large volumes of national government bonds, they were sensitive to the fortunes of their national governments. Vice versa, national public finances were strongly influenced by the health of the financial sector, as bailing out the large banking sectors in many European countries proved to be very costly. The newly introduced, but still incomplete, European banking union has lessened the close ties between banks and governments. And the Single Supervisory Mechanism (SMM) ensures that the ECB, together with national supervisory authorities, carries out banking supervision at the European level. In addition, the Single Resolution Mechanism (SRM) facilitates the resolution of insolvent banks. To protect taxpayers, specific creditors now will bear some of the cost in a bail-in procedure. The banking union has now been functioning for five years, but political discussions on its completion are still ongoing.

Fourth, in a monetary union like EMU national governments proved to be prone to contagion and self-reinforcing liquidity crises. One reason for this was the absence of the central bank's role as the government's lender of last resort (De Grauwe 2011). Redenomination risk (a euphemism for exchange rate risk) also had an impact, through the perceived risk of a country leaving the euro area. Various financial safety nets have in the meantime been created which are to prevent future turbulence, capital flight and contagion. The European Stability Mechanism (ESM) enables contributing members to obtain (conditional) massive temporary financial support funded by national governments. And the ECB can use its program of outright monetary transactions (OMT) under specific circumstances (see below). This welcome set of new rules and institutions is relatively new and have not yet been fully tested.

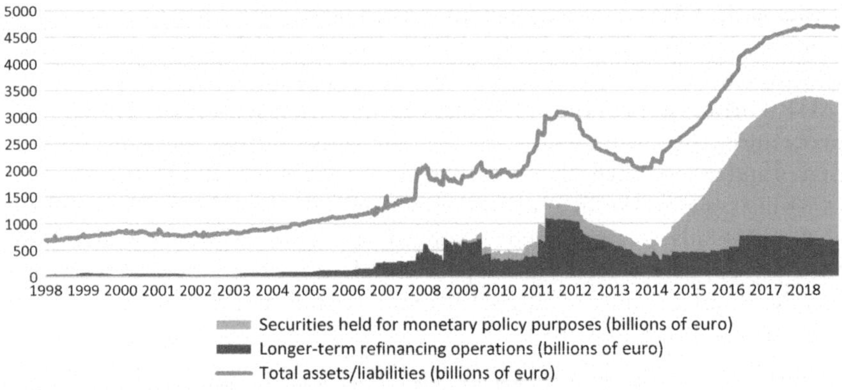

Fig. 10.4 Evolution consolidated balance sheet eurosystem

New Policies and Tasks for the ECB

The crises during the second decade of EMU also had a profound influence on the ECB. The central bank implemented several new policies and formally acquired new responsibilities. These developments were partly driven by exceptional economic circumstances, deflation risks and financial stability concerns. In some cases, they were also partly driven by the fact that other actors in the monetary union were unable to propose solutions for these problems. One of the results of these policies was that the balance sheet of the ECB has expanded significantly since the crisis (Fig. 10.4).

All in all, the ECB has played a crucial role in containing the euro crisis and in strengthening the set-up of the monetary union. The ECB was therefore widely lauded (see for example Blanchard 2019). Yet it sometimes also led to debates, including judicial questions before the European Court of Justice. From a broader perspective, it can be said that the policies of the ECB during the crisis did not differ all that much from those of other central banks in advanced economies. Central bank policies in other countries had to deal with similar dilemmas and discussions (see for example Tucker 2018). At the same time, because the ECB operates in a monetary union, some of these policies are more complicated and this adds to the debate in Europe. Four new policies or task deserve particular attention.

Liquidity Provision to Banks

First, the ECB provided extra liquidity to banks that needed funding during both the financial crisis and the sovereign debt crisis (Hartmann and Smets 2018). It also expanded the list of eligible collateral that banks could use. During the Global Financial Crisis, the ECB started to provide short-term liquidity in unlimited amounts ('full allotment') in September 2018, in order to restore the functioning of the interbank market which threatened to freeze up due to uncertainty about the liquidity and credit risks of other banks.

During the European sovereign debt crisis, roughly between 2010 and 2013, the ECB also started to provide liquidity in longer maturities, up to around three years, through long-term refinancing operations (LTRO's, see Fig. 10.4). At this stage of the crisis, more general concerns about the health of both banks and sovereigns had led to widespread capital flight between euro area countries, resulting in increasing risk premiums and funding difficulties. The aim of the longer-term refinancing operations was to restore the monetary transmission mechanism, by providing banks with a stable longer-term source of funding. In the aftermath of the crisis, the ECB continued to provide long-term refinancing operations, with even longer maturities (up to four years). At this stage, the most important aim of these measures was to contribute to the general easing of monetary and financial conditions, in order to stimulate credit provision and (eventually) inflation.

Liquidity provision to banks is a classic 'lender of last resort' role that was also implemented by many other central banks during the crisis. As history teaches, the lender of last resort function requires a distinction between liquidity problems and solvency problems of banks (Bagehot 1873). While liquidity support can be provided by the central bank, solvency support should preferably be addressed by democratically elected governments financed with taxpayer money. However, especially during crises, it is not always fully clear whether banks are suffering from liquidity or solvency issues. There is always a certain risk that liquidity measures could de facto function as solvency support. This also implies that the support came with financial risks for the central bank. Of course central banks—and also the ECB—are protected against these risks because the liquidity is provided against collateral on which appropriate haircuts (discounts of asset values according to degree of risk) are applied.

An additional complication with respect to the monetary union is that liquidity support has not been provided evenly across all Member States. In general, banks in Southern European countries have made by far the most use of these facilities. Especially during the sovereign debt crisis, these liquidity needs reflected the outflow of private capital from Southern to Northern Europe (a flight to safety). Therefore the provision of liquidity was accompanied by large debit and credit positions within the ECB's Target 2 payments system. In March 2019, for example, credit positions amounted to €940 billion for Germany and €80 billion for the Netherlands, whereas debit positions were largest in Italy (€475 billion), Spain (€402 billion) and Portugal (€80 billion). These positions are temporary snapshots, and can decrease again very quickly once private capital restarts to flow more freely. However, the positions could become difficult to unwind in the very unlikely case of a break-up of the monetary union. This possibility of losses is sometimes seen as a degree of risk sharing between the Member States in monetary union (Council of State, 2017).

(Potential) Liquidity Provision to Governments

Second, since the sovereign debt crisis the ECB has started to (potentially) buy government bonds of countries with financing difficulties (Hartmann and Smets 2018). The sovereign debt crisis led to doubts about the sustainability of public finances in several EMU Member States, which led to a strong increase in risk premiums and long-term interest rates (Fig. 10.3). In several cases, interest rates were higher than could be explained on the basis of fundamentals—an indication of *overshooting* in the market (De Haan et al. 2014). These developments caused disruption of the orderly transmission of monetary policy in various parts of the euro area.

In May 2010, the ECB therefore started the Securities Markets Program (SMP) in which government bonds were purchased from Member States that found themselves in financial distress. The purchases were sterilized to underline that the program was not intended to change the monetary stance. During the same period, EMU Member States also introduced various financial safety nets for governments, including the European Financial Stability Facility (EFSF), the European Financial Stabilisation Mechanism (EFSM) and eventually their successor the European Stability Mechanism (ESM). However, all these programs were not enough to halt contagion and calm financial markets. In the summer of 2012, the ECB therefore announced the Outright Monetary Transactions (OMT) Program—the SMP's successor. Under certain conditions ECB can buy potentially unlimited government bonds from European governments in difficulties. One of the conditions is that the country has a support program from the ESM with strict conditionality. From a monetary point of view, the OMT was necessary to restore the monetary transmission mechanism that was impaired due to 'unfounded fears about the reversibility of the euro' (Draghi 2012). The program has not yet been used so far, but nevertheless was very effective in calming financial markets in the euro area. The sheer announcement of the potential use of ECB money was sufficient to reduce contagion and spillover effects between countries (Gilbert 2019).

In many ways this role of the ECB can be seen as lender of last resort for governments, which central banks are often assumed to fulfill in countries with their own currency (De Grauwe 2011). However, it still led to debates within EMU for several reasons. First, in EMU this lender of last resort role has now been made more explicit than is often the case for other central banks, where this function is often surrounded with 'constructive ambiguity'. Second, it is sometimes questioned whether purchases of specific countries' government bonds are consistent with the prohibition of monetary financing under the Maastricht Treaty. Third, buying bonds of individual Member States is a form of public risk sharing that could give rise to transfers between countries, for which the ECB has no mandate. Therefore, the OMT has been discussed intensively, and has even led to court cases. Following questions from the *Bundesverfassungsgericht*, the German Federal Constitutional Court, the European Court of Justice ruled that the SMP and OMT programs can be considered to be part of the ECB's mandate and do not conflict with the prohibition of monetary financing (Article 123 TFEU).

Unconventional Monetary Policy

Third, in 2015 the ECB initiated large-scale unconventional monetary policies, in particular outright asset purchases and a more extended use of *forward guidance* (Hartmann and Smets 2018). Inflation was low in the aftermath of the crisis, and during 2015 headline inflation briefly turned negative due to declining oil prices, while core inflation dropped below 1 percent (Fig. 10.1). Moreover, inflation expectations also started to decrease, which had until then remained well-anchored, leading to increasing concerns regarding deflation risks and long period of low inflation, also because the policy interest rate had approached the *zero lower bound*.

Like many other central banks in advanced economies, the ECB therefore started to purchase assets under its Asset Purchase Program (APP), a policy also known as Quantitative Easing (see Fig. 10.4). The aim of the APP was to support the monetary transmission mechanism and stimulate overall economic activity and inflation in order to achieve price stability. The APP consisted of several programs for specific types of assets. First, the ECB purchased national and international government bonds under the Public Sector Purchase Program (PSPP). The ECB decided not to apply risk sharing to the purchases of national bonds under the PSPP, unlike with any potential purchases under the OMT. The purchases under the PSPP were undertaken at the risk of the central banks of the Member States (NCBs) themselves. The ECB also bought corporate bonds under the Corporate Sector Purchase Program (CSPP), covered bonds under the Covered Bond Purchase Program (CBPP) and asset-backed securities under the Asset-Backed Securities Purchase Program (ABSPP).

The APP was recalibrated several times under the influence of the economic and inflation outlook. In general inflation remained below the ECB's inflation target for a considerable time, and hence the program was in place for a number of years. Total (net) asset purchases amounted to €60 to 80 billion a month between March 2015 and December 2017, following which purchases were gradually reduced to zero at the end of 2018. In September 2019 the ECB decided to restart the net purchases at a pace of €20 billion per month (see Chap. 14). Overall, the APP is estimated to have had a significant downward effect on long-term interest rates, thereby stimulating economic growth and to a lesser extent bringing up inflation (Hartmann and Smets, 2018). At the same time, the longer the program of unconventional monetary policy was maintained, the more discussion emerged about possible negative side effects. These include the risk of asset price bubbles, excessive risk-taking and other financial imbalances (see also Chaps. 11, 12 and 14).

Banking Supervision

Fourth, since 2014 the ECB has also become responsible for banking supervision in the euro area, with the establishment of the Banking Union. As European banks had become larger and much more internationally oriented, it proved increasingly problematic that the responsibility for supervision and resolution had remained at the Member State level. The European Council therefore decided to establish the Banking Union and the Single Supervisory Mechanism (SSM) in June 2012. The organization of the SSM was fully operational after only 29 months. The SSM started in November 2014 after a comprehensive Asset Quality Review, in order to ensure that there were no legacy issues on the balance sheet of banks. The SSM directly supervises the 116 significant banks in the euro area. This is carried out by Joint Supervisory Teams (JSTs) that are staffed by the ECB and the national supervisors. Banks that are not considered significant (the 'less significant' institutions) continue to be supervised by their national supervisors, in cooperation with the ECB. The ECB can at any time decide to directly supervise any one of these banks when needed.

During the first five years of its existence of the SSM, supervision has clearly been strengthened and has become more comprehensive and intrusive. Due to a more harmonized approach to supervision in Europe, a common supervisory methodology exists and a level playing field in regulation has been established. At the same time, it is clear that the Banking Union as a whole still needs to be fully completed. A European Deposit Insurance Scheme is still lacking, and there is no solution yet for the large quantities of domestic sovereign bonds on banks' balance sheets. Political discussions on the improvement of the Banking Union are currently ongoing in the Council of Ministers.

Several other advanced economies have also brought supervision and monetary policy under one roof, like the Bank of England, after the crisis. Combining the two task may provide synergies for increased effectiveness. But combining supervision and monetary policy in one institution can sometimes also cause complications (see Chap. 9). To a certain extent this potential conflict of interest is acknowledged by separating the supervisory roles within the ECB and placing them with the Supervisory Board.

Conclusion

Twenty years ago, the ECB was a new central bank that had to establish it reputation in the unprecedented institutional set-up of a monetary union. In its first decade, the ECB soon established a solid track record with respect to the core of its mandate—monetary policy. Inflation has been low from the very beginning, and the euro exchange rate remained stable during the turbulence of the Global Financial Crisis and the European follow-up.

In its second decade the ECB implemented new policies and acquired new tasks, both mainly as a result of the crises. These tasks and policies do not necessarily deviate much from those of other central banks, where they have also led to debates. They may have led to even more disputes within EMU, however. This is partly because some of these policies are (politically) more controversial when several Member States are involved, and partly because these policies had to go further than elsewhere due to institutional flaws in the set-up of the monetary union. The strengthened ECB has played a crucial role in solving the sovereign debt crisis and in further strengthening the set-up of the monetary union since then. After two decades, the ECB has become one of the most effective and influential European institutions. One can only speculate on how the ECB's tasks and policies will evolve during its third decade. One issue is how the ECB will fulfill its monetary mandate and design its monetary toolkit in the future. Many of its current policies were implemented at the height of the crises. A key question is: to what extent these measures will be phased out once inflation is on a firmer footing, and which of these instruments will be used on a more permanent basis? A second issue is how the role of the ECB will evolve in the broader context of the monetary union. The role that the ECB currently has in the monetary union is also influenced by the fact that alternative mechanisms were not always present and the fact that Member States and other European institutions were not always able to be decisive. If other parts of the monetary union function better than before, the ECB will be able to focus more on its core mandate and hence will not need to take as many far-reaching measures. Such a situation could, for instance, be achieved if compliance with the EU budgetary rules improves, and if a completed Banking Union limits the interaction between banks and governments more effectively.

The transition of the ECB as not yet fully grown to a mature and respected central bank is encapsulated by Olivier Blanchard as follows: 'It is fair to say that the initial incarnation did not look promising, at least to us on the other side of the ocean. … But as it was tested, the ECB transformed itself, while keeping and indeed reinforcing its credibility. It is hardly recognizable today' (Blanchard 2019).

References

Bagehot, W. (1873), Lombard Street: a Description of the Money Market, Henry King & Co.

Bayoumi, T., and B. Eichengreen. (1993), Shocking Aspects of European Monetary Unification. In: Torres, F. and F. Giavazzi (eds). Adjustment and Growth in the European Monetary Union. Cambridge University Press.

Blanchard, O. (2019), Dinner talk at the ECB forum on Central Banks, Sintra, June 17 2019, www.ecb.europa.eu

Buiter, W. H., G. Corsetti, and N. Roubini (1993), "Excessive deficits: sense and nonsense in the Treaty of Maastricht", *Economic Policy*, Issue 1.

Council of State (Dutch: Raad van State) (2017), The State of the Euro. Advice at the request of the Dutch Parliament, www.Raadvanstate.nl

Décressin, J. and A. Fatas (1995), Regional Labour Market Dynamics in Europe, European Economic Review, 39, 1627–1655.

De Haan, J., J. Hessel and N. Gilbert (2015), Reforming the Architecture of EMU: Ensuring Stability in Europe. In: Badinger, H. and V. Nitsch (eds.), Handbook of the Economics of European Integration, Routledge.

De Haan, L., J. Hessel and J.W. van den End (2014), Are European Sovereign Bond Yields Fairly Priced? The Role of Modelling Uncertainty, *Journal of International Money and Finance*, 47, 239–267.

De Grauwe, P. (2011), Governance of a Fragile Eurozone. CEPS Working Document 34.

Draghi, M. (2012), Introductory Statement to ECB press conference, 6 September 2012, www.ecb.europa.eu

European Commission (2008a), Public Finances in EMU2008. European Economy 4, 2008.

European Commission (2008b), EMU@10. Successes and challenges after ten years of Economic and Monetary Union, European Economy 2/2008.

Feldstein, Martin (1997), "The Political Economy of the European Economic and Monetary Union: Political Sources of an Economic Liability". Journal of Economic Perspectives, 11, 23–42.

Gilbert, N. (2019), Euro area sovereign risk spillovers before and after the ECB's OMT announcement, DNB working paper no. 636.

Gilbert, N. and J. Hessel (2014), "The financial cycle and the European budgetary reversal during the crisis: consequences for surveillance", *proceedings of the 15th Banca d'Italia public finance workshop,* April 3–6, Perugia.

Hartmann, P. and F. Smets (2018), "The first 20 years of the European Central Bank: Monetary policy", Brookings papers on Economic Activity, Fall 2018.

Hessel, J., N. Gilbert and J. de Jong (2017), Capitalising on the euro. Options for strengthening the EMU, DNB Occasional Study 15-2.

Jonung, L. and E. Drea (2009), The Euro: It Can't Happen, It's a Bad Idea, It Won't Last. US Economists on the EMU, 1989–2002. European Economy, Economic Papers 395.

Lane, P.R. (2013), Capital Flows in the Euro Area. European Economy Economic Papers 497.

Obstfeld, M. (2013), Finance at Center Stage: Some Lessons of the Euro Crisis, European Economy - Economic Papers 493.

Pisani-Ferry, J. (2018), Euro area reform: An anatomy of the debate, CEPR policy insight 95.

Reichlin, L. (2019), The European Central Bank, in. G. Amato, E. Moavero-Milanesi, G. Pasquino and L. Reichlin (2019), The History of the European Union. Constructing Utopia, Hart publishers.

Sala-i-Martin, Xavier, and Jeffrey Sachs (1992), Fiscal federalism and optimum currency areas: evidence for Europe from the United States, in M.B. Canzoneri, V. Grilli, en P.R. Masson (eds), Establishing a Central Bank. Issues in Europe and Lessons from the US, Cambridge: Cambridge University Press, 195-219.

Tucker, Paul (2018), Unelected Power. The quest for legitimacy in central banking and the regulatory state, Princeton University Press.

CHAPTER 11

The Global Financial Crisis

Benny Andersen

Central Banking Consensus Pre-crisis

While there were differences, a rough consensus on certain fundamental principles of central banking had evolved prior to the global financial crisis of 2007–09, both in advanced economies and increasingly also in emerging market countries, as described in a comprehensive report of the Group of Thirty (an informal international group of experts) about the lessons from the crisis (Group of Thirty 2015). After the widespread central bank successes in combating the Great Inflation experienced by many advanced countries during the 1970s, the Great Moderation from mid-1980s to around 2007 was characterized by a significant decline in volatility in both growth and inflation, with many countries experiencing the longest economic expansion since the Second World War. While the period was not without challenges, including a number of rather severe economic and financial crises in several emerging market economies, the pursuit of the objective of price stability was remarkably successful across the globe. Policymakers and the intellectual mindset felt reassured that they finally

This chapter draws on De Beaufort Wijnholds (Fighting Financial Fires, Palgrave Macmillan, 2011).

O. de Beaufort Wijnholds, *The Money Masters*,
https://doi.org/10.1007/978-3-030-40041-5_11

got it right and that a general consensus on the fundamentals of sound macroeconomic and financial policies had emerged.

The underlying theory (neoclassical) was that mature economies were generally efficient and self-stabilizing in the allocation of resources, and that following shocks they would relatively soon return to full employment. Prices of financial assets were assumed to be determined by the underlying fundamentals and it was believed that market discipline would largely ensure financial stability. As a consequence, the financial sector barely figured in macroeconomic models, clearly underestimating the important macro-financial linkages in most economies.

This consensus included monetary policy and the converging frameworks focusing on one objective (price stability) and one instrument (short-term policy interest rate). Price stability (low and stable inflation) was considered key to achieving sustainable growth and employment. It became general practice to set the policy interest rate consistent with a forecast for inflation that was on target (generally around 2 percent) over the medium term (typically a two-year time horizon). In its application, a Taylor rule (explained in Chap. 9) was often used, linking interest rate changes to the size of the output gap, and deviations of the inflation rate from the targeted levels. Thus, too high inflation would be an indication that unemployment had been allowed to fall to unsustainably low levels.

Monetary policy during the years of the Great Moderation increasingly focused on using only one instrument, the short-term policy rate. As noted by former IMF chief economist Olivier Blanchard, this choice was supported by the belief that the real effects of monetary policy were transmitted through interest rates and asset prices (not monetary aggregates), and that all interest rates and asset prices were linked through arbitrage and thereby impacted through the setting of current and future expected short-term rates (Blanchard et al. 2010).

Another pillar of mainstream thinking that had gotten more prominence in the 1970s was that central banks should be free from political interference in pursuing their objectives. It was considered key to give central banks independence to facilitate the achievement of the price stability objective. However, the degree of independence varied. In the United Kingdom it is the government who sets the inflation objective and the Bank of England (in effect since 1998) the framework and instruments to achieve it (instrument independence), whereas the ECB and the Federal Reserve also decide what price stability means. In return for independence, it was considered essential that central banks were held accountable for their decisions to the democratically elected politicians and to society, including by ensuring transparency with respect to policy decisions, analysis and considerations. Credibility would be enhanced by clear and open communication.

Furthermore, the role of central banks with regard to financial stability should—according to consensus—overall be limited to their lender-of-last-resort function and crisis management. The successful response to the stock market crash in 1987, the collapse of the huge hedge fund Long Term Capital Management (LTCM) in 1998 and the bursting of the tech stock bubble in the early 2000s had reinforced the view that central banks were well equipped to deal with asset price busts and in encouraging creditor involvement for troubled financial institutions if needed. While central banks' views on financial stability matters were considered appropriate and often supported by academic economists, the primary responsibility rested with other authorities to avoid conflicting objectives for the central bank. And to the extent that central banks had supervisory functions, it was recognized that firewalls were needed to ensure that the primary objective of monetary policy would remain price stability.

The Roots of the Crisis and Why the System Failed

As it turned out, policymakers around the globe were lulled into complacency, neglecting the build-up of several underlying weaknesses that made the global financial system dangerously vulnerable. Those included sharp increases in asset prices, notably in the housing sector, excessive credit growth, a dip in household savings rates to historically low levels, and the emergence of huge imbalances, all supported by an environment of low interest rates, deregulation and technological advances. The sustained low interest rates fueled the appetite for risk taking and led to imprudent lending and leverage by securitizing loans and selling them, thereby reducing capital requirements. These developments constituted a new way of doing business by banks that was inherently very complicated and risky, creating a climate in which regulatory oversight and market discipline were very hard to pursue.

The unfolding events in 2007–09 showed that deep economic and financial disruption can occur even in advanced countries with a strong track record in delivering price stability. When the crisis was triggered, it spread fast and became global. Initially, many policymakers were skeptical about the extent of the problems and were largely unprepared in many areas when the crisis struck. A key underlying reason for the surprises was insufficient attention to the fast changing and less transparent economic and financial landscape through financial globalization and securitization.

The list of vulnerabilities and policy shortcomings was long. The following have been listed as ten key weaknesses (see also De Beaufort Wijnholds 2011).

First, inflated asset prices, notably a massive bubble in the US housing sector that extended well beyond the subprime sector, but also in other markets such as the bond market.

Second, skewed incentives in the financial system whereby a rapid growth of assets were encouraged by risk-awarding compensation policies leading to excessive leverage both in the banking sector but also in other parts of the economy. This was supported by a bonus culture that favored short-term profits. Incentives for traders were in place for them to take risky positions (earning them big bonuses) while sometimes creating large losses to the institution as a whole. Financial institutions were also often excessively reliant on short-term funding sources for long-term investments.

Third was the dismal failure of risk management with 'sophisticated' models based on overly optimistic assumptions and disregard for 'tail events.' Even a fall of the sharply increasing US house prices was not considered to be a tail risk by many.

Fourth, a too relaxed view by those responsible for regulation and supervision, both inside and outside central banks, about the complex securitization of debts, where financial institutions in reality overpaid for financial products. The use of exotic financial instruments that concentrated on risks in particular market segments and enterprises had become much more widespread. This included exotic mortgages that relied on unchanged or falling interest rates together with ever increasing property prices, and often with insufficient analysis of the borrowers' creditworthiness. The most common form of securitization was the origination and selling of mortgage loans, packaged as asset backed securities (ABS) together with other debt of higher quality. Derivatives, collateralized debt obligations (CDO), credit default swaps (CDS) and special purpose vehicles (SPV) all became very complex, and this alphabet soup of financial instruments were often not fully understood by both investors, or by regulators, and supervisors. Princeton professor and former Fed Vice-Chair Alan Blinder talks about 'the crazy-quilt of unregulated securities and derivatives that were built on these bad mortgages' (Blinder 2014, 28).

And in the same vein: 'In retrospect, it is quite astonishing that no action was taken by supervisors to close this lucrative and dangerous loophole' (De Beaufort Wijnholds 2011, 145). Even a healthy degree of self-discipline was lacking with this system of long and complex chain of transactions effectively separating the ultimate lenders from the ultimate borrowers, and as emphasized by a Group of Thirty Report, 'everyone expected someone else to have done due diligence, when in fact no one was doing it' (Group of Thirty 2015, 18).

Fifth, the role of rating agencies in providing the mortgage-backed securities of dubious value with the highest AAA rating. As agencies are paid for their services by the debt-issuing entities, they have incentives to be overly generous in their ratings. And many investors blindly relied on those impressive ratings of asset-backed securities.

Sixth, moral hazard as institutions that considered themselves too big or too interconnected to fail taking higher risks than they otherwise would have done. In the United States there was a widespread belief, supported by practice during the Great Moderation, that whenever key financial institutions or markets got into trouble, the Fed would come to the rescue with ample liquidity support and possibly a lowering of interest rates, including in order to prevent a bear market in stocks. This 'floor' became known as the 'Greenspan Put.' With Ben Bernanke replacing Alan Greenspan as Fed Chairman in 2006 and following a similar strategy, the term 'Bernanke Put' was coined.

Seventh, easy monetary policy maintained for too long as the Fed was overly concerned about the risk of deflation in the first part of the 2000s. This helped supporting the housing price boom and the bubbles in other asset markets.

Eighth, there may have been a general underpricing of risks, with markets increasingly persuaded that better policies had reduced underlying macroeconomic volatility, including the ability of central banks to avert a collapse of financial asset prices.

Ninth, insufficient attention to the linkages between the financial system and the macro economy as well as a need for macroprudential measures to address the inherent risks. In addition, it was often overlooked that financial systems had become progressively more complex and globally integrated.

Finally, the global imbalances with large and persistent balance of payments deficits in the United States mirrored by huge surpluses in China, some Northern European countries and primarily oil-producing countries. This helped to provide liquidity to the US economy and thereby made it easier for the financial system to provide risky credits.

With hindsight, it is surprising and worrisome that so many and such steep vulnerabilities and risks could build up. Despite close surveillance of advanced economies both by national authorities, by markets and private institutions, and by international organizations, very few were drawing attention to the risks and gave timely warning to policymakers.

Among the few who had sounded the alarm bells were some prominent economists speaking before an audience of the central bankers at the annual gathering of governors from around the world in Jackson Hole, Wyoming. Already in 2003, William White, a former Chief Economist at the Bank for International Settlements (BIS), together with his colleague Claudio Borio, drew attention to the inherently pro-cyclical nature of the financial system and warned that 'having won the war, the central bank community may still have some challenges ahead before finally winning the peace' (Borio and White 2004, 32). White later repeatedly warned against the growing imbalances both domestically and externally in many countries, the record asset prices fueled by prolonged easy monetary conditions and the growingly complex securitization practices as well as the dubious task of rating agencies. And then IMF Chief Economist, Raghuram Rajan, in his 2005 lecture at the Jackson Hole Conference, was even more direct by highlighting the build-up of excessive risks in the financial system and arguing that 'If banks also face credit losses and there is uncertainty about where those losses are located, only the very few unimpeachable banks will receive the supply of liquidity fleeing other markets. If these banks also lose confidence in their liquidity-short brethren, the inter-bank market could freeze up, and one could well have a full- blown financial crisis' (Rajan 2005, 345–6).

Furthermore, Nouriel Roubini, a professor at New York University, made very gloomy predictions before the global crisis arrived, foreseeing the worst US housing recession for decades with significant drop in home prices. He also warned that weaknesses in the US subprime mortgage market would cause broader problems in the financial system. At a seminar in September 2006, attended by about 300 IMF economists, Roubini, who cheerfully had given himself the moniker 'Dr. Doom,' elaborated on his view of an imminent consumer burnout now that many consumers are using their home equity as an 'ATM machine,' with a slowdown in the US housing market precipitating a US recession and a global hard landing (IMF 2006, 16). About a year later, Roubini returned to the IMF and in a new seminar reiterated his expectation of a US hard landing and a recession, that the financial turmoil was going to persist and that it would be 'a vicious circle where the real economy gets worse and the financial markets get tighter and vice versa' (IMF 2007b). He also believed that the rest of the world would not be going to decouple. As the moderator and at that time deputy chief economist at the IMF, Charles Collyns, said, 'You certainly have given us lots to worry about, but that is food and drink to us Fund economists' (IMF 2007b).

However, those worries were not mirrored in any official IMF documents. The focus was rather on the global imbalances, the combination of huge current account deficits in the United States and big surpluses in China, some Northern European countries and oil producing countries. An evaluation published in 2011 by the IMF's Independent Evaluation Office regarding the Fund's performance in the run-up to the crisis endeavored to cast further light on why the organization failed to bring the growing risks to the fore. The main conclusion was that the IMF's ability to detect the developing risks had been hampered by a number of factors, including a uniformed mindset that a financial crisis in the largest advanced economies was improbable, group thinking and a mentality with little room or incentives for contrarian views (IMF 2011). Fortunately, all those lessons helped implementation of a much-needed revamp of IMF surveillance and strengthening of the internal corporate culture at the IMF in the following years.

Looking further into the IMF's surveillance of the United States—the epicenter of the crisis—in the preceding years, it is striking to see the equanimity that characterized the assessments, even as late as in the summer of 2007. The discussion of the 2007 US Article IV Report on 27 July 2007 concluded that 'Prospects for the U.S. economy are favorable' and that '[f]inancial innovation and stability have been key to U.S. economic success,' adding that '[t]he financial system has shown impressive resilience' (IMF 2007a). Moreover, the interest of the United States in participating in an IMF Financial Sector Assessment Program (FSAP) to provide an international perspective on financial sector issues appeared to be lukewarm, as reflected by the argument that the IMF's scarce financial resources would be put to better use by focusing on other countries' financial sectors. It was only in late 2009, more than ten years after its inception and at a time when almost 80 percent of the Fund's membership had taken part in at least one such exercise, that the first FSAP discussions with the United States took place. Since the United States had gone through one of the most devastating financial crises, it received considerable criticism for its uncooperative stance.

The Unfolding of the Crisis and the Reaction by Central Banks

The turmoil occurred in stages, each successively believed to be the last one due to professional blindness and lack of imagination. Starting as liquidity crises, market conditions deteriorated to such a degree that in many instances they morphed into solvency crises. In the case of the euro area in 2010, the situation was such that solvency came into play from the start.

The first stage started in 2006 when house prices in the United States began to fall and delinquencies on subprime mortgages rose. However, markets did not react to those developments before early 2007 when credit spreads on structured products, many of which were complex derivatives based on subprime mortgages created by the shadow banks, began to rise. In early August, it was discovered that several European financial institutions had exceptionally large exposures to US subprime mortgages. The cocktail of illiquid long-term assets and illiquid short-term liabilities was poisonous, and money markets started to seize up, first in Europe and soon after in the United States. Two days later, on 9 August, the US mortgage crisis went global (described as the 'day the world changed' by the then Northern Rock CEO, Adam Applegarth, who experienced a run on his bank which was eventually nationalized by the British Government). Banks became distrustful of each other, withdrawing interbank lines and freezing credits. A liquidity crisis was growing with an alarming speed with interbank rates skyrocketing. Huge injections of liquidity by major central banks helped to ease markets, but the situation remained tense for a long time, and a sharply increasing aversion to take risks resulted in huge declines in other assets such as bonds and stocks.

The next phase of the global financial turmoil consisted of a series of solvency crises (Bear Stearns, AIG, Northern Rock etc.), with rescue operations arranged often with central banks in the driver's seat, arguing that the institutions were too big to fail or too interconnected to fail. It raised moral hazard concerns, but as noted by De Beaufort Wijnholds (2011 p.136), '[t]he majority view…was that, in a very serious crisis, moral hazard considerations had to be trumped by stability considerations.' Still, the support for those unprecedented bail-outs was eroding, and on 15 September 2008, the broker dealer and investment bank Lehman Brothers filed for bankruptcy, the largest filing in US history. The failure of Lehman Brothers, where no buyer could be found, unleashed panic around the globe and also criticism of the absence of intervention by the authorities. Stock markets plunged, interbank markets dried up again and the commercial paper market froze. The global financial system was at risk, and authorities were forced to take comprehensive actions to restore confidence and normalize markets.

On Saturday 4 October 2008, the government heads of the four largest European Union countries France, Germany, Italy and the United Kingdom met in Paris to agree on confidence enhancing measures. The meeting was concluded by a rather vague communiqué about coordination, and the markets did not buy into that. Actions spoke louder than words, with more effective unilateral steps taken by Ireland, to give a blanket guarantee on bank deposits, and the Benelux to bail out and partly nationalize their banks. On the other hand, an unusual coordinated interest rate cut of 0.5 percent on 8 October by the Fed, the ECB, the Bank of England and the Swiss National Bank (followed by others, including the Peoples Bank of China) did little to calm financial markets, demonstrating the limitations of central banks to address a severe banking crisis.

A breakthrough came when the G7 finance ministers and central bank governors met in connection with the IMF Annual Meetings in Washington DC on 10 October and issued a plan of action. Former Chairman of the Fed, Ben Bernanke, mentions that 'these big, high-profile international meetings are usually a terrible bore because much of the work is done in advance by the staff. This was not one of those boring meetings. We essentially tore up the agenda and discussed what we should do' (Bernanke 2013a, 74). The statement was brief but powerful. It contained the following commitments:

1. Take decisive action and use all available tools to support systemically important financial institutions and prevent their failure.
2. Take all necessary steps to unfreeze credit and money markets and ensure that banks and other financial institutions have broad access to liquidity and funding.
3. Ensure that our banks and other major financial intermediaries, as needed, can raise capital from public as well as private sources, in

sufficient amounts to re-establish confidence and permit them to continue lending to households and businesses.
4. Ensure that our respective national deposit insurance and guarantee programs are robust and consistent so that our retail depositors will continue to have confidence in the safety of their deposits.
5. Take action, where appropriate, to restart the secondary markets for mortgages and other securitized assets. Accurate valuation and transparent disclosure of assets and consistent implementation of high-quality accounting standards are necessary.

The key players soon put the global agreement into action. Government authorities orchestrated comprehensive guarantees and capital injections into the banking sector to avoid bank runs and default, followed by an overhaul on the regulatory and supervisory front to restore trust in the financial system. But the first responders were the central banks. Through comprehensive and innovative approaches, they took the lead in first halting the crisis, and later helped nurturing a recovery through sustained monetary stimulus.

Their willingness to do 'whatever it takes' led central banks into unchartered waters with a variety of unconventional measures being deployed by the major central banks. While the emphasis differed, for example between the Fed and the ECB, partly reflecting the different importance of the role of banks and markets in their respective financial systems and different monetary policy transmission mechanisms, the major central banks took various unconventional measure. These consisted of drastically lowering interest rates, providing loans for longer maturities, relaxing collateral requirements, introducing quantitative easing, meaning flooding financial markets with liquidity, and forward guidance by means of communicating future policy intentions. These measures are examined more fully in Chap. 12. The measures taken by central banks to restore the functioning of key financial markets are generally assessed to have been effective, whereas the efforts aimed at restoring final demand are generally considered to have been less successful. And there have also been growing concerns about their prolonged use.

International Monetary Cooperation

There is a long-standing tradition of close collaboration between central banks (described in Chap. 12), in recent decades notably through regular meetings—globally as well as regionally—and through a sharing of analyses.

However, only during brief episodes has the collaboration led to coordinated efforts, and in those cases mainly for the purposes of influencing exchange rates through coordinated currency interventions backed up with 'verbal' statements. Key examples are the implementation of the Plaza (1985) and Louvre (1987) Accords. While central banks of smaller open economies have traditionally attached great importance to the impact of global economic shocks, the monetary authorities of the larger and systemically important countries tend hardly to take into account the global impact of their actions.

The global financial crisis brought this collaboration to a new level with the recognition of the surprisingly strong financial sector interconnectedness, and with the IMF and G20 anchoring the necessary political involvement. As noted by former US Treasury Secretary Jack Lew: 'A major reason that the global financial crisis that began in late 2007 never turned into a second Great Depression is that the United States and other countries coordinated their efforts through the IMF and the G-20' (Lew 2016). It is widely acknowledged that the strong leadership at the highest political level was of key importance to the successful outcomes of the cooperation.

In addition to the coordinated and implemented plan of action, the currency swap agreements between major central banks from late 2008 played a key role, with some lines even left untouched as a sign of a return of confidence. Capital flows in general recovered sharply, whereas restoring bank lending proved to be more challenging. The establishment of a swap network between central banks, in which one central bank grants funding in its currency to another central bank, to allow the receiving central bank to provide liquidity in the originating central bank currency to banks located in the receiving banks jurisdiction, became a very visible and effective instrument of central bank cooperation during the crisis. The swaps granted by the Fed were by far the most important. A limited number of major central banks (ECB, Bank of England, Bank of Japan and the Swiss National Bank) were authorized by the Fed to draw an unlimited amount of dollars with up to three months maturity under the swap agreements. And those swaps were made reciprocal. Another ten central banks could draw sizeable but limited amounts. Some of those central banks decided to make part of those amounts available to other central banks.

The swap network was entering new territory. To have access to such swaps for the purpose of liquidity management, rather than only for foreign exchange operations, was unusual. At the peak of the crisis, the amount of swaps drawn exceeded more than half a trillion dollars with the lions' share taken by the ECB. Essentially, the key central banks with unlimited access were giving up control over their own balance sheets. As noted in a comprehensive analysis of the network by Papadia, 'the size and the scope of the swap network support the view that it can be seen as an episode of global monetary policy' (Papadia 2013, 6).

At the global level, the G20, which together with the IMF eventually became the main forum of international financial and monetary cooperation during the crisis, pledged at its meeting in November 2008 to implement a greater degree of policy coordination and followed this up at its London meeting in April 2009 by announcing a $1.1 trillion package of financial resources (including to treble the resources available to the IMF to $750 billion and to support a $250 billion allocation in newly created SDRs (special drawing rights in the IMF)) to support countries seriously affected by the crisis, anchored in IMF financial support programs and providing confidence to other countries without an immediate financial need.

The G20 was established in September 1999 as a group of Central Bank Governors and Finance Ministers recognizing the growing importance of key emerging market economies in the global economy, and to better address the widening crisis in several of the emerging market countries. The aim was to broaden the dialogue on economic and financial policies among systemically important countries, although the G20 policy agenda remained dominated by the key G7 members and their policy priorities. Moreover, while the G20 together with the IMF played a key role in preventing that the crisis morphed into a full-fledged and prolonged depression, the call for sustained and enhanced coordination of macroeconomic and financial policies among the key players in the global economy very much remains a work in progress. As concluded in a 2019 report by the IMFs Evaluation Office, 'the G-20 seems to have become a less efficient forum for policy cooperation after the initial heat of the crisis passed' (IMF 2019, 4).

The crisis led to a closer collaboration between national central banks bilaterally, regionally and globally—again with the IMF at the core—to strengthen the global financial safety net with huge amounts made available through special borrowing arrangements, in addition to the regular IMF credit facilities based on members' quota subscriptions.

Regional Financial Arrangements (the European Stability Mechanism, the Chiang Mai Initiative Multilateralization credit lines among Asian countries and the BRICS' Contingent Reserve Arrangement) were developed and expanded, contributing to a more comprehensive Global Financial Stability Net (GFSN) and with a noteworthy increased importance of key emerging market authorities. These arrangements have an aggregate size comparable to that of the IMF, but to reach the full potential of the GFSN, its fragmented layers still needed to be stitched more closely together. 'It is highly uneven in scale and coverage across regions, has major components that are untested in crisis, and lacks coordination' (G20 2018, 21). While there is strong evidence that the joint and cooperative actions of central banks initially helped to shorten the crisis and mitigate its effects, the collaboration also resulted in a patchwork with different layers, uneven coverage with many left behind, inadequate incentives for countries to adopt strong policies unless anchored under an IMF financial assistance program and sometimes costly excessive self-insurance through reserves building.

Spillovers from the unconventional policies in advanced economies have challenged international policy cooperation, with many emerging market authorities expressing concern about the financial spillovers and volatile capital flows, especially as the growth benefits from the unconventional monetary policy measures became less evident with time. When the Federal Reserve announced its intention to taper the pace of asset purchases in 2013, a number of emerging market countries experienced heavy capital outflows and sharp market volatilities ('taper tantrum'). Emerging market economy authorities repeatedly argued in favor of having advanced country central banks recognize and acknowledge spillovers of their actions and take them into account when making monetary policy decisions. However, to more directly respond to international spillovers may have been in conflict with central banks' mandate in many cases. Furthermore, according to Ben Bernanke, differences in growth prospects and swings in investor sentiment are more important than interest rate differentials due to differences in monetary policies in inducing cross border capital flows (Bernanke 2013b). In 2014, the then central bank governor of India, Raghuram Rajan, in a Bloomberg TV interview claimed that 'international monetary cooperation has broken down,' and despite a number of initiatives by the IMF to address the concerns (on spillovers, capital flows, surveillance, external sector reports etc.), the IMF's Independent Evaluation Office has concluded that 'these new approaches have generally been regarded as technically well-founded but have not succeeded in making multilateral concerns an effective influence on members' policy decisions' (IMF 2019. 26).

Side Effects and Exiting to a New Normal

While the central banks played a key role in helping diffuse the threats of a systemic collapse of the financial system and a prolonged global economic depression, including through exceptional and unconventional measures, strengthened coordination and collaboration, their actions were not without unwarranted side effects.

The prolonged period of extremely low or negative policy interest rates (described more fully in Chap. 12) may have contributed to misallocations of real resources, reduced potential output and led to unsustainable increases in some asset prices. Another side effect of unconventional monetary policies was the already mentioned spillovers to other countries, notably strong and volatile capital flows. Furthermore, easy monetary policies may have lost their effect over time, as the main effect of such policies is to bring forward debt-creating consumption and investment, and the headwinds of such debt rises over time.

In addition, the importance of building up policy space and maintaining an arsenal of instruments to potentially address future crises strengthens the case for timely exits that have been slow in coming in some central banks. Such policy room is limited if interest rates are already at or near the zero bound, government debts are excessive and structural reforms are not being implemented. The latter are often considered too slow to deliver and therefore politically unattractive for policymakers focusing on the objective of being reelected and drawing comfort from the short-term support from central banks. Indeed, an unfortunate consequence of the response to the crisis by both fiscal and monetary policy authorities has been insufficient attention to pro-growth structural reforms, hampering long-term growth potential. Much remains to be done by governments to address structural weaknesses which are outside the remit of central banks, but who nonetheless often point to the urgent need for such policies.

Concerns have also been expressed that the benefits from unconventional policies are limited to such an extent that they may not justify the moral hazard they create, as demonstrated by prolonged economic weakness in a number of countries. Moreover, when treasury paper and other liquid funds yield zero or even negative interest rates, the search for yield may lead to increases in share prices and those of other financial assets that thereby become delinked from the underlying real fundamentals. As a result, new asset bubbles may be building up.

At the political level, far-reaching public guarantees were issued for the troubling banking sector to avoid bank runs and default spirals and contagion. Furthermore, comprehensive action was taken overhauling the regulatory and supervisory framework to restore trust and build resilience. In addition, many countries placed more emphasis on macroprudential policy frameworks. However, questions remain about the extent to which authorities have the tools to fight the next financial crisis. As concluded in a 2018 Group of Thirty report, 'the net result is an enhanced ability to deal with certain kinds of problems (the failure of individual institutions, modest shocks) and a degraded ability to deal with other kinds of problems (systemic shocks, international contagion, threats from new vectors such as cyber attacks)' (Group of Thirty 2018, 27).

Several prominent economists have voiced concerns about the prolonged use of loose monetary policy as the only game in town to support growth. As a result of the very loose monetary conditions and continued search for yields, vulnerabilities have been allowed to accumulate, including in housing and other asset markets. In addition, overall debt levels in relation to GDP are now considerably higher than before the crisis erupted. As noted by the Group of Thirty: 'While the short-term benefits associated with conventional and unconventional monetary policies are self-evident, the costs of the unintended consequences are not. Only time and further policy measures will reveal the magnitude of such costs' (Group of Thirty 2015, xi). There may also be a tendency to exiting too late in view of the great uncertainties about the effects of a tightening cycle.

Moreover, the monetary policy space generally remains very limited to address possible future economic downturns and deflationary risks. BIS senior economist, Claudio Borio, summed up the prevailing criticism in his media briefing at the release of the September 2018 *BIS Quarterly Review*:

> With interest rates still unusually low and central banks' balance sheets still bloated as never before, there is little left in the medicine chest to nurse the patient back to health or care for him in case of a relapse. Moreover, the political and social backlash against globalization and multilateralism adds to the fever. Policymakers and market participants should brace themselves for a lengthy and eventful convalescence. (Borio 2018)

Harvard professor and former Treasury Secretary, Larry Summers has put further into perspective the resources needed in the medicine chest, arguing in a Bloomberg TV interview in 2018 that: '[d]ownturns happen, ... When they happen, the normal playbook is to cut interest rates by 500 basis points, but there's not going to be that kind of room'. In fact, as shown in a 2018 IMF Working Paper by Assenmacher and Krogstrup, only three OECD countries (Iceland, Mexico, and Turkey) had policy space in excess of 250 basis points in 2017 (Assenmacher and Krogstrup 2018, 4).

A key reason behind the limited space is the existence of the lower bound of zero interest rates. The alternative of holding cash effectively prevents central banks from cutting policy rates significantly below zero. Instead of depositing funds at banks at a negative interest rate, one can simply hold cash earning zero interest rates, and it is only because of the inconvenience and other costs (e.g. storage and insurance) of holding large cash amounts that central banks only have been able to move policy rates slightly into negative territory such as in the euro area, Denmark, Sweden and Switzerland. Proposals to overcome these limitations are discussed in Chap. 13.

Central Banking More than a Decade After the Crisis

In spite of the recognized undesirable side effects of the unconventional measures and the perceived need for central banks to exit to a new normal, with inflationary pressures negligible in most countries, monetary policy remained very accommodative for more than a decade after the crisis erupted.

Together with repeated rounds of quantitative easing, it has helped economies to recover and, in the case of the Eurozone, the actions by the ECB have prevented the crisis in the euro area peripheral countries from spinning entirely out of control.

While key central banks eventually started (slowly) to roll back the extraordinary large asset purchases, renewed growth concerns, weak inflationary pressures and trade and technology tensions implied that uncertainties remained about the direction and timing of future policy changes. Indeed, renewed global growth concerns in 2019 first fueled speculation and later in the year action by the ECB concerning a possible re-launch of more monetary stimuli, even in view of the growing evidence that the effects of unconventional monetary policies seem to have diminished over time 'as the novelty wore off' (IMF 2019).

Still many of the key foundations of central banking from the Great Moderation are considered fully valid even ten years after the crisis erupted, such as the importance of ensuring price stability as the key contribution central banks can make to support strong and sustainable growth, that central banks must remain independent of political pressure to provide stimulus or other actions inconsistent with the core mandate of the central bank, and that transparency and accountability remain key to the effectiveness of monetary policy. In other areas, a new consensus seems to have emerged. This includes the promotion of financial stability where central banks have a pivotal role in identifying systemic threats in the financial sector and are obliged to play a key role in the management and resolution of financial crisis, and are given authority over macroprudential instruments (discussed in Chap. 12), as well as the power to deploy unconventional monetary policy instruments such as quantitative easing, forward guidance and off-balance sheet commitments.

During the crisis and its aftermath, central banks have emerged as the most prominent players in the global economic policy arena. They play a key role in ensuring that credit-driven crises are prevented by carefully monitoring the build-up of systemic risks and ensure that measures are taken to prevent or offset them. However, there is no consensus about which instruments—conventional monetary policy, unconventional monetary policy, macroprudential instruments (or combinations) are best for this purpose.

While central banks have played a crucial role in managing financial crises and limiting their short-term costs, they cannot substitute for the necessary policy actions by governments, including structural reforms and sustainable fiscal policies. Central banks cannot on their own restore health to an economic and financial system if it is characterized by over-indebtedness and a level of aggregate demand that is unresponsive to monetary stimulus. And broadening the mandate of central banks beyond the pursuit of price stability can easily complicate the relationship between central banks and governments. Moreover, the longer term effects of the wide area of unconventional instruments applied by central banks are still untested, including the degree to which they encourage excessive risk taking and fuel new price bubbles and imbalances, impacts income distributions and the extent to which central banks have the necessary means to counter such risks.

There is a growing concern that the role of central banks has been overstretched by endowing them with too many responsibilities and thereby compromising their pursuit of the essentials (further discussed in Chap. 13). And an important question that has gained traction is whether recent experience teaches that policymakers should be more humble about their knowledge of how economies and financial systems work and about the effects of their policies over time. Another question is whether it is justified to continue labeling measures as unconventional or 'not normal' after more than a decade of existence and with increasing prospects of even more to come.

These are some of the main questions and challenges that central banks will have to grapple with in years to come and which are addressed in Chap. 13.

References

Assenmacher, Katrin and Krogstrup, Signe (2018): "Monetary Policy with Negative Interest Rates: Decoupling Cash form Electronic Money", IMF Working Paper 18/191, August 2018.

Bernanke, Ben S. (2013a), The Federal Reserve and The Financial Crisis. Lectures by Ben S. Bernanke. Princeton. 2013.

Bernanke, Ben S (2013b): What should economists and policy makers learn from the financial crisis. London School of Economics and Political Science, March 25, 2013.

Blanchard, Olivier, Dell'Ariccia, Giovanni, and Mauro, Pablo (2010). Rethinking Macroeconomic Policy, IMF Staff Position Note, SPN/10/03, 12 February 2010.

Blinder, Allan S. (2014), After The Music Stopped, The Financial Crisis, The Response, And The Work Ahead, Penguin Books. 2014.

Borio, Claudio and White, William (2004): Whither monetary and financial stability? The implications of evolving policy regimes. Presented at the Federal Reserve Bank of Kansas City's Symposium on "Monetary Policy and Uncertainty: Adapting to a Changing Economy" at Jackson Hole, Wyoming on 28–30 August 2003. BIS Working Papers no. 147, February 2004.

Borio, Claudio (2018), BIS Quarterly Review, September 2018 – media briefing remarks. September 23, 2018.

Group of Thirty (2015), Fundamentals of Central Banking, Lessons from the Crisis, Group of Thirty, October 2015.

Group of Thirty (2018), Managing The Next Financial Crisis, An Assessment of Emergency Arrangements in the Major Economies, Group of Thirty, September 2018.

G20 (2018), Making The Global Financial System Work For All, Report of the G20 Eminent Persons Group on Global Financial Governance, October 2018.

IMF (2006), Forum by Prakash Loungani, Meet Dr. Doom, IMF Survey Vol. 35 Issue 19, October 17, 2006.
IMF (2007a), "United States: 2007 Article IV Consultation", IMF Country Report No. 07/264, August 2007.
IMF (2007b), Transcript of IMF Seminar 13 September 2007 – The Risk of a U.S. Hard Landing and Implications for the Global Economy and Financial Markets, Featured Speaker: Nouriel Roubini, Moderator: Charles Collyns. IMF, September 2007.
IMF (2011), IMF Performance in the Run-Up to the Financial and Economic Crisis: IMF Surveillance in 2004-07, Independent Evaluation Office of the International Monetary Fund, 2011.
IMF (2019), IMF Advice on Unconventional Monetary Policies, Independent Evaluation Office of the International Monetary Fund, Evaluation Report 2019.
Lew, Jacob J. (2016). America and the Global Economy: The Case for U.S. Leadership." Foreign Affairs, April 11, 2016.
Papadia, Francesco (2013), "Central bank Cooperation During the Great Depression", Bruegel Policy Contribution Issue 2013/08. July 2013.
Rajan, Raghuram G. (2005), "Have Financial Developments Made The World Riskier?" Jackson Hole, Federal Reserve Bank of Kansas City (August). https://www.kansascityfed.org/publicat/sympos/2005/pdf/rajan2005.pdf
Wijnholds, Onno de Beaufort (2011), Fighting Financial Fires, Palgrave Macmillan, 2011.

CHAPTER 12

Modern Monetary Policy

At the time the global financial crisis was still raging, central banks effected drastic changes in their monetary policies, introducing hitherto untried new measures. As Agustin Carstens, General Manager of the BIS, observed in 2018 in a speech at the BIS Annual Meeting: 'In the modern era, central banks have never pursued such an unconventional monetary policy and certainly not for so long'. Such a 'revolution' in new approaches and instruments defines the end of the complacency which characterized much of the great moderation of the 1990s and early 2000s.

In the early years of the twenty-first century, the framework within which monetary policy was conducted was largely unchanged from that of two decades before. Central banks pursued a defined goal, usually price stability, sometimes—as in the case of the Federal Reserve—coupled with maximum employment. However, financial stability was seldom explicitly included in the remit of the monetary institutions. Direct inflation targeting had replaced money supply targets as best practice, delivering satisfactory results in most instances. The main instrument to arrive at the targeted rate of inflation—generally around 2 percent in advanced economies—was steering short-term interest rates. Direct limits on credit expansion were applied only in countries where well-functioning financial markets were lacking. The tools used to deliver the desired interest rate and to ward off domestic liquidity squeezes had undergone little change over the decades. There were *standing facilities* that could be tapped at an official rate—the Bank rate, or policy rate—which could be adjusted when a tightening or

O. de Beaufort Wijnholds, *The Money Masters*,
https://doi.org/10.1007/978-3-030-40041-5_12

easing of short-term rates was indicated. Besides the central rate for advances there has generally been a somewhat higher rate—Bagehot's penalty rate—charged at the discount window, for a long time known as the Lombard rate. The Federal Reserve operates on the basis of three facilities for liquidity support: the primary, the somewhat more expensive secondary and the cheaper seasonal credit facility. The rate at which banks can borrow through the primary facility is usually ½ to ¾ percent higher than the federal funds rate, the rate at which sound banks extend credit to each other. In all cases eligible collateral is required. At the European Central Bank the 'penalty' rate is called the marginal lending facility. Similar instruments of lender of last resort support nowadays exist at most central bank.

Open market operations had remained an important part of central banks' toolkits, but besides outright transactions in short-term government paper, repos (repurchase transactions, usually overnight) were often favored, also increasingly in emerging countries. Less frequently applied, *minimum reserve requirements,* sometimes considered to be ineffective and disruptive when frequently adjusted, have remained important in some countries where financial markets are not yet fully developed, as a means to influence commercial banks' liquidity. While often dormant at some central banks, the Peoples Bank of China (POBC) has relied heavily on adjustments of its minimum reserve requirements to steer money market rates.

New Instruments

The tried and trusted tools, however, did not always deliver the effect that was sought. New instruments were developed, especially at the Fed and the Bank of Japan. In 2006 the American Central Bank was authorized to *remunerate* banks' reserves held with the institution, both with respect to their required and their excess reserves, following Congressional pressure to eliminate the implicit tax that reserve requirements impose on depository institutions. In practice this action provided an additional tool for the conduct of monetary policy as the Fed can steer the banks' liquidity position by adjusting the rate of remuneration paid on excess reserves. In more recent times influencing excess reserves has become its operational channel of choice. And in 2001 the Bank of Japan, when it concluded that traditional monetary policy did not deliver the goal of boosting domestic demand, experimented with an instrument that came to be known as *quantitative easing*. This approach entails large scale purchases by the central bank of government securities thereby flooding financial markets with liquidity. The Japanese initiative proved to be a harbinger of things to come.

The tremendous impact of the global financial crisis of 2007–09 led to a dramatic reordering of the international monetary and financial architecture, including an increased role of central banks as crisis managers and protectors of financial stability. After the worst of the turmoil was over, the world's money managers faced a stark new reality. No longer was maintaining inflation at a steady low rate considered a necessary condition for sustainable economic growth, their first concern, their focus having shifted to supporting economic growth more directly by aiming at raising the low rate of inflation rather than preventing it from exceeding their inflation target as in the past. Since the global financial debacle spawned a deep recession, the immediate challenge facing governments and central banks had become the prevention of further economic shrinkage and a return to healthy levels of growth and employment. The fear that what became to be known as the Great Recession would turn into another Great Depression would drive economic policy for a decade after the outbreak of the financial upheaval. While some degree of confidence in the financial system returned after 2009, there was an urgent need to exit from a stagnant low growth environment. Most central banks were spurred into aggressively easing monetary policy. In situations such as the post-crisis recession, a large role for fiscal policy is generally considered appropriate. However, the application of fiscal stimulus was often constrained by the existence of large budget deficits and sometimes by unsustainable levels of government debt. Moreover, under the European Stability and Growth Pact, many countries had already surpassed the upper deficit level of 3 percent of GDP that constitutes the central requirement of the Pact.

Besides serving as the main catalyst for restoring demand, central banks had to address other serious challenges in the aftermath of the crisis, in particular the fragility of the banking system and the need for stronger supervision and regulation of private financial institutions. Financial stability became a prime concern of central banks and its interaction with the aims of monetary policy a new source of uncertainty. This development is discussed in Chap. 13.

Dealing with Recession

Since the Korean War caused a jump in prices in the early 1950s, central banks generally focused more on keeping inflation in check than directly supporting economic growth. And because the mandate of monetary policy has overwhelmingly been the pursuit of price stability, or a variant thereof, this posture was justified. While the outright pursuit of full employment has also been a consideration and has sometimes been part of central banks' mandate—the Fed being the prime example of having a dual mandate, though only since 1978—in practice, containing inflation had been the predominant feature of monetary policy before 2007. While recessions, which were mostly mild, did usually lead to monetary easing, it was practiced for a short time only and limited in scope. This process was drastically reversed during the global financial crisis and the deep recession that followed it. As the rate of price increases shrank to very low levels, central banks fully concentrated on dealing with a lack of economic growth and burgeoning unemployment. Avoiding deflation and the debt-deflation process became a major preoccupation for policymakers in a large part of the world.

In the United States inflation fell from an average of 2.8 percent in the first seven years of the 2000s to an average of 2 percent in the immediately following years and stayed under the Fed's—initially informal—inflation target of 2 percent until 2017. Anemic economic growth led to unemployment reaching an alarming 10 percent in 2010. A worse picture marked the European economic landscape, featuring low inflation and two instances of serious recession. Unemployment in the euro area peaked at 11 percent in 2013. Whereas the United States was able to restore its real GDP to its pre-crisis level relatively quickly, it would take the euro area several years longer. (The United Kingdom succeeded in reaching this benchmark somewhat earlier.) Many other advanced economies, foremost Japan, experienced poor economic growth and virtually no inflation. The new economic powerhouse China did not suffer the same fate, although its rate of economic growth fell back somewhat to a still impressive 5–6 percent and inflation stayed above zero.

If inflation targeting had been predominantly a matter of keeping annual price increases at around 2 percent, the objective was now the opposite—*raising* inflation to the 2 percent level. Meeting the target in a symmetric fashion, that is, also during a recession, was deemed crucial to avoid sliding into deflation. All central banks in advanced countries came to pursue this goal, some earlier than others. When the ECB slightly raised its main operational rate in 2008, it soon reversed course as it became clear that the euro area was sliding into a serious recession. However, among the emerging market countries several monetary institutions were initially not in a position to follow a similar approach. Several of the BRICS (Russia, Brazil and South Africa) were still suffering from inflationary problems, as did Argentina, Turkey and Ukraine. But on a wide scale the *pursuit* of higher inflation—unheard of for most of monetary history—became the standard monetary policy stance.

The need to return to inflation of around 2 percent almost became an article of faith among central bankers. Ben Bernanke, who took over from Alan Greenspan as Chairman of the Board of Governors of the Fed in 2006, was convinced that if central banks did not aggressively loosen monetary policy, the serious mistakes of the 1930s were likely to be repeated Bernanke (2013b). He went so far as publicly apologizing for the erroneous policy stance of the American Central Bank some 80 years earlier and was adamant that the Fed would not this time allow the economy to slide into deflation and depression. Other prominent central bankers, such as the Bank of Japan's Haruhiko Kuroda, Mervyn King of the Bank of England, Mark Carney of the Bank of Canada (later of the Bank of England), Stefan Ingves of the Swedish Central Bank and with somewhat less missionary zeal, Jean-Claude Trichet of the ECB and Philip Hildebrand of the Swiss National Bank, shared the Bernanke philosophy. Mario Draghi, who succeeded Trichet as the head of the ECB in 2011, showed himself to be a strong champion of the need for higher inflation. At the same time, the Governor of the Peoples Bank of China, Zhou Xiaochuon, whose country continued on the path of rapid economic transformation, played a crucial role in ensuring that sufficient fiscal and monetary support was forthcoming to stave off recessionary forces in his country. But as explained by Professor David Dao Lui of Tsinghua University in Beijing, the route taken by the Chinese Central Bank differed significantly from that of Western central banks, in view of the unique characteristics—a blend of a market and a command economy—of the Chinese economic system (Dao Liu 2013).

Zero and Negative Interest Rates

The obvious monetary tool to influence the rate of inflation is adjusting the policy interest rate, as central banks have done for centuries, beginning with the Bank Rate in England. While an aggressive loosening of monetary policy by way of lower interest rates normally poses no technical problems, a new challenge arose because the 'natural' lower bound of money market rates was zero, or so it seemed. In the United States the notion of negative interest rates, which had only existed during brief periods in Germany and Switzerland at the time of the dollar crisis of the early 1970s, was considered unrealistic. The consensus view was (and is) that for the United States there is a *zero bound* to interest rates. Charging banks to hold unremunerated balances at the Fed, instead of compensating them with a small fee, would imply that commercial banks would have to pay practically no interest on their clients' time and savings deposits if they wanted to avoid incurring losses on an important part of their funding. However, very low rates allow banks to provide credits at attractive rates, thereby stimulating the economy and eventually pushing up prices. But what if businesses and households are not applying for credit, even at such low rates, because of a weak economic outlook? Economists are quick to point out that the problem has to be viewed in terms of *real* interest rates. With the federal funds rate in the United States at zero and inflation tending to move into negative territory, the real rate would still be positive, whereas some prominent economists suggested that negative real interest rates would be needed to bring back bank lending to satisfactory levels. And a few European central banks became convinced that they should explore the once unthinkable step to take their policy rates into negative territory. The Swedish Central Bank, where the influential former academic economist and strong adherent of negative rates, Lars Svensson was a member of the policymaking team, lowered its policy rate to slightly below zero. Others, including the Danish, Norwegian and Swiss central banks, followed the Swedish example. Commercial banks passed on part of this bounty, but the effects on credit demand were generally muted.

As most central banks did not consider it feasible or desirable to enter negative interest rate territory, they looked for other ways to achieve an inflation rate of 2 percent. But here they could encounter an additional complication. Central banks normally conduct open market operations to steer short-term interest rates, yet it is uncertain whether these changes translate into similar adjustment of long-term rates. In fact, modern central banks are often largely powerless to bring about significant changes in longer term bond prices by raising or lowering their policy rates. And since long-term interest rates have the greatest impact on the real economy, the implication is that monetary easing by lowering short-term interest rates provides only a limited degree of stimulus. Fed Chairman Alan Greenspan described this phenomenon as a *conundrum* for central banks in testimony before Congress in 2005. However, as Fig. 12.1 shows, a combination of aggressive monetary measures, discussed below, not only brought down short-term interest rates, but long-term rates as well. In Germany and Japan, 10-year bond yields fell to zero or even slightly below zero. (Safe haven considerations also played a role.) However, while long-term rates also declined in the United States, they remained well above zero, fluctuating around 2 percent in recent years.

Quantitative Easing

While the Fed and most other central banks ruled out bringing their policy rates to levels below zero, a few others (Scandinavian central banks and the Swiss National Bank) set their (nominal) policy rate at negative levels in the conviction that real rates below zero were needed to sufficiently

Fig. 12.1 10-year Government Bonds Interest Rates (1991–2019)

stimulate demand. They did not believe that modest negative rates would lead to a large scale demand for converting bank deposits into banknotes, pointing out that there is a cost (storage, insurance, transportation) to taking such action and that it would be profitable only at relatively large negative rates, sometimes estimated at 2 percent. But outside of this small group, central banks did not wish to break the zero barrier. Therefore, in order to overcome this constraint, but still provide sufficient stimulus to the economy, they adopted a policy of ***quantitative easing*** (QE). Such a policy, consisting of massively purchasing capital market assets against central bank money would, they argued, allow them to surmount the conundrum. Their main aim became to flood financial markets with so much liquidity that banks would be willing to extend more credit to firms and households than they otherwise would. The Bank of Japan which had experimented with quantitative easing (QE) as early as 2001 started buying Japanese government bonds in the secondary market on a massive scale, thereby creating plentiful liquidity. While such indirect monetary financing of the government had long been considered anathema in many countries, the concern about deflation trumped fixed principles in the world of central banking after the global financial crisis. There were exceptions to this change in philosophy, especially from the German Central Bank and the Netherlands Bank in their capacity as members of the Euro System. But while resistance from those quarters delayed the application of quantitative easing (QE) by the ECB, a majority of the 18 national central banks within the Euro System have been in favor. Subsequently, the ECB Council announced that it would be charging banks 0.4 percent (increased to 0.5 percent in 2019) on their deposits with the central bank as a disincentive to commercial banks to hoard their excess liquidity and an incentive to use it for extending credit. Thus a variant of negative interest rates was introduced by the world's second largest central bank. The Bank of Japan charged their banks 0.2 percent and the Danish National Bank 0.6 percent on the commercial banks' deposits. Penalizing deposit holders in order to incentivize them to extend more credit to the private sector became an additional instrument in central banks' toolkit. However, there is no consensus on how effective this measure has been, especially since its impact is hard to separate from other factors determining commercial banks' lending activities.

Bernanke's Role

Ben Bernanke, who became Chairman of the Fed in 2006, is a strong believer in quantitative easing, a practice he had earlier studied with respect to Japan (Bernanke 2015b, 41). In his opinion a host of financial assets lent themselves to large-scale purchases by the central bank, thereby giving the bond markets and commercial banks a boost. In addition to long-term government bonds, the Fed started buying up massive amounts of asset-backed securities (ABS) and other capital market assets in 2008, while maintaining the federal funds rate at zero. (Although it was sometimes advocated, the American central bank did not buy equities, recognizing that serious complications could emerge, such as maintaining fairness in such purchases.) The Bank of England followed soon after, as did other central banks in advanced countries. At the same time, the Bank of Japan, confronted with stubbornly low inflation, stepped up its capital market purchases from its already high levels. And despite considerations of fairness, the Japanese Central Bank also bought large amounts of equities, long considered by central banks to be undesirable.

The Fed followed up its initial QE program, which amounted to purchases of mortgage-backed securities of $600 billion, by a second round of QE in November 2010 with asset purchases of $30 billion per month. After a pause the Fed saw a need for a third round of QE in September 2012, pumping liquidity into the market at a rate of $40 billion per month and soon increasing its monthly purchases to $85 billion, until it started tapering its operations the following year. Eventually the Fed's purchases totaled $4.5 trillion. Between March 2009 and July 2012 the Bank of England bought 375 billion pounds sterling ($470 billion), mainly government bonds on the secondary market. Concerned about the effects of the Brexit announcement, the British Central Bank purchased an additional 70 billion pounds in August 2016. The Bank of Japan's QE operations have continued longer and have been larger in terms of its balance sheet than that of other central banks. The ECB entered into QE transactions later than other practitioners, after it had introduced a series of very large long-term credit facilities (up to four years) in order to supply the euro area banks with ample liquidity. But by 2009 the ECB had concluded that more had to be done and embarked on a QE program, initially limiting purchases to €60 billion of so-called covered bonds. After a long pause, in part reflecting opposition within its Council, the ECB announced an expanded asset purchase program in January 2015, including obtaining bonds issued by euro area governments and official European institutions. In a next step it extended the list of eligible assets to corporate bonds, which did not sit well with all members of the euro area, some considering that such purchases constituted a form of money creation—an area that a central bank should not enter. Moreover, they felt that such transaction would be too risky, but their reservations did not carry the day. At its peak the ECB's monthly purchases amounted to €80 billion. These transactions are described more fully in Chap. 10.

The verdict on how successful QE by the Fed has been is not unanimous, although there is general agreement that the first round of QE was effective, even if it had been based only on its psychological impact. And the majority opinion was that QE had led to lower borrowing costs for the private sector thereby giving a (limited) boost to consumption, supporting housing prices, pushing up stock prices, as well as the rate of inflation and inflation expectations. The second round has also been regarded by most observers as engendering (limited) positive results, but many were more critical of the need for a third round of QE in September 2012. David Lindsey, a former high official at the Fed, wrote that Jeremy Stein, a Governor of the Fed Board at the time, 'drove an [...] analytical nail in the coffin of QE3' (Lindsey 2013, 239). Stein questioned the positive effect on fixed investment of reductions in the term premium on interest rates for long-term security purchases, as opposed to declines in the expected path of the federal funds rate. More concretely, he voiced concerns that bond markets would overheat as a result of the open-ended nature of QE 3 ('Stein to Step Down as Fed Governor,' *Financial Times*, 3 March 2014).

Exiting from QE proved to be somewhat problematic. When the Fed announced that it was starting to gradually reduce ('taper') its monthly purchases in 2013, financial markets reacted fiercely, expecting that such cutting back would be followed by higher interest rates and thereby putting an end to 30 years of falling rates. These fears turned out to be overblown, the market after a while letting up on its 'taper tantrum.' The Bank of Japan's exit from QE was first mentioned in guarded terms in early 2018, but did not result in any different course of action. It has also intervened in the longer end of the bond market (yield curve intervention) to overcome the Greenspan conundrum. The massive purchases by the Bank of Japan have suited the government, since they reduced the cost of financing its deficits. The macroeconomic downside is that the process removes the incentive for the government to stabilize the national debt which reached the staggering level of 250 percent of GDP in 2019. While Japan is different in that its institutional investors and public display a very high degree of 'home bias' in their portfolio decisions, such a bias is much weaker in the Americas and Europe. Coming rather late to QE, the ECB stepped up its monthly purchases at a time the Fed was entering a new phase and reducing and then terminating its buying program. Low inflation also proved to be more stubborn in the euro area than in the United States, sometimes remaining below 1 percent. By contrast to the United States, extreme monetary easing was fully transmitted to European capital markets. Huge purchases by the ECB of euro area government bonds (allotted among the various countries on the basis of their share in the capital of the ECB, with the exclusion of debt-ridden Greece), in combination with large inflows of capital from abroad, pushed sovereign bond yields into negative territory in several countries, foremost in Germany and the Netherlands. And even in countries with high debt ratios, such as Italy and Spain, rates on short end of the yield curve turned slightly negative. This previously almost unthinkable scenario continued for a while.

Mounting Concerns

As monetary easing continued and nominal interest rates remained very low or turned negative following the Great Recession, doubts emerged about the wisdom of such prolonged accommodation. In this vein, critics increasingly warned that by continuing to maintain (very) loose monetary policies year in and year out, central banks were allowing their governments to delay necessary fiscal adjustment and structural reforms. Moreover, as Claudio Borio of the Bank for International Settlements pointed out, such 'financial repression' could entail the risk of (again) increasing leverage in the financial sector, resulting in undesirable asset inflation (Borio 2014). Another criticism of prolonged application of monetary easing was that it led to unwanted capital inflows and appreciation of the currencies of emerging countries who felt compelled to resist this process by means of lowering their own interest rates. And Raghuram Rajan, then President of the Indian Reserve Bank, suggested that the industrial countries welcomed the depreciation of their currencies which resulted from their loose policies. He complained that the emerging countries were subjected to 'competitive monetary easing' (Rajan 2014). However, advanced country central banks saw this effect as a by-product of a policy that was supporting economic growth in their economies which benefitted economic recovery on a global scale. The issue is an important one, illustrating the potential spillover effects of monetary policy decisions in large advanced countries. Over the years the American Central Bank—and more recently the ECB—have been regularly exhorted to take into account the effects of their policies on other countries. But such considerations have seldom moved the largest central banks to mitigate their focus on their domestic economies. In an interesting twist, the President of the United States criticized the ECB in June 2019 for keeping its policy interest rate lower than that of the Fed, suggesting that the ECB was deliberately maintaining a low rate of the euro.

Exiting from Extreme Easing

Around 2012 economic prospects in the United States were deemed to have improved sufficiently to start withdrawing monetary stimulus to the economy. But making an actual decision to move toward modest tightening can be complicated. And the Federal Reserve did not want to move prematurely and have to reverse course later. Subsequently the Fed started to reduce its balance sheet by not reinvesting securities that had reached maturity. It also began very gradually to sell some of its accumulated assets in the market. This process did not cause any market volatility. In the meantime the Fed began raising the federal funds rate from zero in small steps ('baby steps') of ¼ percent as the signs of satisfactory growth and higher inflation became clear. At the end of 2018 the federal funds rate was set at between 2 and 2½ percent. With inflation around the 2 percent target, implying that the real interest rate stood at zero, monetary policy was still on the loose side. But as the outlook for growth became less buoyant and inflation did not rise beyond its target, the Fed announced that it would refrain from further hikes for the time being. And in the course of 2019, after it detected signs of a possible slowdown of the economy, it lowered its policy rate in a few small step to between 1.5 and 1.75 percent. A potential downside to this reversal is that the still low interest rates would prevent the Fed from moving aggressively enough in the event of a recession.

A Data-Driven Approach

The recent experience of changing monetary course in the United States is instructive and a good example of a successful exit strategy. Discretionary monetary policy is forward looking and *data driven*. It does not depend on following the development of a single economic variable such as the money supply, but considers a range of factors reflecting the state of the economy, on the one hand through its econometric forecasting models, on the other hand based on a more judgmental interpretation of the data. Many of the variables are readily available, but others are not measurable and involve considerable guesswork. Economic growth, the rate of inflation, wages and unemployment, as well as the growth of productivity are readily available data, as is the capacity utilization in industry, although interpretation of such data is not always obvious. Inflation can be measured in various ways (headline vs. core), but more importantly, the extent to which changes in the price level are temporary or more permanent is notoriously difficult to gauge. A case in point is the price of energy which represents an important element in the measurement of headline inflation. Looking at core inflation (excluding energy and food) is the way this problem is usually addressed. Since the outlook for inflation is of central importance, the Fed (mainly through the regional reserve banks) conducts surveys of inflation *expectations*. The process involves inquiring about the expectations of consumers with respect to inflation, both in the short term and longer run, as well as of professional forecasters. In addition, the difference between the nominal yield on Treasury bonds and the real yield on inflation indexed bonds issued by the Treasury (TIPS) is regarded as an indicator of market sentiment. Finally, surveys are conducted to gauge inflation *perspectives* by asking respondents' views regarding present and past inflation rates. Similar surveys are conducted at other central banks.

As to the other variable directly linked to the American central banks' mandate, the officially measured level of unemployment is announced with little delay. But there are other factors that need to be taken into account, such as the level of wages, the participation rate of the workforce, the number of workers on disability and the size of unfulfilled job openings. Complicating the picture is the lack of clarity as to the causes of the prolonged deterioration of productivity growth and its implications for the degree of joblessness. Then there are the data that cannot be measured directly but are important in evaluating the state of the economy. Potential output and thereby the output gap can only be estimated. Furthermore, the natural or neutral interest rate, the real short-term rate at which inflation is low and stable and economic growth in line with potential cannot be measured directly. The natural interest rate is not a constant number either and is subject to changes caused by shifts in structural factors over time, as discussed in Box 12.1 on monetary theory. Also considerable uncertainty exists about the natural rate of unemployment. Because achieving conformity of both the actual levels of interest rates and unemployment to their (estimated) natural rates will in theory bring about stable and low inflation and unemployment, it is an overarching goal of the Fed and in line with its dual mandate. In recent years the Fed has been quite successful in achieving that happy state of affairs even though the actual rate of unemployment fell below 4 percent, considerably less than contemporary estimates of the neutral level of around 5 to 6 percent (See also the section on forward guidance and the misreading of the natural level.) The foregoing illustrates how difficult it can be for the Federal Reserve (as well as its sister institutions) to formulate monetary policy under the uncertainty in the real world.

Monetary Policy and Financial Stability

The Fed, like other central banks, can, in addition to the aforementioned economic factors, also be influenced by concerns about financial stability, although so-called macroprudential measures have been developed to separate monetary and financial considerations. (This major issue is discussed in Chap. 13.) Furthermore, under extreme conditions such as major political upheavals, the exchange rate of the US dollar can be taken into account in decisions on monetary policymaking. It is sometimes suggested that since the Fed's actions have consequences for the distribution of income of the public, the central bank should pay heed to this process. Indeed the very low interest rates that prevailed for a decade in the United States benefitted debtors and hurt savers whose bank accounts have generally produced less income than the rate of inflation. Pensioners and other persons with fixed incomes in the United States (and elsewhere) have also complained of unfairness. However, it is not part of the remit of central banks to deal with the political distribution issue. Concern expressed by pension funds and insurance companies about their solvency is another matter. The business model of these institutions is different from that of banks in that their capacity to pay out pensions and insurance claims depends importantly on the income from and value of their bond holdings. When interest rates are very low, these institutions frequently experience a shortfall of the ratio of their assets to their liabilities. The result can be that pension funds cannot meet their payouts and that insurance companies are in danger of insolvency. Since institutional investors are very big players in financial markets, their health should not be endangered, as the case of insurance giant AIG has demonstrated. But because the majority of members of the US Congress are critical of bail-outs of individual nonbank entities, the Dodd-Frank bill prohibits the central bank to repeat such actions. This is an unfortunate legislative decision based mainly on populist considerations and renders the Fed less capable of dampening the fires of future serious financial crises.

Other central banks that pursued an aggressive loosening of monetary conditions since the global financial crisis also gradually moved away from forceful monetary stimulus. The Bank of Canada, recognizing the strength of the Canadian economy, started raising rates in 2017, whereas the Bank of England announced in January 2018 that its focus had shifted to containing inflation which had risen to 3 percent, thereby surpassing its target. But a year later, the uncertainty surrounding Brexit led to a reversal of course. After a long time of sluggishness in the euro area, a surge of economic growth in 2017, despite inflation remaining well under 2 percent, shifted the debate within the ECB toward lessening its stimulus. In the course of 2018 it began tapering its bond purchases, while suggesting that it would not raise interest rates until the second half of 2019. Subsequently, when it became concerned that the economic outlook for the euro area was deteriorating, the ECB retracted its intention concerning interest rates. In Japan, where low inflation has been the most stubborn among the major economies, bond buying by the central bank continued without interruption, in addition to which it bought a sizeable chunk of Japanese equities. But in academic and political circles doubts were increasingly expressed about the continued effectiveness of the Bank of Japan's program.

The Peoples Bank of China (PBOC), while not having embarked on a bond buying scheme, which was not necessary as growth remained satisfactory and the risk of deflation relatively remote, steered the economy through traditional monetary policy responses. Reflecting the differences in the structure of its financial system from that of other major economies, the PBOC's instrument of choice has been adjusting its minimum reserve requirements.

Why Have Interest Rates Remained So Low?

Having exited the phase of extremely accommodative monetary policy, interest rates in the United States remained unusually low, including long-term rates. Acknowledging that such low rates at a time of relatively robust economic recovery was problematic, the Fed explained that while it could raise the federal funds rate more rapidly, factors beyond the control of the central bank contributed to the prolonged period of low rates. Vice-Chairman Stanley Fischer (2016) cited three reasons to be concerned about the then prevailing monetary conditions. The first factor was that very low long-term rates could be a sign that the long-run outlook of the economic growth was a cause for concern. A second element was that low rates diminished the Fed's ability to deal with adverse shocks as its room for lowering its policy rate would be limited when a recession was on the horizon. And a third worry was the threat that prolonged low rates could pose for financial stability. The main consideration of the Fed to keep interest rates low was to sustain the level of domestic demand that is needed to meet its dual mandate of maximum employment and price stability. This means that the equilibrium, or neutral, interest rate, defined as the rate in the longer run, is considerably lower than in the past, implying that the balance between savings and investment has shifted (think of the IS curve described in Chap. 5). In this context it has been suggested that a global savings glut exists.

In enumerating the reasons for a weaker economic outlook for the US economy for coming years, Fischer emphasized low productivity growth which he related primarily to a slowdown in innovation, an aging population leading to higher savings and lower wage growth, coinciding with a continuation of the relatively low rate of investment of recent years. The reduced appetite for investing could, according to Fischer, be due to increased uncertainty or the possibility that the US economy has become less capital intensive, which could be explained by stagnant or low wage growth. And finally, he pointed to a slowdown in growth in other countries which often are dealing with the same longer term economic challenges.

Fischer's analysis can be interpreted as a plea for a somewhat more rapid pace of the Fed's small-step approach to raising interest rates, but at the same time explaining the limits of the American Central Banks' capacity to meet the economy's structural challenges. These challenges are sometimes judged to be of a chronic nature and therefore imply an environment of *secular stagnation* (Summers 2018).

Exchange Rates and International Reserves

A country's exchange rate and its central bank's monetary policy can be closely connected when it pursues a degree of stability in the former. For the United States this link is hardly a factor since the dollar is a floating currency free of intervention by the authorities, except in extreme circumstances. The role of the Fed with respect to the dollar rate is generally limited to the operational aspects. Moreover, in the rare case that a need for currency intervention arises, the Fed follows US Treasury instructions. Whereas the Fed's Governors can differ in their opinion from the government on whether a downward slide of the dollar has gone too far, it cannot on its own take action to prevent it from falling further. Pronouncements on the position of the dollar are made from time to time by high officials, mostly stating that a strong dollar is in the interest of the United States. Talking down the dollar, as was done by the US Treasury Secretary in 1977, is risky and can result in undesirable undershooting. Under the Trump administration, the stance regarding the exchange rate has been hard to interpret.

At the opposite end of the spectrum, monetary policy was subordinated to maintenance of the exchange rate under the gold standard, as is the case in modern times for countries that have permanently pegged their currency to a reserve currency, a practice that is nowadays limited to Denmark, which closely tracks the euro, Hong Kong and to small developing countries. Since the breakdown of the Bretton Woods System in the early 1970s, all major currencies and many others have let their exchange rate float. However, a full free float, as enjoyed by the US dollar, is much less common since many governments, mostly emerging and developing countries, manage the movements of their currencies. Such managed floating can be justified when foreign exchange markets are thin and over- and undershooting of the currency rate is a concern. While for many years a few countries claimed that they were floating without any intervention from their monetary authorities, they later encountered situations in which they felt a need to enter the markets, sometimes on a massive scale, to prop up or slow down a rise in their currencies.

At the outbreak of the Latin American and Asian financial crises of the 1990s, many of the affected countries held relatively modest amounts of international reserves, forcing them to take strong adjustment measures and rely on the IMF for large injections of usable foreign exchange. As a result, the hard-hit countries built up their reserve stocks in the aftermath of the crises, as a means of *self-insurance* against out-of-control depreciation of their currencies. While Latin American central banks accumulated foreign exchange roughly in line with measures of optimal levels of reserves, several Asian countries went beyond self-insurance. A striking example is that of China, whose international reserves reached almost $4 trillion, equaling around one third of its GDP. An important factor in this process was the Chinese policy of keeping its exchange rate low by means of large-scale intervention in the foreign exchange market, in order to foster export-led growth. But when the Chinese authorities shifted their stance to no longer keeping the renminbi exchange rate artificially low and large amounts of capital went abroad after capital controls were eased, the tide turned and the POBC spent close to a trillion dollars to support the exchange rate.

Central banks in countries pegging their currency to the dollar, hold very large reserves, while some free floaters retain comparatively small stocks of international reserves (Table 12.1). The Bank of England and the ECB belong to that category. Other free floaters comfortable with holding relatively small amounts of reserves are Canada (5 percent of GDP), Sweden (10 percent) and the United Kingdom (6 percent). Since the US dollar is by far the main reserve currency in the world and can draw on its sizable foreign currency swap lines with other central banks, it can afford to keep relatively very modest reserves (less than one half of a percent of GDP). But while useful as a measure of the degree to which a country is 'invested' in official reserves, the level of reserves as a percentage of a country's GDP is not a reliable indicator of the adequacy of a country's reserves. Factors such as economic openness, the scope of capital controls, the level of short-term government debt, the degree of access to international capital markets and official swap lines as well as country-specific factors need to be taken into account.

Under a regime of fully floating exchange rates, central bank intervention in the foreign exchange market is in principle absent. However, over time, so-called free floating currencies were eventually steered by official intervention. Abandoning their stance of non-intervention, central banks stepped in when faced with a rapidly and deeply depreciating (and sometimes appreciating) currency, usually backed up by raising (or lowering as the case may be) short-term interest rates to stem extreme capital flows. Such an event took place in 2000 in the early days of the euro as its weakness became a cause for concern. More recently, an instance of massive intervention to stem an unwanted appreciation concerned the Swiss Franc.

Table 12.1 International reserves (in $billions) and Forex regimes

	Reserves	*% of GDP*	*Forex regime*
China	3113	24	MF
Japan	1256	26	FF
Switzerland	800	118	FF/MF
Euro area	768	7	FF
Saudi Arabia	489	71	$ peg
Russia	460	30	MF
Hong Kong	431	126	$ peg
India	411	16	MF
South Korea	402	26	MF
Brazil	380	19	MF
Singapore	288	89	$ peg[1]
Thailand	249	55	MF
Mexico	173	15	MF
United Kingdom	164	6	FF

Source: IMF, reserves and GDP based on end 2017 or mid-2018 numbers

FF free floating, *MF* managed floating, *$ peg* keeping the domestic currency rate fixed (between narrow margins) against the US dollar

[1]Until 2018

The Swiss National Bank, which had maintained a free float of its currency for decades, started to buy massive amounts of euros against its swiftly appreciating currency in September 2011. The strong upward pressure on the Swiss Franc was the result of persistent large inflows of foreign capital, mainly of money in search of a safe haven in turbulent times. Applying capital controls to ward off excessive capital would be anathema for an international financial center like Switzerland. And as lowering short-term rates to zero proved to be insufficiently effective, the central bank decided to intervene heavily in the foreign exchange market. In the process the central bank's holdings of foreign currencies (mainly euros) reached a level of $730 billion in 2015, equal to 110 percent of Swiss GDP, far beyond what would be a reasonable stock of reserves. Although large scale intervention by an advanced country is generally frowned upon, as it tends to make its currency cheaper and thereby strengthen its competitiveness in an artificial way, the Swiss action was seen as justified in light of its special circumstances as an international financial center and its currency's role as a safe haven. Eventually the central bank introduced negative interest rates, which had a substantial impact. The independent Swiss National

Bank was in the driver's seat in this instance of manipulating the exchange rate to make its domestic monetary policy effective, the Swiss government acquiescing in the unorthodox action.

The ECB constitutes a special case with respect to the link between the exchange rate and monetary policy. The ECB is fully independent in its conduct of monetary policy and does not have a target rate for the euro. But adjusting its policy interest rate or making decisions on the size of its quantitative easing can have an impact on the exchange rate of the common currency. Movements in other major currencies, in particular the dollar, also have an impact on the euro rate. The ECB is adamant that it refrains from influencing the common currency through intervention. Only in 2000, at the very beginning of its existence, did joint intervention with the US authorities take place when the euro slid from its initial dollar rate of 1.17 to a mere 88 cents. Even though the amount of purchases was relatively modest, the euro started to recover immediately. Despite having a fully free floating common currency since then, European politicians and entrepreneurs from time to time complain when they fear that the euro has become too strong and threatens the currency zone members' competitiveness. The central bank seldom enters this discussion, but has on occasion downplayed the significance of movements in the euro exchange rate. It has described such movements as a mere side effect of its policy of attaining and maintaining price stability. And when President Trump complained that the low euro exchange rate against the US dollar gave European countries an unfair competitive advantage, the head of the ECB Mario Draghi, answering questions of journalists emphasized that: 'We [the ECB] don't target the exchange rate' (reported by CNCB on 18 June, 2019).

While the responsibility for allowing large fluctuations in the dollar rate resides with the US Treasury, the situation with respect to the euro is open to interpretation. In the parlance of the media, the question is 'who is Mr. Euro?' In other words, who deals with the US authorities when questions arise about the position of the euro and the US dollar? The easy answer is of course that there is no target rate for the euro and, secondly, that the Statutes of the ECB proclaim that it must operate without any political influence. Nevertheless, the then President of the European Commission, Jean-Claude Juncker, at the time claimed the title for himself, as did the President of the ECB at the time, Jean-Claude Trichet. In the view of the media and central bankers, the honorific belonged to the Central Bank President.

Central banks manage the stock of their countries' *international reserves*. They determine the composition of this buffer, within the constraint of the countries' currency regime. They are also free to invest the reserves in the assets of their choice, mostly determined by liquidity, safety and yield. The US dollar has remained the most popular as a reserve, vehicle and intervention currency. The share of the euro in global official reserves rose rapidly after its introduction as a result of European countries outside the euro area deciding to hold significant amounts of the currency of their largest trading partners. Considerations of portfolio diversification also generated interest in the euro. Its share has remained around one quarter of global officially held foreign currency reserves. Suggestions that the euro might challenge the dollar as the major reserve currency have proved to be baseless. In fact, the ECB is not in favor of such a development which could hamper its monetary policy actions. And a substantial international role for the Chinese renminbi is yet to arrive, although its inclusion in the basket of currencies constituting the SDR indicates its increasing importance.

Box 12.1 Optimal Reserves

Before the breakdown of the Bretton Woods System, an important issue concerned the optimal size of global reserves and that of individual countries. Whether there was enough gold and how it was distributed continued to be a central question under the gold standard. Central banks played a crucial role in the late 1960s in negotiations concerning the creation of a new reserve asset, the SDR (special drawing rights in the IMF), to avoid the effects of a shortage of gold and to reduce the role of the dollar. After the link between gold and the dollar was severed in 1971, and with the advent of floating exchange rates, the reserves issue lost part of its relevance for the world's largest economies. By enjoying full access to international financial markets, they can tide over periods of balance of payments deficits by borrowing from commercial banks and issuing bonds. If they experience difficulties in raising enough funds, they can turn to the International Monetary Fund or the European Stability Mechanism. But as borrowing from the IMF and ESM come with policy conditions, countries relatively prone to running external deficits (except for the United States which can borrow in its own currency) prefer to hold a certain amount of reserves so as to avoid having to take abrupt adjustment measures or turning to the IMF. For emerging and developing countries practicing managed

(*continued*)

Box 12.1 (continued)

floating with no or uncertain access to international financial markets, the question of adequate reserves remains of central importance. There exists a vast literature on this complicated matter which has led to refinements of the crude 'three months of imports' rule of thumb, but no formula has been accepted as the single standard. Factors that are usually included are the openness of the economy, the size of short-term external liabilities (remaining maturity of one year or less), that share of the money supply that can at short notice be mobilized as capital outflows and the costs of holding reserves (De Beaufort Wijnholds 2007). The IMF analyzes the adequacy of the reserves of countries whose economies it examines (mostly emerging and developing countries) and usually includes target levels for reserves as one of the conditions for countries that borrow from it.

Communication

Traditionally, central banks were reluctant to share information about their actions. Reacting to mounting criticism that such 'secrecy' was no longer acceptable in a changing world, central banks gradually moved toward more transparency. Within the central banks themselves, younger officials expressed similar complaints. An early and outspoken advocate of more openness and better communication, Alan Blinder, then Vice-Chairman of the Fed, got into to 'a bit of conflict' with Alan Greenspan, whose lack of transparency in communicating Blinder considered to be no longer appropriate. Blinder resigned not long afterward.

In tandem with taking aggressive monetary action, many central banks further streamlined their communications in recent years, recognizing that providing clear and transparent information and explanations of decisions taken is of great importance for maximizing the effectiveness of their actions. Surprising financial markets is generally undesirable as monetary policy decision-making is normally focused on managing market expectations. When market participants are caught off guard, the result can be unwanted disruption. There are, however, exceptions, such as aggressively defending a currency in a nosedive, requiring a sudden, extremely large raise in short-term interest rates making it very expensive for market participants to short the currency, known as a *bear squeeze,* as well as attracting capital from abroad. But such extreme rates can only be maintained for a limited time to prevent damage to the economy. An example of pushing up interest rates to exceptional levels concerns Argentina, where in mid-2018 the central bank raised short-term rates to 60 percent (about 30 percent in real terms) to defend the rapidly falling peso. Most of the time, however, transparency through effective communication is vastly preferred over surprises.

Although informing national parliaments, through either issuing periodic monetary reports or testifying at hearings, both a decades-long practice, an aura of secrecy still surrounded central banking decision-making until approximately the turn of the century in the case of the Fed and somewhat later in other countries. The American Central Bank, under pressure from Congress and laws such as the *Government in Sunshine Act*, had become more transparent by periodically providing a considerable amount of factual information. But during most of his tenure (1987–2006), Chairman Greenspan's *modus operandi* consisted of deliberate obfuscation. By expressing himself in oracular terms, which were difficult to pin down, he earned a reputation for avoiding clear policy pronouncements whenever he felt a need for a degree of secrecy. But as shocks flowing from sudden actions, such as the large hike in the federal funds rate in 1994, became controversial, the Fed responded by measures such as shortening the period between FOMC meetings and the publication of its minutes, thereby providing market participants and the public a better understanding of its considerations. Even more important was moving from issuing bland announcements on the occasion of a change in the Fed's target rate to providing short statements after every FOMC meeting, setting out the central bank's interpretation of economic conditions and its reasons for changing its policy rate or keeping it unchanged. But as is customary in official circles, the language in which these messages were written was often perceived as dense. The market reaction was to increase the activity of so-called Fed-watchers who are kept busy parsing every word and comma these statements contain.

The FOMC Opens Up Fully

A novel element in communication was added when FOMC members decided in 2012 to publicly present their individual short-term and longer-term expectations for real GDP growth, the level of unemployment, core inflation (the personal consumption expenditures price index) and the level of interest rates (designated the appropriate policy rate). The information shows the mean, median and the range of the projections (Understandably FOMC members are not identified by name.) These forecasts, officially known as the Summary of Economic Projections (SEP), are also presented in a plotted graph, allowing interested parties to absorb in a glance what the range of thinking is within the Fed about future developments. These 'dot plots' are unique among central banks and sometimes questioned as to the desirability of not only reporting how individual FOMC members voted (by name) on proposed monetary actions, but also revealing each member's forecasting skills or predilections and how they differ from those made by the Fed staff. It is also not clear what the extent is to which such exercises contribute to influencing inflation expectations, especially when the range of forecasts is wide. Addressing such concerns the Feds' then Vice-Chair, Stanley Fischer, stated that 'one may say that the SEP shows the basis from which each participant in the FOMC discussion is likely to start. But the task of moving from information to an interest rate decision is not simple and requires a great deal of analysis and back-and-forth among FOMC participants at each meeting' (Fischer 2017).

Greater transparency has also become the norm at other central banks. At the Bank of England, in addition to its periodical inflation and financial stability reports, the position of each member of the Monetary Policy Committee is published whenever a policy decision is made. Different from the practice at other central banks, the London-based institution nowadays includes two outside experts (i.e. not part of the Bank of England management or staff), among the eight members of its monetary policy committee (the same holds for the highly independent Financial Policy Committee). The outside members are respected monetary economists from academia, think tanks and corporations. They have full voting rights, reside in London during their term and are supported by a small staff. Bringing in such external experts provides an opportunity to benefit from views developed outside the confines of the central bank, where 'group think' can influence decision-making.

The European Central Bank's approach from the start of its actual inception as supranational policymaker in 2000 was to have its President present an oral statement to the media after each monetary policy meeting of the ECB Council, followed by a period of question and answer. Supplying immediate background information on its decisions was welcomed by 'ECB watchers' and other observers and was later adopted by a number of other central banks. But at the beginning of its activities, the ECB declined to publish the minutes of its Council's deliberations. It feared that as an institution working on the basis of a consensus reached by members of different nationalities, identification of the views expressed by its individual members could politicize the process of decision-making. The Bank later revised its position and decided to make publicly available comprehensive minutes of its deliberations, but without mentioning names. However, in most instances observers are able to discern what the various positions were.

Limits

In practice central bank independence and accountability tend to go hand in hand. Hence a high degree of transparency has become the norm for most countries. At the same time, it is widely recognized that there are limits to transparency. As Blinder has observed: '[t]ransparency can and should stop short of voyeurism' (Blinder 2004, 8). For instance, central banks cannot disclose confidential information about commercial banks. It is also obvious that in the case of imminent currency devaluations and revaluations no substantive information can be released. The same holds for deliberations among central bank officials outside regularly scheduled meetings, such as those of the FOMC and the ECB Council. Officials often meet informally, for instance over dinner the night before a scheduled meeting, to get a sense of where various policymakers stand. (There is no need, to paraphrase Blinder, to report the informal conversation nor the dinner menu to the public.) Avoiding surprises is common practice within and between monetary institutions. To insist on making the exchange of views expressed at such informal gatherings public will only lead to finding other informal ways of communication among central bankers.

This brings us to the practice of *leaking*. Providing confidential information to outsiders is pervasive in many countries, especially in the political arena. Leaking to the media by government officials is often the norm rather than the exception, foremost in the United States. Although leaks are officially frowned upon, attempts to stop unwanted leaks are generally fruitless. And often 'unauthorized' releases of information are deliberate and used as a tool, for instance as a trial balloon regarding new policies, or to undermine the position of opposing parties. Leaking should not be considered as an acceptable form of transparency as it implies passing on information on a selective basis and breaches confidentiality rules. It is at best an unfair practice and can at its worst cause considerable damage. While it cannot be maintained that central banks never leak, it is quite uncommon, as claimed by Princeton professor and former Fed senior official, Alan Blinder (Blinder 2017, 117). Much of what makes central bankers credible resides on trust and leaking tends to abuse it. Maintaining a reputation for soundness and reliability is crucial for the credibility of official monetary institutions.

Box 12.2 Negotiations and Communication

Negotiations are a special form of communication among a limited group of participants. In the domain of economic policy, central bank officials and government representatives meet regularly. A common practice is for the heads of the central bank and ministers of finance to meet regularly, sharing information and sometimes discussing the mix between monetary and fiscal policy. When a central bank is independent such get-togethers (usually in a good restaurant) are an excellent form of cooperation, but do not amount to actual negotiations, each player respecting the other's particular responsibility. The dynamic changes when a president or prime minister (plus high-ranking civil servants) meets with the head of their central bank. It is often a way to exert pressure on the central bank to take a certain action (usually on interest rates) and can become more of a negotiation which tends not to be made public, but the gist of which usually becomes known to the outside world. Absent a directive, the central bank can object or propose an alternative course of action. For instance, as related in Chap. 8, Fed Chairman Arthur Burns, pressed by President Nixon to go slow on fighting inflation, suggested to introduce price and wage controls. When these measures were not a success, Burns had to revert to traditional policy, which he executed halfheartedly.

Besides domestic negotiations on economic policy, a large number of negotiations are of an international, or regional (the euro area), character. The number of such meetings has ballooned in recent decades. Central banks are practically always involved in the monetary and financial negotiations. Some of such meetings are held among central banks, usually in the mode of 'sitting around a table.' Apart from discussing policy matters, they can constitute formal negotiations, ranging from monetary reform to financial support operations. Usually gathering at the BIS, they have from time to time negotiated the amounts and terms of so-called bridge loans to countries with serious payments problems, in order to tide over the period between a loan application and the disbursement of IMF loans. Such gatherings tend to take place in a non-confrontational manner, culminating in 'fraternal agreements.' However, meetings on major monetary reforms involve significant political considerations, making government participants the ultimate deciders. However, independent central banks, who usually possess superior analytical and technical knowledge, when combined with well-developed diplomatic skills, are often able to exert considerable influence on the outcome of negotiations.

Central banks' behavior in negotiations on international monetary policy and reform can differ significantly from that of governments who as political entities tend to act more assertively and are generally more focused on short-term solutions than more strategic considerations. Since central bankers on average serve considerably longer than senior government officials, they have the 'luxury' of being able to focus on the longer run.

Based on observations by the authors over several decades, some general strategies and modes of behavior encountered in international decision-making are identified. It is important for inexperienced central bankers to be aware of such matters. The points below are intended to provide some advice to them.

1. All central bank officials who regularly attend policy-oriented meetings should be able to deal with journalists without falling into traps. Media training for such officials should be compulsory. On-the-job training only is generally insufficient.
2. Central bankers should as much as possible avoid participating in purely (often time consuming and boring) procedural discussions. They should leave it to treasury officials when governments are also represented at the meeting. Treasury persons are usually more adapt in these matters.
3. Negotiations tend to continue longer than necessary, not so much because of the oratorical tradition of some countries, but chiefly due to participants' wish to demonstrate to the home front that they have fought hard, even if they can show little for it. With

regard to international meetings consisting of representatives from both monetary authorities, there is not much that central bankers can do about it and are often condemned to listen patiently or cool their heels in the corridors.

4. Thorough preparation can make the difference between a weak presentation and one that is listened to. Central bankers tend to spend more time on analysis and often possess more technical knowledge than government officials, whom they can help prepare a strong and well-reasoned national position if needed.
5. Building trust delivers results over time. This is generally easier for central bankers who often have known each other for a long time and tend to be less confrontational than political appointees.
6. Forming coalitions is usually essential to achieving meaningful results in dealing with the most powerful players, such as the United States. A lack of cohesion among European countries has in the past often led to failure. For instance, this happened from time to time at the IMF when despite collectively having a greater share of the votes than the United States, disagreement between Germany and France and their supporters resulted in an unnecessary European loss. The best that central banks can do to foster coalition building is to caucus among themselves and strive to inform their governments where the various parties may come out.
7. Timing is important. There is a tendency among certain negotiators to put all their cards on the table at the beginning of a meeting while signaling that their position is immutable. Such a tactic can lead to becoming isolated and having to backtrack in order to achieve a compromise. Seasoned central bankers may counsel newly appointed government officials to avoid such a scenario.
8. Countries who want to camouflage that they are the actual sponsors of a certain proposal may approach a friendly participant to introduce it. For instance, the United States from time to time requested Canada to put forward a position developed in Washington, while the same is true for Germany and the Netherlands. The junior partners are, however, not always prepared to play such a role on demand and may expect some 'reward' from their powerful neighbors at some point.
9. Central bankers can play a useful role as honest brokers in disputes between third parties. For instance, for those of us who served on the Board of Executive Directors at the IMF and represented mul-

tiple countries, it was common practice to act on behalf of a country involved in negotiating a credit with the Fund, while at the same time keeping in mind best practices supported by the IMF.

10. Central banks are usually less inclined to take rigid positions than governments, also because they lack the political power to impose their will. But in case they are very powerful (such as the German Bundesbank was), their full support of their government's negotiating position can be crucial. A classic case where a rigid, but well thought out, position by a government backed-up by its central bank led to important concessions by its opponents pertains to the negotiations culminating in the Treaty of Maastricht establishing the European Economic and Monetary Union in 1992, which seven years later led to the founding of the European Central Bank. France was very eager to gain influence over European monetary policymaking in order to avoid the effects of tough anti-inflation policies à la Germany's Bundesbank, fearing that it would slow down its domestic economy. The French government hoped to achieve this through a European common monetary policy strongly influenced by France. However, Germany successfully resisted the French ambitions. As Andre Szasz, a former Executive Director of the Netherlands Bank and participant in the EMU project explained: 'Germany attached conditions to EMU which France had no choice but to accept,' referring to the prohibition of governments to influence the future European Central Bank's monetary policy decisions, rendering it fully independent (Szasz 1999, 213–28). On top of that France accepted to have the ECB situated in Frankfurt, Germany.

Strengthening Accountability

An essential condition for central banks to maintain their independence is to be accountable. The increasing role and broad implications of central bank policies in recent years has not only led to more openness but also to a need for full accountability. There is a strong need to clarify to internal and external stakeholders the objectives, strategies and the decisions taken by central banks. While accountability has already been observed for a considerable time with regard to monetary policy, banking supervisors, including central banks, have entered into serious discussions with regard to strengthening accountability mechanisms (BIS 2015).

A well-designed system of accountability can enhance the operational position of central banks (Cœuré 2017). In line with international practices and research, a distinction can be made between institutional independence, regulatory independence, operational independence and budgetary independence. An accountability arrangement should ensure sufficient room for central banks to act within their mandate and discretion to exercise their powers and judgment, while explaining relevant observations and policy decisions.

Forward Guidance

Monetary policy is by its nature forward looking and market participants benefit from any information that might help them to make better decisions. While quantitative easing was judged to be partially successful, central banks felt that by providing indications or even commitments about the future path of interest rates, they could influence expectations directly. As such, forward guidance would enhance the impact of QE or replace it as part of an exit strategy from QE. Whereas transparency informs about past discussions and decisions, forward guidance informs stakeholders about the likely *future* course of monetary policy. In the past such information was seldom provided in a clear fashion. But the Greenspan approach of silence or puzzling comments gave way after his departure to aiding financial markets and other actors to make decisions partly on the basis of general or even specific indications of the future path of monetary policy.

The central banks of Norway and Sweden were the first to provide explicit indications of the future path of interest rates in their countries, a move that was generally well received. However, there are limits to the effectiveness of forward guidance. Care has to be taken to avoid falling into the trap of pre-commitment and the associated risk of time inconsistency, as the experience of the Fed and the Bank of England demonstrate. After Ben Bernanke took over from Greenspan as Chairman of the Fed in 2006, he departed from his predecessors' oracular style by announcing in 2008, at a time that interest rates had already been lowered to close to zero, that rates would remain low 'for some time.' And in 2011 the Fed stated in a further step toward commitment, that low interest rates would be 'warranted' until mid-2013. Ratcheting up his rhetoric, Bernanke declared in December 2012—inflation was still significantly below the 2 percent target—that the Fed would keep interest rates close to zero until US unemployment would fall below 6.5 percent, a decline of 1.2 percent from the then prevailing rate. Linking monetary policy directly to the level of joblessness was an untested experience which did not work well. The 6.5 percent number also smacked of being a commitment. Less than a year later, Mark Carney, Governor of the Bank of England, announced a similar link to the unemployment rate, putting the threshold for the UK at 7 percent. The inspiration for these moves may have come from the influential academic Michael Woodford, as described in Box 12.3 on monetary theory. However, in both cases the unemployment triggers were reached considerably earlier than foreseen by the central banks, demonstrating that the level of joblessness alone is not a good indicator of the state of the economy, and that this kind of near commitment carries a considerable risk of time inconsistency. Apart from the aforementioned—probably not to be repeated—outlier, forward guidance has mostly taken the form of stating intentions with respect to monetary policy actions on the basis of the current state of the economy as a whole and of economic forecasts. For instance, by suggesting that they will keep interest rates (very) low for the foreseeable future, central banks hope that markets will adjust their expectations accordingly. But announcements of intentions without a clear time frame are unlikely to be effective as unforeseen circumstances can occur and render expectations obsolete. Therefore, indications of intended changes in policy interest rates in the near future, as well as the likely size and number of such changes over the coming months, have become the most common form of such statements. For instance, after shifting to a stance of modestly reducing the degree of monetary stimulus, following the cessation of its asset purchases in 2013, the Fed now regularly announces its general intentions with respect to the future path of interest rates. For example, it announced in 2018 that it *expected* to raise interest rate three or four times with ¼ percent in the coming 12 months. On account of indications of a weakening of the economy, a different route was taken, but that does not mean that forward guidance is not useful. A degree of flexibility in policymaking is part of modern monetary policy.

The Bank of England has, in addition to quantitative easing, also made active use of forward guidance and has described its approach in detail (Bank of England, *Forward Guidance*, 2014). Smaller central banks in advanced economies have in recent years also practiced a high degree of transparency with respect to their policy intentions. As for the ECB, in view of the tardy recovery of the euro area economy, it signaled for many years that it would maintain a very accommodating monetary policy as long as the objective of bringing up inflation to its target was not met. And in Japan the central bank also emphasized the need for continuing to aggressively ease its policy as inflation was stubbornly stuck at a very low level. But after many years of failing to hit the target, commentators and officials within the Bank of Japan started questioning the wisdom of continuing to strive to bring up inflation exactly to 2 percent.

International Collaboration

There is a long history of collaboration between central banks. Sister institutions such as the Bank of England and the French Central Bank supported each other from time to time with loans to overcome periods of reserve losses under the gold standard. And after the First World War, European Central Banks were in close contact with each other, focused on returning to normalcy, initially to stabilize the wrecked economy of Belgium, but also as parties involved with the payment of reparations by Germany. During much of the 1920s, the major European Central Banks and the Federal Reserve Bank of New York entertained close ties, including providing each other with temporary financial support. As described earlier, this informal network started to dissolve with the demise of the gold standard.

Following the Second World War the tradition of cooperation between central banks was resumed and took on a more formalized character. Regular meetings of the heads of central banks at the Bank for International Settlements proved fruitful ground for confidential discussions cum negotiations. And the establishment of the International Monetary Fund gave a further boost to the formal involvement of the worlds' monetary experts. Central bankers have since played an important part in the governance of the IMF, either through their heads having been appointed members of the Board of Governors (the highest tier of decision-making) or as members of its Executive Board. In most cases central banks share the responsibility of their countries' IMF membership with their ministries of finance. Within the IMF, informal groupings, which include representatives from central banks, caucus among themselves. The main categories are nowadays the Group of Seven (formerly the Group of Ten richest nations), the European Union members and the Group of Twenty-Four developing countries. The International Monetary and Financial Committee (IMFC), a body comprised of ministers of finance and central bank governors, meets twice annually to discuss economic developments and policies. The Committee consists of 24 principles, representing the 24 country constituencies that constitute the Executive Board. In parallel, a self-invented non-treaty based body, known as the Group of Twenty (G20), was called into being in 1999, to satisfy a need felt by advanced and emerging countries to discuss monetary and financial issues of mutual interest in a more informal and confidential setting than the IMFC. Membership of the G20 deviates from that of the IMFC in that some smaller European countries are not represented (the ECB and the European Commission, however, participate in meetings), whereas emerging countries play a bigger role. Low income developing countries are not represented, but play a major role in the World Bank's Ministerial Development Committee. Much discussion has taken place about the respective roles of the IMFC and the G20 and the composition of their membership, in light of the considerable overlap between the two bodies. Central Bank officials fully participate in the meetings of all these groups.

Central banks have an important stake in the international monetary system. Their knowledge of the workings of the system is deep, in many instances backed by a team of international experts. But while they have a strong voice in the management of that system, the ultimate decisions are of a political nature. There are, however, instances where central banks have lead in taking decisive action to ward off dangerous threats to the system. As was described in Chap. 11, it was the world's central bankers who stepped in boldly at the time of the global financial crisis to prevent a financial meltdown. The astute management of the crisis was received very positively around the world by most political and monetary institutions, as well as the financial markets, strengthening the position of the monetary institutions. Christine Lagarde (2013), then Managing Director of the IMF, conveyed this sentiment when stating that 'central bankers have been the heroes of the financial crisis.' (However, in the Unites States and some other advanced countries, the general public was highly critical of bail-outs of commercial banks; a case of 'Main Street' vs. 'Wall Street.')

Central banks, like other policymakers, cannot rest on their laurels. Their actions are closely scrutinized and their prominent position often challenged, as is discussed in the final chapter which reflects on the future of central banks.

* * *

What are the main conclusions regarding monetary policy in the post Great Recession years and what lessons can be drawn from the slow moving recovery? The following enumeration draws on a comprehensive analysis by a team of IMF staffers (Bayoumi et al. 2014) and other insights described in previous sections.

1. Despite the emphasis on restoring economic growth after the Great Recession, long-term price stability should continue to be the ultimate goal of central banks. The consensus view is that best practice is direct, symmetric inflation targeting. Although changes to IT have been proposed (we will return to possible improvements in the final chapter), so far no change has been undertaken, reflecting the view expressed by John Murray, former Deputy Governor of the Bank of Canada, that there is strong evidence that IT 'improves economic performance and is less prone to destabilizing attacks than other monetary frameworks' (Murray 2017). But in view of the far-reaching changes in the global economic landscape, additional intermediate goals, such as financial and external stability, may be needed as well as a more intensive use of macroprudential measures, while capital controls and foreign exchange intervention should not be ruled out. Leaning against the wind, that is adjusting interest rates to counter financial instability (see Chap. 13 for a full discussion) should be carefully considered when financial bubbles appear.
2. There are gaps in the understanding of the monetary transmission channels. Besides the interest rate and exchange rate channels, as well as the effect of interest rate movements on equity markets and on lending activity, there is an incomplete understanding of how very low policy rates influence risk taking by banks. Also, the apparent changed relationship between inflation and unemployment (Phillips curve) requires further analysis. In this regard the IMF staff suggests the need for reconsidering the role of econometric models (at least until they better reflect the post-Great Recession world) and advocate 'more art and less science,' in monetary policymaking. In other words, a greater role for qualitative judgment and market feeling is desirable. This runs counter to the conclusion reached by Frederic Mishkin, then member of the Governing Board of the Fed, just before the Global Financial Crisis erupted, that monetary policy needed to be 'more science and less art' (Mishkin 2007).

3. When the economies of advanced countries fell into a tailspin in 2008 and central banks' policy rates were lowered in response until they reached the zero interest rate lower bound (or even below), central banks developed new instruments to further loosen monetary policy. These unconventional tools, such as massive financial asset purchases and forward guidance, but also reaching and sometimes broaching the lower zero bound, involved costs which tended to increase with prolonged use. While generally considered helpful in raising inflation toward the 2 percent target, a consensus developed that these costs were bound to cause disruption in the bond markets, adversely affecting institutional investors, as well as a misallocation of resources. In the absence of crises, the costs of QE and extremely low interest rates exceed the costs, according to the IMF staff. By contrast, forward guidance is also a useful instrument in calmer times.
4. Central bank independence is crucial for maintaining price stability. Expanding monetary institutions' mandate carries risks of political interference to the detriment of keeping inflation low.
5. Deep financial crises are transmitted swiftly in an interdependent world. But should international turmoil be countered by greater policy coordination among nations? The IMF staff does not make the distinction between international cooperation and coordination. There is a long history of comprehensive *cooperation* in the monetary domain, both with respect to the exchange of views and advice on countries' domestic monetary policies, as well as on the functioning of the international monetary system. International fora such as the International Monetary Fund and the Bank for International Settlements have successfully facilitated international monetary cooperation over the years. Policy *coordination* entails two or more countries' central banks and—in the fiscal domain governments—agreeing to take certain measures such as interest rate changes and intervention on currency markets simultaneously and are made public to enhance the effect. Such instances are, as we have seen in the foregoing, limited to extreme situations where strong action is in the interest of all participating countries. But concerns about giving up some sovereignty and uncertainty about the outcomes make it unlikely that 'rules' about policy coordination can be agreed on.
6. Avoiding overburdening monetary policy—a tempting 'solution' for politicians to many problems—is of the essence. Central banks are not able, with the tools they have at their disposal, to heal all ills of an economy. When government finances are chronically out of order and

necessary structural reforms are not implemented, the costs will exceed the benefits of central banks' QE and extremely low interest rate.

Box 12.3 Monetary Theory

A long-standing debate concerns the degree to which academics influence monetary policymaking and, conversely, how much central bankers help to steer academic theories toward more operational results. No doubt cross fertilization has been very useful in bringing theory and practice closer through a process of iteration, although measuring these tendencies can only be done on an anecdotal basis. During the first centuries of central banking history, monetary institutions tended to be run exclusively by practitioners, a situation that in some cases lasted into the twentieth century. For instance, the Bank of England did not recruit economists until the 1960s, a far cry from the situation in the present day where large numbers of highly qualified economists (some foreigners) populate the Old Lady, among which a significant proportion hail from academia or pursue their further careers at universities. The same is true for many other central banks. There is evidence that these academics return to their teaching position with an improved insight in real world problems. Another sign of an increase in the role of academics in central banking is the appointment of theoretical economists to top positions at central banks. For example, Mervyn King became Governor of the Bank of England in 2003, Ben Bernanke chaired the Board of Governors of the Federal Reserve System from 2006 to 2014 when Janet Yellen, another prominent former academic, took over. Stanley Fischer, who began his career at MIT, served as Vice Chairman of the Fed after being the Governor of the Bank of Israel and occupying senior positions at the World Bank and the IMF. Axel Weber went from academia straight to the top of the German Central Bank and Lucas Papademos served as Vice President of the European Central Bank after having started out in academia.

A good example of cross fertilization between academia and monetary practitioners is the widespread adoption of inflation targeting from 1990 on. A similar breakthrough was achieved around the same time as when the inverse relationship between central bank independence and inflation was empirically established. The result was a spectacular increase in the degree of independence enjoyed by central banks.

In terms of pure theory, a plethora of New Keynesian macroeconomic models were developed during the 1990s and 2000s, spanning a range of variations, with models including micro foundations arguably being the most innovative. Research economists working at central banks and international organizations—the number of which grew substantially over the years—were equally active in developing up-to-date models. Best known are comprehensive models such as Dynamic Stochastic General Equilibrium Models (DSGEM). While these and other sophisticated models owe much to developments in monetary theory, it is less clear to what extent they have played a role in actual monetary policy decision-making. Skeptics include Gregory Mankiw (an academic with policy experience) who stated that new macroeconomic concepts developed in the past several decades 'had little impact on macroeconomists who are charged with the messy task of conducting actual monetary and fiscal policy'(Mankiw 2006, 44).

Synthesis

In 2003 Professor Michael Woodford, a foremost theoretician, published an influential book *Interest and Prices: Foundations of a Theory of Monetary Policy* (Woodford 2003) and presented a synthesis of various theories in which the management of expectations about future monetary policy actions play a central role. He also emphasized the need for central banks to effectively communicate what they are doing in a world in which the transmission of information and the execution of financial transactions are instantaneous. He furthermore provided a framework for designing an optimal inflation-targeting regime by central banks. And a few years later Woodford argued that a convergence of macroeconomic theories had led to 'fewer fundamental disagreements among macroeconomists now than in past decades' and that a new synthesis had emerged which was helpful in influencing policymakers (Woodford 2008).

Applying Monetary Theory

Central bankers and academics have long struggled to develop reasonably reliable estimates of the natural—or neutral—interest rate, the real rate of interest—at which inflation and unemployment are both in equilibrium. The importance of this unobservable number is that deviations from the neutral rate indicate economic imbalances that may require monetary policy action. It is now generally recognized that the neutral rate is not a fixed number, but can vary between roughly ½ (or even less) and 3 percent, depending on the prevailing economic conditions. In their seminal paper, Thomas Laubach and John C. Williams (an academic and central banker) found a close link between the neutral rate of interest and the trend economic growth rate, but warned that estimates of the neutral rate are imprecise and subject to considerable real-time measurement errors (Laubach and Williams 2003).

Some central banks attach a high importance to the estimated level of the neutral interest rate in their countries. Such an approach has been followed by the Federal Reserve for many years. Defining the neutral real interest rate as the longer-run federal funds rate minus long-run inflation (r*, or r star), the natural rate of unemployment (u*) reflects the corresponding output gap. Together with the Fed's inflation objective p* or (p star) they are the lodestars of American monetary policy. Actual outcomes can, however, substantially diverge from r* and u*. Lower than expected inflation in the United States in recent years can be attributed to having succeeded in anchoring inflation expectations and the related flattening of the Phillips curve.

As to unemployment, actual levels have deviated considerably from u*, rendering it an unreliable indicator as a result of which the Fed has been placing less emphasis on u*. Fed Chairman Jerome H. Powell admitted as much in a speech before a gathering of central bankers at their annual palaver at Jackson Hole, Wyoming (Powell 2018). Deemphasizing the role of u* is in line with the analysis of that of Professors Taylor and Woodford on robust rules for monetary policy (2011). In addition, a few weeks after Governor Powell's speech, the FOMC (the policy setting organ of the Fed) announced that it was also downgrading the role of the neutral federal funds rate (FOMC, *Minutes* of meeting on 25, 26 September 2018). Decisions on the stance of monetary policy would henceforth be guided mostly by incoming information pertaining to the economic outlook, with the neutral federal funds rate being only one among many factors in its policymaking. This important pronouncement can be interpreted to emphasize that monetary policy at the Fed will in the future be truly data driven. After so many years of searching for the neutral short-term interest rate, this major adjustment in the FOMC's decision-making approach is likely to influence other central banks and diminish academic interest in their quest for a reliable estimate of what has been an important analytical tool for the American central bank.

Monetarism RIP?

Having played a central role in monetary policy in the past, most central banks nowadays do not pay much attention to the money supply based on the finding that the relationship between money and prices has broken down. Most academics too reject a role for M in setting monetary policy. Woodford opines that 'while it is always possible that monetary targeting might yet discovered to have unexpected virtues, there is little ground for presuming that such virtues must exist simply because of familiarity with the hypothesis.' The only role Woodford sees for tracking monetary aggregates is that they could be part of a large number of indicators that are used by central banks in preparing their macroeconomic projections. (Woodford 2007). However, some respected academic economists did not share this negative view. Nobel laureate Robert Lucas defended the European Central Bank's use of monetary aggregates, remarking that he was concerned that the already widely held opinion 'that the monetary pillar is superfluous and [would] lead monetary analysis back to the kind of muddled eclecticism that brought us the 1970s inflation' (Lucas 2007, 168).

While the role of the money supply has virtually vanished from the practice of monetary policy in United States, the United Kingdom and most other central banks, this is not the case for the European Central Bank. It follows a two-pillar approach in which a comprehensive monetary analysis is conducted alongside an economic analysis, the latter representing the same variables as used in the models mentioned heretofore. The monetary analysis' role is to cross check the picture resulting from the economic analysis. Convinced of the continuing usefulness of closely following the course of monetary aggregates and credit, the ECB conducted a lengthy study some years ago in order to enhance its monetary analysis (European Central Bank: Monetary Analysis at the ECB, 2010).

As a point of departure it cites 'the overwhelming consensus regarding the empirical long-run relationship between money and prices' which, it argues, provides a reliable nominal anchor for monetary policy. The ECB sees this as an approach distinct from the short-termism and fine-tuning practiced elsewhere, believing that monetary developments can signal inflation risks beyond the business cycle. In that sense committing to closely studying monetary trends serves as an 'insurance devise' (ECB 2010). By ignoring the role of money in the New Keynesian macroeconomic models, it argues that other central banks failed to pick up signals of the impending financial crisis of 2007 and beyond. Monetary analysis as practiced by the ECB not only provides indications of future price developments but can also furnish evidence of a build-up of financial imbalances, for instance deviations in the trend growth of credit, which is generally lacking in the models. An example is the rapid increase in M3 and credit to the private sector, such as financing mortgages, and the following sharp drop in these aggregates at the time of the Global Financial Crisis. By being able to discern unusual patterns in the monetary and financial sphere, the ECB considers it to have been better equipped than others to see financial storms developing in the distance. Recognizing the limitations to the accuracy of early warnings concerning financial stability, the Bank acknowledges that not all major financial crises of the past have been preceded by sharp deviations in money and credit growth trends, '[b]ut every major economic crisis in the 20th century was preceded by the emergence of monetary imbalances'.

The European Central Bank's enhancement of its monetary analysis has inter alia consisted of improving money demand models, by including elements such as wealth, developing money-based indicators of inflation risks and by incorporating money and credit into structural general equilibrium models by means of a fully articulated banking sector. The ECB cautions that while its structural models provide a comprehensive view across various sectors of the economy, they do not represent a full explanation of how the real economy is affected by money. As always, there are areas in which further research is needed, while some older debates continue in more or less intensity. First there is the perennial issue of what approach is superior: rules versus discretion. And the difference of opinion on the role of money is yet to be bridged. A major challenge is to successfully incorporate the financial sector into New Keynesian models.

The ECB has since its inception maintained its two-pillar approach, despite criticism from various quarters. However, there has been a shift in emphasis in its analysis from growth of the money supply to a comprehensive analysis of credit growth and its components, underpinned by an extensive loan survey.

Only the Central Bank of Argentina has abandoned inflation targeting and opted for a target for the growth of base money (Mo). This switch was made in the midst of an exchange rate crisis. With the Argentine peso in an almost free fall and after substantial sales of dollars by the central bank, followed by engineering a sharp increase in the short-term interest rate, failing to stem the outflow of capital, the Argentine government turned to the IMF for a credit of in total $57 billion (the largest credit ever granted by the Fund). As part of the economic program agreed with the IMF, the central bank—in a surprising move—replaced its IT with a target for base money. Since a change in base money directly affects the central bank's ability to create money, and by keeping the amount of Mo unchanged for the initial period of the program, the expectation was that such a drastic measure would turn the tide.

Modern Monetary Theory

Calling it Modern Monetary Theory, a few academics supported by a fringe of politicians, promote the view that monetary financing of large scale government spending, for instance on the environment, is an appropriate way to avoid having to raise taxes. The gist of this unorthodox 'modern' theory is described by *The Economist* as follows:

> A government that prints money and can borrow in its own currency cannot be forced to default, since it can always create money to pay creditors. *New* money can also pay for government spending; tax revenues are unnecessary. Governments, furthermore, should use their budgets to manage demand and maintain full employment (tasks now assigned to monetary policy, set by central banks.' (*The Economist*, 16 March, 2019, 67)

The notion that government need not raise taxes to pay for increased spending and can engage in monetary financing of budget deficits has been repudiated by leading mainstream economists such as Larry Summers who has termed the novel theory 'voodoo economics' (Summers 2018). And it is hard to imagine the world's independent money masters signing off on a piece of magical thinking.

Integrating the Financial Sector

Hyman Minsky, a professor at Washington University in St. Louis, argued in the 1980s, at a time when financial crises were largely absent, that in a capitalist society there was a strong likelihood of that at some point major financial crises would materialize (Minsky 1982). His theory, which was also seen as an ideological screed, received little attention at the time. It got another look at the time of the Global Financial Crisis, demonstrating the need for increased insight into the systemic side of the international financial system. And after the elevation of financial stability as a major policy goal in the mid-2000s, there were attempts to successfully integrate the financial sector into contemporary macroeconomic models. However, the domestic and global financial interconnections and their relevance to monetary and economic conditions are so complex that those efforts so far have produced little of note. As a consequence the role of officials with a significant understanding of markets (market 'feeling') has—once again—become more prominent. So far, therefore, as regards financial markets, the art of central banking has been more useful than the science.

Box 12.4 Behavior and Narrative Economics

A relatively new branch of economics, *behavior e*conomics has become widely practiced, filling a gap caused by an almost complete lack of the application of psychology to standard economic analyses. The rational expectations theorem, useful as it was in the development of several branches of economics, by definition excluded irrational behavior of economic agents. Behavior economics has demonstrated the limitations of the rational expectations theorem and enriched economic theory in such fields as decision-making by consumers and investors as well as the stock market. Without referring explicitly to behavior economics, Alan Blinder, writing in 2004, highlighted the changes in central bankers' attitudes that had taken place in previous years. He characterized these adjustments as a quiet revolution, reflecting an initial lack of awareness among academics of such an important shift in the practice of central banking. First, he mentioned the striking move toward greater transparency by central banks. Second, he explained how central banks were abandoning the 'single decider' model by which the heads of monetary institutions practically singlehandedly made the decisions on all monetary policy actions. This model was being increasingly replaced by monetary policymaking by committees in what came to be called a 'collegial' approach. Blinder argued that making decisions by a team was arguably more difficult, but led to better results. Third, he examined the complex relationship between central banks and financial markets, raising the question: 'Who shall be servant and who shall be master?' Warning against a tendency for central banks to not only follow the markets, but also taking advice from them could lead to short-termism and bad policy. Blinder concluded that 'fundamentally, the markets need to be led, not followed' (Blinder 2004, 95).

Two behavioral economists and Nobel Prize laureates, George Akerlof and Robert Shiller, have also focused on the role of markets, stressing the importance of 'animal spirits' as a driving force on financial markets (Akerlof and Schiller 2009). Although acknowledging the power of central banks, they did not attempt making a contribution to the behavioral aspects of monetary policymaking.

However, Shiller's introduction of *narrative* economics, which postulates that stories can have an important influence on economic outcomes when they go 'viral,' includes a section on inflation. In most instances inflation causes anger among the public, leading to narratives about its 'immorality' and where to place blame. The most common narrative on inflation in modern times has been the existence of a wage-price spiral and the 'evil' labor unions who are 'behind it.' And, so the narrative went on, while the unions were claiming that they represented all workers, 'politicians and central bankers were selfishly perpetuating the upward spiral of inflation which impoverished real working people not represented by powerful unions' (Shiller 2019, 258). 'The moral imperative here was strong' (Shiller, 261) and provided central banks with ample support to drastically bring down inflation and interest rates by means of central bank independence and inflation targeting. At the time of writing (late 2019), the narrative seems to be the exact opposite. Heather Long reports that in a listening tour by the Federal Reserve, 'the overwhelming message from the hundreds of people at 14 events has been: "[t]he nation isn't really at full employment"' (*Washington Post*, 30 October 2019), despite the fact that at 3.5 percent civilian unemployment is at its lowest in 50 years. As mentioned in Box 12.2, measurement problems may have contributed to an underestimation of the joblessness rate.

References

Bank of England, *Forward Guidance*, 2014.

Bayoumi, Tamim et al, "Monetary Policy in the New Normal", *IMF Staff Discussion Note*, International Monetary Fund, April 2014.

Bernanke, Ben: "The Federal Reserve and the Financial Crisis", *Lectures,* Princeton University, Princeton NJ, 2013a.

Bernanke, Ben: "What Should Economists and Policy Makers *Learn* from the Financial Crisis? *Lecture,* London School of Economics and Political Science, London 25 March, 2013b.

Bernanke, Ben "The Taylor Rule", Brookings Institution, 2015a.

Bernanke, Ben: *The Courage to Act: A Memoir of a Crisis and its Aftermath,* W.W. Norton, New York, 2015b.

Blinder, Alan: *The Quiet Revolution: Central Banking Goes Modern,* Yale University Press, New Haven, 2004.

Blinder, Alan: *Advice and Dissent: Why America Suffers when Economics and Politics Collide,* Basic Books, New York, 2017.

Borio, Claudio: "Monetary Policy and Financial Stability: What Role in Prevention and Recovery?" BIS *Working Paper* 440, January 2014.

Borio, Claudio et al: "The Costs of Deflation: A Historical Perspective", BIS *Quarterly Review*, March 2015.

Cœuré, Benoît: "Independence and Accountability in A Challenging World", *Introductory Remarks* at the Transparency International EU Event, Brussels, 28 March, 2017.

De Beaufort Wijnholds, J.Onno: "Reserve Accumulation: Objective or By-product?" European Central Bank, *Occasional Paper Series* no 73, September 2007.

Dao Liu, David; "Chinese Monetary Policy in the Global Context" *Paper* presented at the Federal Reserve Bank of Kansas City Symposium, Jackson Hole WY. August, 2013.

Economist, The: "Modern Monetary Theory", 16 March, 2019, 67.

European Central Bank: Monetary Analysis at the ECB, 2010.

Fischer, Stanley: "Why are Interest Rates so Low?" *Speech* at the Economic Club of New York, 17 October, 2016.

Fischer, Stanley: "Monetary Policy Expectations and Surprises", *Speech* at Columbia University, New York, 17 April, 2017.

Lagarde, Christine: *Speech* at the Federal Reserve Bank of Kansas City, Symposium, Jackson Hole WY, 23 August, 2013.

Lindsey, David: "A Century of Monetary Policy at the Fed", Palgrave Macillan, Basingstoke, 2013.

Long, Heather: "Americans Urge the Federal Reserve to Boost the Economy", *Washington Post*, 30 October, 2019.

Laubach, Thomas and John Williams: "Measuring the national Rate of Interest", *Review of Economics and Statistics* vol 85 issue 4, 2003, 1063–70.

Lucas, Robert, "Econometric Policy Evaluations: A Critique" in Karl Brunner and Alan Meltzer (eds), *The Phillips Curve and the Labor Markets*, Carnegie-Rochester Series on Public Policy Series, vol 1, 1972, 19–46.

Lucas, Robert: "Central Banking: Is Science Replacing Art?" in European Central Bank, (ed) *Monetary Policy: A Journey from Theory to Practice*, Frankfurt, 2007.

Mankiw, Gregory: "The Macroeconomist as Scientist and Engineer", *Journal of Economic Perspectives*, Fall 2006. 29–40.

Minsky, Hyman: "Can it Happen Again?" *Essays on Instability and Finance*, M.E. Sharpe, Armonk NY, 1982.

Mishkin, Frederic: "Will Monetary Policy Become More of a Science?" The Federal Reserve Board, *Finance and Economics,* Discussion Series 44, Washington DC, 2007.

Murray, John: "Inflation Targeting after Thirty Years: What have we Learned?" Norges Bank, *Arbeidsnoted* 217/4, Oslo, 2017.

Powell, Jerome: "Changing market Structures and Implications for Monetary Policy", *Speech* at the Federal Reserve Bank of Kansas City Symposium, Jackson Hole WY, 24 August, 2018.

Rajan, Raghuram: "Competitive Monetary Easing: Is It Yesterday Once More?" *Remarks* made by the governor of the Reserve bank of India, Brookings Institution, Washington DC, 10 April, 2014

Shiller, Robert: *Narrative Economics: How Stories Go Viral & Drive Major Economic Events,* Princeton University Press, Princeton NJ, 2019.

Summers, Lawrence: "Fed Bashing is Foolish", *Washington Post,* 6 November, 2018.

Szasz, Andre, *The Road to European Monetary Union,* Macmillan, London 1999.

Woodford, Michael: *Interest and Prices: Foundations of a Theory of Monetary Policy,* Princeton University Press, Princeton NJ, 2003.

Woodford, Michael: "How Important is the Role of Money in the Conduct of Monetary Policy?" National Bureau of Economic Research, *Working* Pape 13328, August 2007.

Woodford, Michael: "Convergence in Macroeconomics: Elements of a New Synthesis", *Presentation* made at the annual meeting of the American Economic Association, January 2008.

CHAPTER 13

Maintaining Financial Stability

Marco van Hengel and Paul Hilbers

Defining Financial Stability

Financial stability is a very generic concept that—in contrast to price stability—is difficult to define and observe. Financial stability tends to be taken for granted in good times and is only fully appreciated at those moments when it is not achieved.

There is no international, uniform definition of financial stability. It is typically described as a situation where there are no impediments to the normal functioning of the financial sector. For the purposes of this chapter, we will use the following definition (The Netherlands Bank 2014): '*A stable financial system ensures an efficient allocation of resources and is able to absorb shocks, without any disruptive effects on the real economy.*'

The definition distinguishes three elements.

First, the relevance of financial stability hinges on the impact on the real economy. In normal times, financial institutions channel investments and savings to the economy and provide insurance against risks that individual participants cannot take on themselves. To safeguard these essential functions, developments in the financial sector need to be sustainable. This means that there are no negative effects on the economy or society and that no excessive risk-taking takes place. In other words, financial stability

O. de Beaufort Wijnholds, *The Money Masters*,
https://doi.org/10.1007/978-3-030-40041-5_13

provides the stable conditions in which the financial sector can effectively fulfil its intermediary role and contribute to long-term economic growth.

The second important element of financial stability is its focus on the absorption of shocks. This recognizes the fact that financial and economic shocks can occur, because of the inherent characteristic of financial institutions to take on risks. Risks may materialize from time to time, which is part of a normal functioning of the economy. The objective of financial stability is to mitigate the effects of these shocks in the financial sector and ensure a stable economic environment.

The third element states that financial stability supports an efficient allocation of resources. Business and households make investment decisions and can do this more effectively in a sound and predictable environment. In an unstable financial system, resources are misallocated into less profitable projects or sectors. As a result, the economy will grow below its potential and vulnerabilities may develop.

The Evolving Role of Central Banks

Financial stability has always been an integral part of central banking, but has gained a more explicit position in recent years. After the global financial crisis, the so-called macroprudential perspective of supervisory policy developed into a separate responsibility with its own objectives and instruments. This field of expertise is relatively new and continues to evolve.

Microprudential Perspective

Traditionally, financial stability has been an implicit, but slumbering element of the activities of central banks. Standard thinking on central bank activity tended to highlight three elements. Monetary policy would focus on price stability and a sound functioning of the payments system. In addition, in its role as provider of liquidity to the financial system, the central bank acted as a lender of last resort during periods of stressed liquidity. These tasks were complemented by microprudential supervision aimed at ensuring that individual institutions are sound. The conventional assumption was that—taken together—these three elements create the necessary conditions for a stable macroeconomic environment in which the financial system can operate efficiently and financial stability is automatically achieved.

However, this assumption has been proven wrong. Risks may emerge from *systemic* developments within the economy or financial system *as a whole*. To illustrate the point, a parallel can be drawn with the safety of cars and traffic. Microprudential supervision can be compared to regulations for safe cars, such as brakes, crumble zones and airbags. This ensures a proper functioning of the car and reduces the chance and impact of an accident on the car and its passengers. Macroprudential policies (see below), however, are more like traffic rules such as speed limits and traffic signs that make the roads and traffic safer. To avoid accidents you need both safe cars and effective traffic rules, just like microprudential supervision and macroprudential policy are needed to maintain financial stability.

Macroprudential Perspective

The term 'macroprudential' first emerged in the late 1970s (Clement 2010), but the concept did not gain much popularity in subsequent years. Unfortunately, important lessons were learned only through the experience of financial crises.

The Asian crisis of 1997–98 primarily emerged from vulnerabilities related to too much lending within the economy and the financial sector, together with adverse economic developments and unsustainable exchange rate policies. The crisis erupted in July 1997 and escalated because of a sudden loss in confidence among international investors and a sudden reversal of capital flows, which created severe capital account problems. As a consequence, the Asian region greatly suffered from contagion both through direct and indirect effects.

In the wake of the Asian crisis, macroeconomic linkages and the stability of the financial system received more attention. The International Monetary Fund (IMF) played a leading role in the strengthened analysis of vulnerabilities to the financial system with the introduction of Financial Soundness Indicators (IMF 2002), a set of sector-wide indicators on the soundness of financial institutions. In addition, the IMF developed the Financial Sector Assessment Program (FSAP). This is a structured analysis of the stability of the financial system which the IMF performs in different jurisdictions. The FSAP program has proven to be a welcome addition to the traditional macroeconomic surveillance of the IMF, by concentrating more than before on financial developments and system-wide aspects.

These developments fostered a crucial international policy debate, involving both central banks and national treasuries. The Bank of

International Settlements, acting as a catalyst in the discussion, pointed out (Crockett 2000) that the focus on financial stability introduces two distinctive new elements to supervisory analysis. First, financial stability monitoring—in contrast to microprudential supervision—does not examine the likelihood of a single failure, but concentrates on systemic risks and the impact on the functioning of the financial system. Second, risks can emerge endogenously, because the financial sector operates as a network, where the failure of a single institution can cause contagion effects to other institutions.

The global financial crisis of 2008–09 triggered a major wake-up call about the relevance of financial stability, as it struck at the core of the financial system. Within a couple of months, the financial system became highly dysfunctional. Liquidity in the market dried up rapidly and banks were no longer prepared to lend to each other. As a result, individual financial institutions that were in their core fundamentally sound ran into serious financial problems. Authorities, including central banks, intervened with unprecedented measures. For example, among many other interventions, the Federal Reserve felt obliged to rescue insurance giant AIG, because it was too large to ignore and too interconnected with many different counterparties. A failure of AIG would have caused a severe disruption within the global financial system and the world economy.

The Financial Crisis Inquiry Commission in the United States concluded that the financial crisis could have been avoided and was to a large extent the result of widespread failures in regulation and supervision (FCIC 2010). The Dodd-Frank Wall Street Reform and Consumer Protection Act (Dodd-Frank Act) led to an overhaul of the financial regulatory system and included the creation of the Financial Oversight Council (FSOC) to monitor and evaluate systemic risk.

Evaluation reports in Europe about the lessons of the global financial crisis (De Larosière 2009; Turner review 2009) also emphasized the need for regulatory and supervisory repair and particularly included the creation of a separate pillar of macroprudential policy to monitor and safeguard the stability of the financial system. It was assumed that the monetary authorities would play a leading role in this context.

The growth of financial markets and the increasing interconnectedness between the different financial centers also highlighted the need for closer international cooperation (Box 13.1).

Box 13.1 Financial Stability Board (FSB)

The Financial Stability Board (FSB) was established in 2009 to create a structure of cooperation between central banks, treasuries and supervisory agencies to share expertise and discuss relevant developments in global financial markets. The FSB replaced the Financial Stability Forum (FSF) thereby strengthening its institutional setting, increasing its membership and strengthening its coordinating role in regulation and supervision.

The FSB plays a leading role in discussing and assessing vulnerabilities to the global financial system. The FSB promotes international financial stability by coordinating national financial authorities and international standard-setting bodies toward developing strong regulatory, supervisory and other financial sector policies. Its analyses are directed at developing best practices as well as standards and codes in regulatory policy. The FSB also monitors the implementation of regulation in different jurisdictions.

The secretariat of the FSB is located within the Bank for International Settlements (BIS) in Basel. The organization is a member-driven organization that decides on the basis of consensus between 25 participating jurisdictions as well as 10 international organizations and standard-setting bodies. The FSB has a coordinating role toward national and international supervisory bodies and international financial institutions, such as the IMF, and standard-setting bodies.

During the global financial crisis of 2008–10, the FSB was responsible for developing a comprehensive action plan to address the structural vulnerabilities in the global financial system. This reform program proved essential to restore international financial stability.

Source: www.fsb.org/about

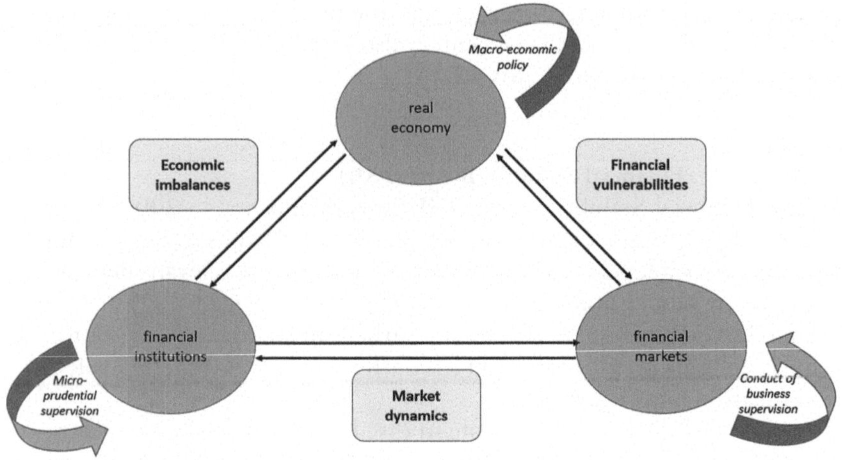

Fig. 13.1 Interactions within the financial system

Design of Macroprudential Policy

After the global financial crisis, many central banks enhanced their capacity to explicitly focus on the stability of the financial system.

Macroprudential Perspective

Macroprudential policy complements financial supervision, because it does not concentrate on specific segments, but on the interactions between the real economy, financial markets and financial institutions (Fig. 13.1).

Economic Imbalances

There is an important and direct relationship between the developments in the real economy and the solidity of financial institutions. Economic imbalances can undermine the solidity of financial institutions, since they lead to unexpected losses, causing firms and households to be less capable to meet their redemptions and interest payments. At the same time, imprudent or unproductive lending within the financial sector leads to suboptimal investments and misallocation.

Such interactions may also have a dynamic effect. If the capital position of a bank deteriorates, it may further reduce its lending to the economy in order to repair its balance sheet. Moreover, the decline in credit supply leads to even slower economic growth and further deterioration of the economic cycle, amplifying the initial effect.

Financial Vulnerabilities

Risks to the financial system can also occur as a result of interactions between the real economy and financial markets. Financial vulnerabilities and an unsustainable policy mix may ultimately trigger a financial crisis. Sound fiscal and monetary policies are therefore an important precondition for financial stability. For example, loose fiscal policy can lead to a sovereign debt crisis if a country is not able to meet its obligations, causing capital flight and an increase in yields. In the same way, an incompatible monetary policy mix leads to high inflation and pressure on the exchange rate that can morph into a currency crisis.

Conversely, conditions in the financial markets can affect developments in the real economy. A clear example from recent year is the existence of excess liquidity in financial markets within an environment of low interest rates. The resulting search for yield leads to distortions in price setting in financial markets and increases risks of asset price inflation. Finally, when financial bubbles burst, the economic costs can be very high. Well-known examples are the Latin-American debt crises of the 1980s and 1990s, the Asian financial crisis of the 1990s and the Global Financial Crisis of 2008–09.

Market Dynamics

The financial market itself can also be a source of instability. Financial developments are often driven by sentiments which may easily change after unexpected events. Market dynamics can lead to financial turbulence and herd behavior. Such financial shocks undermine an adequate functioning of financial institutions. Market volatility or liquidity stress increases risk premiums and reduces financing available to the economy.

Problems in financial institutions can spread to other institutions as a result of direct or indirect contagion. The extent of which depends on the structure of the market. In addition, structural developments within the

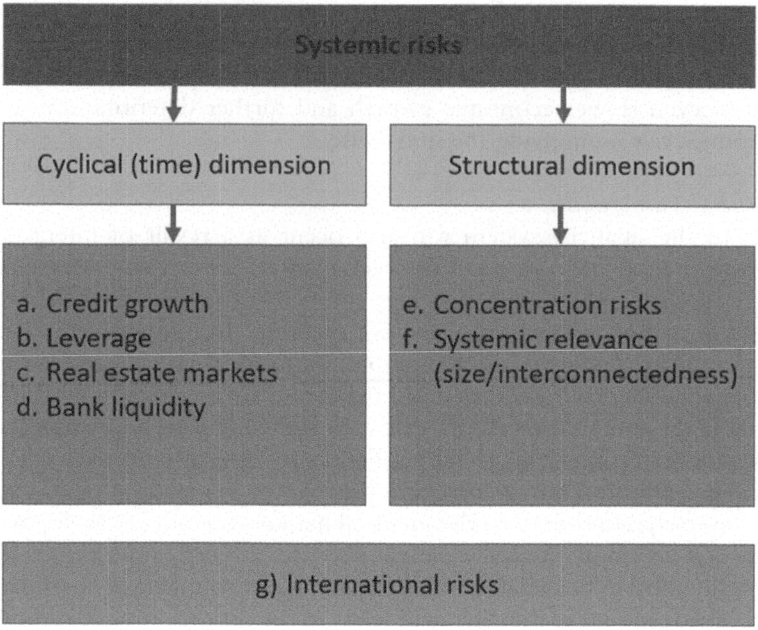

Fig. 13.2 Types of systemic risks

financial sector or shifts in financial intermediation can cause risks to emerge elsewhere within the financial system.

Systemic Risk

To achieve financial stability, central banks focus on developments that may threaten the financial system and could ultimately affect the real economy. These systemic risks can occur through various channels.

Policymakers typically distinguish two dimensions (Fig. 13.2; DNB, 2010). The cyclical dimension includes types of risks that emerge during the economic cycle and usually follow a pattern where vulnerabilities build up in periods of high growth and losses occur during a downturn. The structural dimension includes risks that derive from the more fundamental characteristics of the financial sector.

a. Credit growth
Financial stability is closely related to credit growth in the economy. If credit growth is above its long-term trend, it is generally an indication that vulnerabilities may be building up.

There is extensive literature on the financial cycle (Borio 2012). It follows a classic pattern. A structural shift in risk perception leads to an economic boom and a self-reinforcing period of credit growth. This drives up property and asset prices and constitutes the basis for further credit growth. The financial cycle ends when the economic cycle turns and risk perceptions suddenly shift. At that moment, many investments turn out to be unprofitable and loans are not fully paid back. This leads to reallocations and deleveraging with negative economic consequences. The financial cycle typically has a longer trend than the regular business cycle and is closely correlated with financial crises.

b. Leverage
Too much debt financing (leverage) can make the financial sector and economy vulnerable to financial shocks. The leverage ratio measures the amount of capital to total assets. History has shown that prior to a crisis, the leverage ratio tends to fall because total lending increases and banks do not hold adequate capital buffers to absorb unexpected losses. Such losses can and do occur when a class of assets or investments is initially deemed relatively safe, but turn out to be much more risky. At that moment, financial stability is at risk, the financial position of institutions is being undermined.

c. Real estate markets
Developments in the real estate sector have a direct economic impact on housing and business activity and also play an important role in portfolio investments and as collateral.

Real estate is subject to large price fluctuations. Prices can strongly increase during an economic boom, when high demand is met by ample availability of credit. The relative inelastic supply of new houses and office buildings fuels further price increases. On the other side, the correction in real estate prices during an economic crisis is also sharper. Experience shows that real estate markets often have a triggering or amplifying role in financial crises. An evident example includes the house pricing boom and bust in the US subprime markets.

d. Bank liquidity

Liquidity problems can crucially undermine the proper functioning of the financial sector and hamper financial intermediation. This is the implicit result of the business models of banks to attract short-term funding to finance longer term lending. When short-term funding stops during stress, there is a risk that banks cannot provide lending and meet the demands of households and companies.

Liquidity is an elusive concept. While, it is available in a stable and well-functioning financial system, it can disappear quickly and unexpectedly and directly lead to financial problems. A good example is the British bank Northern Rock, which was one of the first victims of the global financial crisis. Its vulnerable business model depended too much on long-term mortgage investments funded by short-term borrowing. When doubts about its financial position arose, liquidity suddenly dried up, triggering a bank run and a government bail-out. When an individual bank cannot meet its obligations, it can produce contagion effects within the rest of the sector.

e. Concentration risks

A financial sector that is dominated by relatively few large financial institutions is more vulnerable to economic and financial shocks than a more diversified sector with more and smaller institutions. Within a concentrated financial system, problems in a single financial institution will more likely have systemic effects. Moreover, a concentrated sector also leads to more uniformity within the financial sector which makes it more susceptible to common shocks. There are also indications that a concentrated sector leads to less efficiency and less innovation, because it is difficult for new parties to enter the market.

f. Systemic relevance (size/interconnectedness)

The global financial crisis has also shown that the size and dominant position of financial institutions can create problems for the effective functioning of the financial sector and the economy as a whole. A large financial institution can be so important and interconnected within the financial system that its failure will have direct and severe negative economic consequences. Authorities will eventually feel obliged to prevent such a failure. However, this 'too-big-to-fail' problem has other negative consequences. Most importantly, it creates moral hazard within institutions to take on more risks than warranted, based on the premise that they will in the end receive a government bail-out if problems were to arise. Such expectations lead to imprudent lending with negative consequences for financial stability and economic growth.

g. International risks
Risks to the financial sector can also emerge as a result of international economic developments, especially in the case of small open economies. Because of the international character of financial markets and financial institutions, turbulence within the global economy can have destabilizing effects on the rest of the world.

Box 13.2 International Cooperation: Herstatt Affair

The Herstatt affair is a classic example of the interactions within the international financial system.

Herstatt was a relatively small, privately owned German bank with a significant position in the foreign exchange market. As a result of increased volatility in the US dollar in 1973–74 and adverse developments in its position in the market, Herstatt suffered great losses. In June 1974, it was eventually forced to file for bankruptcy. This created a shock to the financial system, because the bank failed to settle its contracts on that day. US banks had delivered German marks to Herstatt. However, as a result of the immediate suspension of its activities at the end of the German business day and the time difference with US market, Herstatt was not able to deliver the US dollars in return. This created significant contagion effects and disturbance in the international banking and currency markets.

The international and system-wide consequences of a failure of this single institution underlined the need for international coordination and regulation among financial supervisors. As a direct result, the Basel Committee of Banking Supervision (BCBS) was established to enhance financial stability by improving the quality of banking supervision world-wide and to serve as a forum for regular cooperation between its member countries on banking supervisory matters. The Committee contributes to financial stability through a microprudential perspective by developing international standards for banking regulation.

Over the years, the BCBS has become the authority for the supervision of internationally active banks. The BCBS sets the international standards for banking supervision through the Basel Capital framework which constitutes the basis for national legislation in different jurisdictions.

Table 13.1 Financial stability indicators

Credit and leverage	*Concentration risk*	*Liquidity and maturity mismatch*	*Systemic importance*
Credit/GDP-ratio Trend credit/gdp ratio Trend deviation credit/gdp-ratio Credit to households Credit to non-household corporations House prices Commercial property prices Loan-to-value ratio first-time buyers Loan-to-income ratio first-time buyers Long-term interest rate BAA-AA risk premium Leverage ratio banks Basel capital ratios for banks	Concentration exposures of banks	Loan-to-deposit ratio Proportion of short-term market funding Risk premium in money market Risk premium on senior unsecured bank obligations	Size of bank balance sheet to gdp Share of G5 banks Rating uplift

Source: DNB (website)

Financial Stability Indicators

In order to structure the monitoring framework of systemic risks, supervisors have developed indicators of financial stability. Table 13.1 provides an overview of indicators that are most widely used.

The broad scope of indicators reflects the many dimensions of financial stability. The assessment of vulnerabilities can be quite difficult. For example, the overall picture generally can provide mixed signals. Moreover, the occurrence of a financial crisis depends on many different factors and specific circumstances. Supervisory judgment is thus required to provide an eventual assessment of financial stability. More prosaically, it can be said that macroprudential analysis is 'more an art than a science.'

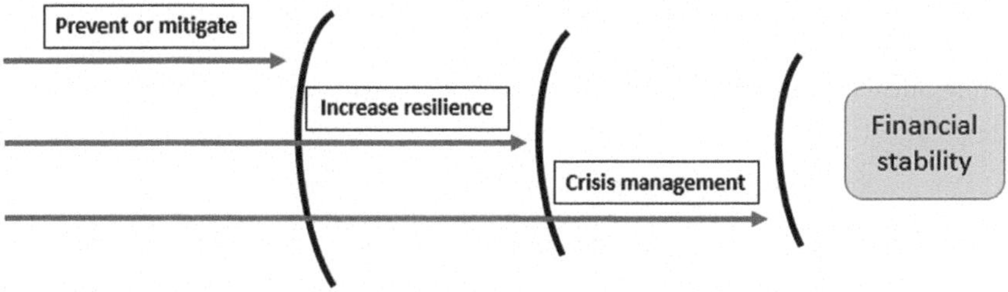

Fig. 13.3 Three lines of defense. (Source: the Netherlands Bank (2014))

Strategy

It is important to overcome the *inaction bias* in macroprudential policy, which is the presumed tendency of supervisors and regulators to take a 'wait and see' perspective on how risks develop. Such behavior reflects the fact that the costs of mitigating actions are upfront and directly visible, whereas the long-term effects of preventing a financial crisis are more difficult to measure (ESRB 2014). Macroprudential authorities should therefore be operationally independent to ensure timely intervention.

The approach to achieve the objective of financial stability, generally depends on a three-step strategy (Fig. 13.3).

The first line of defense is preventing or mitigating the build-up of systemic risks, requiring an early identification of vulnerable developments, timely warnings and mitigating measures to eliminate or reduce any imbalances and potential shocks. To this end, central banks publish regular (mostly semi-annual) reports on relevant developments with respect to financial risks and issue warnings and recommendations. The aim is to create awareness of potential vulnerabilities in the financial system among financial stakeholders, the public and policymakers. However, as indicated earlier, risks cannot always be fully avoided.

The second category consists of measures to increase the resilience of the financial sector to absorb shocks. This can be realized through higher capital buffers or more specific measures that limit the impact when risks materialize. It is also important to prevent the financial sector itself from generating or amplifying risks.

The third category of measures focuses on adequate crisis management to prevent an escalation of risks and contagion toward other institutions. Typical measures that are in place within the financial system are deposit insurance, liquidity support and recovery and resolution measures. The latter means that critical functions of the financial sector are maintained, while allowing an orderly resolution of an institution.

Macroprudential Policy in Practice

Since macroprudential policy has been generally recognized as a necessary complement to monetary policy and microprudential supervision, it has been developed as a separate pillar of responsibility within central banks. An effective organization of macroprudential policy consists of several elements (IMF-FSB-BIS 2016).

Organization

A clear legal basis provides a solid basis for the macroprudential authority and supports its ability to act when financial stability risks emerge. To this end, several countries have adopted legislation which explicitly embeds financial stability as a formal objective with a designated macroprudential authority. Central banks need to be closely involved, either in the form of an internal organizational branch or as part of a separate committee with its own statutes. Its membership consists of relevant stakeholders and may include external academic advisors.

A macroprudential authority should be able to take relevant measures. Such measures include the use of formal macroprudential instruments as well as 'soft' powers in the form of warnings and recommendations. The effectiveness of such powers depends on the position and authority of the macroprudential authority.

In order to ensure timely intervention, a macroprudential authority should be operationally independent, much like a central bank with respect to monetary policy. On the one hand, risks to financial stability should not be addressed too late. Vulnerabilities may then have already developed and measures could at that stage even be counterproductive. On the other hand, a macroprudential authority should also be careful not to act too soon, the downside being that it could obstruct dynamic developments and innovation within the financial sector. To counterbalance the strong mandate and operational independence, there needs to be a clear mechanism of accountability, requiring the macroprudential authority to explain how the measures taken contribute to financial stability.

There exists a great variety in the governance of the macroprudential function among jurisdictions. On the one hand, there is a formal approach, like in the United Kingdom, where the Financial Policy Committee (FPC) has an independent position with 'powers of direction.' It can give direct orders for certain defined changes in regulation. In other countries, including the United States and the Netherlands, the focus of the macroprudential authority is primarily on coordination and information sharing (Table 13.2).

Table 13.2 Different organizational structures of macroprudential authority

	US [a]	*UK* [b]	*Netherlands* [c]
	Financial Stability Oversight Council	Financial Policy Committee	Financial Stability Committee
Role/mandate	The FSOC is charged with identifying risks to financial stability, promoting discipline and responding to emerging risks.	The FPC identifies, monitors and takes action to remove or reduce systemic risks to protect and enhance the resilience of the UK financial system. A secondary objective is to support the economic policy of the government.	The role of the FSC is to identify risks to financial stability and to make recommendations with respect to these risks.
Tasks/powers/ instruments	The main task is to facilitate coordination and promote information sharing and collection. The FSOC can recommend further action for more intensified supervision.	The FPC has powers of direction to direct regulators to: Set the countercyclical capital buffer Set sectoral requirements Set a leverage ratio Set LTV and debt-to-income limits Set LTV and interest cover ratio The FPC also has power of recommendation to anyone to reduce risks to financial stability.	The FSC has the power to issue warnings and make recommendations. The use of relevant macroprudential measures remains with the responsible organizations (after discussion in the FSC).

(*continued*)

Table 13.2 (continued)

	US [a]	*UK* [b]	*Netherlands* [c]
	Financial Stability Oversight Council	Financial Policy Committee	Financial Stability Committee
Institutional governance	The FSOC has a macroprudential mandate, but limited formal powers. The secretary of the Treasury chairs the FSOC.	The FPC is the macroprudential authority and has formal powers. The governor of BoE chairs the FPC. The FPC strives for consensus.	The FSC is the designated macroprudential authority. It derives its authority from its expertise, membership and analysis. The central bank chairs the FSC. The committee strives for consensus.
Members	The FSOC has 10 voting members from Treasury, Fed, OCC, CFPB, SEC, FDIC, CFTC, FHFA, NCUA and 1 independent member + 5 non-voting members from state organizations.	The FPC contains 13 members, of which 6 from the Bank of England (incl. Governor and board members); 5 external experts; the chief executive of the FSC and one non-voting member from HM Treasury.	The FSC consists of 8 members, of which 3 from the central bank, 2 from the conduct of business authority, 2 from the Ministry of Finance and 1 from the Bureau of Economic Policy analysis (as an external expert).
Independence/ accountability	The FSOC publishes an annual report and, where appropriate, reports on specific risks. The chairman provides an annual testimony to congress.	The FPC publishes a summary of its meetings twice a year and a record of the meeting in the financial stability report.	Warnings and recommendations are public, unless there are risks to financial stability. The minutes are published and sent to parliament.

[a] https://www.treasury.gov/initiatives/fsoc/about/Pages/default.aspx

[b] https://www.bankofengland.co.uk/financial-stability

[c] https://www.financieelstabiliteitscomite.nl/en/about_fsc

The effectiveness of a macroprudential committee depends on the quality of its analyses and its expertise to identify systemic risks as well as its authority toward responsible agencies to follow-up on its warnings and recommendations. For example, the Dodd-Frank Act does not solve the patchwork quilt of regulatory institutions in the United States. As a result the FSOC has too large a membership without a clear macroprudential commitment from the members nor great authority from its analyses. This can be seen as a missed opportunity to develop a strong macroprudential power. Or as the former US Secretary of the Treasury, Timothy Geithner, remarked, 'you can't convene a committee to put out a fire'(Geithner 2014).

In Europe, the macroprudential authority resides with the national jurisdictions, with the European Systemic Risk Board (ESRB) in a monitoring and coordinating role.

Macroprudential Instruments

Following the risk identification process, the next step is to prevent or mitigate the emergence of systemic risks. Several different macroprudential instruments are available for this purpose.

When implementing these measures, policymakers have to strike a balance between the intended outcomes and unintended effects or 'leakages.' Effective policy may also require a combination of tools, when a single measure does not address the full nature of the problem.

Buffers

The macroprudential toolbox includes different types of capital buffers.

SIFI-Buffers

Banks that are considered 'too-big-to-fail' are required to hold extra capital buffers. The Financial Stability Board has an annual process to establish which institutions are systemically important in a global context, the so-called global systemically important banks (G-SIBs). The 2014 framework established by the Basel Committee has a quantitative basis, wherein systemic relevance is determined on the basis of five criteria: (a) size, (b) interconnectedness, (c) substitutability, (d) complexity and (e) cross-jurisdictional activity. The FSB list currently includes approximately 30 institutions and comprises the largest banks from the United States, United Kingdom, Europe, China and Japan (inter alia, J.P. Morgan, Citigroup, Deutsche Bank, HSBC, Bank of America, Bank of China, Mitsubishi UFJ).

In addition, national jurisdictions have their own process to determine whether other institutions are systemically important for their domestic markets, the so-called domestic systemically important banks (D-SIBs). This D-SIB framework is more principle-based and allows national supervisors to take into account national considerations. Within the European framework, this D-SIB buffer is referred to as other systemically important institution or O-SII buffer and is bound at a maximum.

Countercyclical Capital Buffer

The countercyclical capital buffer is aimed at addressing the cyclical dimension of systemic risk. It is a tool to strengthen the capital position of a bank in good times and release capital in an economic downturn. This strengthens the resilience of a bank and can help to curb lending during an economic boom. Conversely, when the countercyclical buffer is released in the economic downturn, banks have more resources to continue their lending activities. The idea is that this reduces procyclical effects within the financial sector. The activation of the countercyclical buffer strongly relies on the development of the credit-to-GDP ratio and the deviation from its long-term trend. However, credit growth may not be the only good indicator of the financial cycle. Particularly, after the global financial crisis and the resulting unconventional monetary policies and excess liquidity, the development of credit growth may not be a good reflection of underlying developments and vulnerabilities. Therefore, authorities can also take into account other relevant variables and qualitative information.

Systemic Risk Buffer

The systemic risk buffer (SRB) is an extra buffer that is imposed on banks to address systemic risks of a long-term, non-cyclical nature that are not covered by the European capital requirements regulation. It addresses risks that are related to more structural characteristics of the financial sector that may affect the stability of the system as a whole. Examples are risks stemming from the structural characteristics of the banking sector, risks stemming from propagation and amplification of shocks within the financial system and risks resulting from vulnerabilities to external shocks. The level of systemic risk buffer may vary across institutions and sets of institutions. The focus of the SRB will change under new European legislation, scheduled to enter into force in 2021, to prevent and mitigate macroprudential or systemic risk not covered by the European capital requirements regulation and by the SIFI-buffers or countercyclical buffer.

Capital Conservation Buffer

In addition to the SIFI-buffer, countercyclical buffer and SRB, which are typical macroprudential instruments, banks are also required to hold a capital conservation buffer.

The capital conservation buffer is a capital buffer of 2.5 percent core equity capital. It allows banks that are fundamentally sound but are hit by a severe shock to absorb losses, without a direct formal breach of their pillar 1 and pillar 2 capital requirements. If the capital conservation buffer is used, a bank has time to rebuild its financial position, using profits and retained earnings. A bank may also choose to raise new capital, if possible. The regulatory framework also places proportionate restrictions on certain payments that affect the capital position of banks, such as dividend payments and bonuses.

Leverage Ratio

The leverage ratio, defined as the ratio of available capital to total exposures, is a non-risk-weighted measure, which means that it does not take into account the characteristics of the loan portfolio. This compares to the regular micro-prudential capital requirements that are risk-weighted, which means that they are based on the expected losses of the exposures. Within the overall framework, the leverage ratio is a useful complement and a good indicator for financial stability risks, because a financial crisis typically occurs when a class of assets or investments are deemed relatively safe in an upward cycle (reflected in low risk weights), but turn out to be much more risky in a downturn. In those cases, risk-weighted capital requirements do not adequately capture the risks. The leverage ratio then serves as a useful backstop.

Other Measures

Macroprudential supervisors can also take more targeted measures to address specific vulnerabilities, such as placing limits on intra-financial large exposures, increasing liquidity requirements, imposing higher risk

weights or requiring public disclosure. In European legislation, this is referred to as the flexibility package (ESRB 2018a, b).
An important set of measures impose limits on lending within the real estate sector. For example, many countries apply loan-to-value (LTV) or loan-to-income (LTI) limits to mitigate price increases and prevent excessive lending in the housing market. Such limits also increase the resilience of households against sharp declines in housing prices. Another measure would be to introduce higher capital risk weights for lending to specific sectors. The benefit of such detailed measures is that it directly addresses the potential causes of systemic risk. At the same time, it can also be a disadvantage, because these measures have a limited scope and can often be politically unattractive.

Stress Tests
Stress tests are an important macroprudential instrument to identify the resilience of financial institutions and stability of the financial system as a whole. The use of stress tests has increased strongly after the global financial crisis. Their aim is to gain insight into the effects of a ***severe but plausible*** economic downturn on the solvency position of individual institutions. Such a scenario usually consists of a combination of lower economic growth, rising unemployment and a fall in asset and housing prices. The calculated results of a stress test show how vulnerable institutions are to these shocks and the impact of the losses they would incur on their capital position and profitability. Such analyses can be the basis for preventive as well as remedial action.

Communication and design are important in stress tests. There should be a clear follow-up to the stress test to indicate how the vulnerabilities identified would be addressed and how any capital shortfalls would have to be corrected. The experience in the United States is a case in point. Shortly after the global financial crisis, a comprehensive stress test took place (Federal Reserve System 2009). Banks that did not meet a pre-specified threshold of capital after stress were required to recapitalize, either in the market or through a government program. This strategy worked well and played an essential role in restoring confidence in the US financial sector as a basis for the economic recovery after 2008–09. Stress tests in other parts of the world have also proven to be valuable, as long as the tests and scenarios are sufficiently robust and credible.

Box 13.3 Climate Stress Test[a]

As part of its work on sustainability, the Netherlands Bank has developed a climate stress test, which attempts to capture the financial and economic effects of climate change.

Authorities have signed an international climate agreement in Paris. The stress test develops four scenarios that analyses the effects to meet these international requirements.

The stress test calculates the effects on the economy within the different financial sectors, depending on technological changes and government policies. It shows the impact of changes in economic conditions and losses from asset exposures to different economic sectors, depending on their energy-intensity. Under certain conditions, a disruptive energy transition can lead to substantial losses for financial institutions. It indicates that the risks of climate change should be more structurally integrated into the general risk management of banks.

[a]Vermeulen et al. (2018).

Challenges

Financial stability is a broad concept that encompasses many different dimensions. As a result, the actual implementation of macroprudential policy poses several challenges.

Limited Toolbox

A macroprudential authority has to act within its mandate which is constrained for the following reasons.

Potential vulnerabilities can emerge anywhere within the real economy or the financial system. The macroprudential authority does not always have full authority on all relevant aspects where systemic risks may emerge. There is an unresolved discussion on what falls under the scope of macroprudential policy. For example, risks can occur in the more traditional fields of the housing market, commercial real estate, asset markets, but also from fiscal policy, the tax system or any other government policies for that matter. In addition, potential measures to protect the stability of the financial system can also have broader implications for the economy and possibly interact with other policy objectives of the government, including housing market policies or socio-economic policies. There is a trade-off whether policies should be brought within the sole responsibility of the macroprudential authority, giving priority to financial stability, or whether broader considerations prevail and decision-making is considered part of a political process.

If the macroprudential toolbox is too limited, macroprudential authorities cannot always fully and effectively address the underlying risks. For example, the Bank of England's Financial Policy Committee has an array of tools at its disposal, but the US authorities have limited macroprudential instruments. A debate with strong political overtones took place in Sweden in the 2000s where record-high house prices raised concerns at the central bank of an impending correction. The central bank considered macroprudential action essential, but needed government consent, requiring a tense atmosphere. Finally, after several years of discourse the Government introduced a tougher amortization requirement for mortgage loans.

Finally, it is important to realize that macroprudential measures are not automatically as effective as monetary policy actions. Central banks have full control in setting interest rates, which has a direct impact on inflation because it 'gets into all the cracks of the financial system' (Stein 2013). The impact of macroprudential instruments is more complex and diverse and only affects a part of the financial system through indirect effects.

Interaction Monetary Policy and Financial Stability

Monetary policy and macroprudential policy are closely linked. In most circumstances, they support and reinforce each other, since financial stability benefits from price stability and monetary policy is more effective when the financial system is sound.

Following the global financial crisis, monetary policy has played a prominent role within the financial system. Central banks have significantly eased monetary conditions through interest rate reductions and unconventional policies to support their objective of price stability and promote effective financial transmission. These measures have generally been effective in averting the risk of deflation and stabilizing lending rates within the European Union, the United States and elsewhere. The decisive actions taken by central banks have also neutralized negative sentiments in the market.

At the same time, very loose monetary conditions also create external effects, which may grow stronger over time, inter alia, leading to a search for yield and asset price inflation. Moreover, very low interest rates can lead to a build-up of private and public debt, because of reduced incentives to deleverage. Experience teaches that the theoretical view that monetary policy can be solely aimed at price stability, while macroprudential policy ensures financial stability is flawed. This is also characterized as a Panglossian fallacy (Knot 2017). For these reasons, it is important that monetary policy also takes into account unintended side effects.

European Integration

Microprudential supervision in the euro area has been shifted to the Single Supervisory Mechanism, so that supervision of individual banks is now organized at the European level under the responsibility of the European Central Bank. By contrast, macroprudential supervision remains a national responsibility. This reflects the specific nature of systemic risk, which depends on local developments in, for example, the housing market and the different cyclical positions of member countries. Moreover, macroprudential measures often also have broader, economic, implications which remain a national mandate. At the same time, the increasing integration of the European financial market makes coordination and cooperation on macroprudential policies increasingly important.

The European Systemic Risk Board (ESRB) has been created to coordinate the oversight of the EU financial system. It monitors and assesses systemic risks within the European financial system and fulfills a catalytic role. Where appropriate, the ESRB can issue warnings and recommendations to all their members or to a single jurisdiction to mitigate vulnerabilities. These warnings and recommendations are subject to a comply-or-explain procedure with the ESRB (ESRB 2014).

In addition, there is a coordination mechanism to enhance the effectiveness of macroprudential policy within the EU. National authorities that wish to take macroprudential measures have to notify the ESRB, which is subject to a non-objection process. Moreover, there is a so-called reciprocation procedure. Measures that are taken by a specific country to address risks within their jurisdiction are complemented by supportive measures of other jurisdictions. For example, a measure to increase risk weights that is taken by a specific country only applies to the banks within that Member State. With reciprocation, other countries also apply that same measure to the exposures of their banks in that country. This enhances the effectiveness of macroprudential policy within the EU and promotes a level playing field.

Systemic Risks Beyond Banking

Macroprudential policy is traditionally limited to the banking sector. However, risks to financial stability can also emerge in other sectors of the financial system (ESRB 2016). Importantly, after the global financial crisis there has been a strong increase of lending outside the banking sector. Such lending, used to be labeled 'shadow banking,' is currently more accurately called 'non-bank financial intermediation.' The advent of this intermediation in recent years can be the result from the strengthening of regulation within the banking sector, which induces activities to emerge elsewhere in the system. This is also referred to as the waterbed effect.

Risk outside the banking sector can affect financial stability through various channels. It can lead to too rapid credit growth in that part of the financial system, which is not adequately captured by supervision and regulation. In addition, the growth of non-bank finance can lead to increased leverage within the financial system, which may lead to losses in a downturn. These losses may spread to other sectors as a result of contagion or interconnectedness. Finally, a strong increase in lending can cause a liquidity mismatch, which can lead to fire sales during a market correction and shocks to financial stability.

It is therefore important to take a comprehensive approach and also address systemic risks beyond the banking sector. This should start with collection of data and a good monitoring process. In practice, this has proven to be a difficult task, absent a clear definition and delineation of the non-banking sector, where flows and end users are not easily identified. In this context, the FSB has taken important steps through its annual monitoring report to provide a good basis to identify relevant developments and follow liquidity within the system as an indicator of possible future vulnerabilities.

European legislation after the global financial crisis, such as the Alternative Investment Funds Managers Directive (AIFMD) and the European Market Infrastructure Regulation (EMIR), explicitly include macroprudential instruments. At the same time, macroprudential policy beyond banking remains a field that needs to be further developed, because lending outside the banking sector becomes increasingly more important and may lead to new risks for financial stability that authorities should be able to adequately address.

References

Borio, Claudio. (2012), *The financial cycle and macroeconomics: what have we learnt?*, BIS working papers, no. 395.

Clement, Piet: (2010), *The term "macroprudential": origins and evolution*, BIS Quarterly Review, March 2010.

Crockett, Andrew: (2000), *Marrying the micro- and macro-prudential dimensions of financial stability*, remarks before the eleventh international conference of banking supervisors.

De Nederlandsche Bank (2010), *Towards a more stable financial system; macroprudential supervision at DNB.*

De Nederlandsche Bank (2014), *DNB's financial stability task.*

De Larosière, Jacques: (2009), *The high-level group on financial supervision in the EU*, report to the European Commission.

European Systemic Risk Board (2014), *Flagship report on macroprudential policy in the banking sector.*

European Systemic Risk Board (2016), M*acroprudential policy beyond banking: an ESB strategy paper.*

European Systemic Risk Board (2018a), *A review of macroprudential policy in the EU in 2017.*

European Systemic Risk Board (2018b), *The ESRB handbook on operationalising macroprudential policy in the banking sector.*

Federal Reserve System (2009), *The Supervisory Capital Assessment Program: overview of results.*

Geithner, Timothy: (2014), *Stress test: reflections on financial crises*, Crown Publishers, New York, 2014.

IMF (2002), *Financial soundness indicators: analytical aspects and country practices*, IMF occasional paper.

IMF-FSB-BIS (2016), *Elements of effective macroprudential policies: lessons from international experience.*

IMF (2010), *The making of good supervision*: 'learning to say no', IMF Staff position note 10/08.

Knot, Klaas (2017), *Modesty in times of uncertainty*, speech at Business Economists' Annual Dinner, London (29 November 2017)

Stein, J. (2013). *Overheating in Credit Markets: Origins, Measurement, and Policy Responses.*

The Turner review (2009), *A regulatory response to the global banking crisis*, Financial Services Authority.

Vermeulen R., Schets E., Lohuis M., Kölbl B., Jansen D.J. and Heeringa W. (2018), *An Energy Transition Risk Stress Test for the Financial System of the Netherlands*, DNB Occasional Studies.

CHAPTER 14

An Uncertain Future

Modern central banking consists of the following elements:

1. Maintaining price stability and sometimes also maximum employment, as its central mandate.
2. Gearing monetary policy toward an intermediate goal, usually inflation targeting.
3. Independence from the government, at a minimum concerning operations.
4. Acting as lender of last resort.
5. Ensuring financial stability, in cooperation with government agencies.
6. Supervising the soundness of individual commercial banks and certain other financial institutions, in cooperation with governmental agencies tasked with prudential supervision.
7. Deploying macroprudential (macro-pru) policies when the pursuit of price stability and financial stability is in conflict. Cooperation of the government may be needed. More controversial: use monetary policy to foster financial stability when macro-pru instruments cannot deliver the required results ('leaning against the wind').
8. Practicing as much as possible openness without divulging highly sensitive information and communicating effectively.
9. Advising the government on exchange rate policy and implementing such policies. This is not spelled out in the case of the European Central Bank.

O. de Beaufort Wijnholds, *The Money Masters*,
https://doi.org/10.1007/978-3-030-40041-5_14

10. Managing an efficient payments system.
11. Holding and managing an adequate but not excessive stock of international reserves.
12. Participating actively in overseeing the international monetary system (together with the government) through the International Monetary Fund. Working closely with other central banks on matters of mutual interest, for instance through the Bank for International Settlements.
13. Engage in close contact with the government without compromising independence.
14. Hire highly qualified staff, mainly economists, market specialists and lawyers.
15. Collect economic and financial statistics and regularly publish reports on the economic and financial outlook.
16. Maintain a research department that is not overly occupied with building econometric models.
17. Larger central banks provide technical assistance to developing countries, either directly or through international organizations.

Most of the tasks listed above as being part of modern central banking are not set in stone. In a rapidly changing global financial system, a resurgence of protectionism and rising international political tensions, the future of central banking can face sudden new challenges without having fully dealt with earlier imperfections.

The following areas are most likely to require central banks' close attention. First and foremost is the existential question of central bank independence. Closely related are the shape and scope of monetary policy in the future and the design and maintenance of financial stability, as well as the interaction between these crucial central bank activities. Payments systems and *fintech* (new financial technologies) are likely to undergo important changes and could drastically impact other central bank functions. Risks and opportunities associated with new developments regarding the international monetary system, international cooperation between central banks, the Euro System, the global trade rules and the domestic and geopolitical landscape are also examined. Finally, central banks need to analyze and prepare for the potentially very large economic and financial consequences of climate change and their role in coping with the fallout.

Central Bank Independence

The substance of central bank independence and the world-wide movement toward greater autonomy for monetary institutions from their governments was treated in Chap. 9. During the 1990s the existence of a central monetary institution, separate from the government, was fully accepted in most countries. But it had taken a long time before that stage was reached. In the early days of central banks, they were mostly established for providing services to governments, while running their own commercial business, and were owned by private shareholders. Those central banks that were established as state banks, such as in France and Germany, without private shareholders, were not independent in the modern sense of the word either. And when the need for a central bank for the United States was discussed in the early twentieth century (recall that earlier attempts had been squashed on political grounds), there was a sizable faction that was strongly opposed to the idea. Only when President Wilson came out in favor of establishing a bank of banks (which he later regretted) did the Federal Reserve arrive. There is still a small group of adherents to the view, especially in the United States, that there is no good reason to have a central bank. These radicals are generally to be found among politicians from the far right, such as Ron Paul, who wants to abolish the Federal Reserve (Paul 2009) but have no followers among mainstream politicians and policymakers.

While some European central banks, such as the Bank of England, the Netherlands Bank and those in Scandinavia, gained a measure of de facto independence around the 1920s, the concept was not identified as such. And as we saw in Chap. 4, the Federal Reserve found it difficult at first to establish a positive reputation. But by the 1920s, it too wielded considerable influence. However, in none of these cases, in one form or another, was autonomy enshrined in a law. The earliest instance of legislation explicitly granting autonomy to a central bank dates from 1922. Upon insistence of the Allied Command after the First World War, the Weimar Republic politicians passed a law that made the *Reichsbank* to some extent independent from the government, the German Chancellor no longer heading the central bank (Marsh 1992). Still its actual degree of freedom was limited, although following the hyperinflation of 1923, the influence of the German central bank increased significantly under the leadership of Hjalmar Schacht. When the Nazis came to power ten years later, the central bank became increasingly hamstrung, although Schacht who, after a period of being in and out of his job resigned in 1939, was one of the very few individuals who dared to disagree with the Fuehrer.

History repeated itself after the Second World War when the Allies insisted on the creation of an institution in Western Germany that would ensure monetary stability. As recounted earlier, an interim provisional institution served as central bank until the Bundesbank was erected in 1957 and granted the highest degree of independence of any central bank in the world. Elsewhere, the relationship between the central bank and the government was formalized in those countries where the former had been nationalized after the War, such as the Bank of England and the Netherlands Bank. The degree of autonomy varied considerably, the aforementioned banks being subject to a directive from the government in the event of a conflict. In practice, the most independent central banks, that is those enjoying instrument independence, were, besides the Bundesbank, the central banks of Switzerland, the Netherlands, Belgium and the Scandinavian countries. (The Federal Reserve only regained a high degree of autonomy in 1951, as related earlier.) Little change took place from the 1950s until around 1990 when the world-wide movement toward (more) independence took off. The evidence that countries with the most central bank independence maintained relatively low inflation after two major oil crises had clearly left an impression on those countries struggling with rapid price increases. Moreover, advances in monetary theory also played a role, especially the finding that inflation was lower in countries where central independence was stronger (Alesina and Summers 1993). Often overlooked, the role of the International Monetary Fund in strengthening the position of central bank was also substantial, particularly outside the advanced countries. A good example is that of Mexico, which received a very large credit from the IMF in the wake of its severe financial crisis of 1994–95. Among the reforms implemented on the basis of the economic program agreed to with the IMF, the Bank of Mexico attained a significant degree of autonomy with respect to both monetary policy and banking supervision.

Despite laws protecting central banks from undue pressure exercised by the executive and legislative branches of government, official monetary institutions have been subjected to strong criticism and attempts to undermine the independence they enjoy. Even the highly respected German Central Bank came under fire during its 40 years existence, mainly from the government. These skirmishes were often settled 'behind closed doors,' partly because the German public was inclined to back the central bank when such disagreements came into the open. Elsewhere, when conflicts concerning monetary policy flared up, governments (the Netherlands and the United Kingdom are examples) refrained from giving a directive to their central bank, as these could be challenged by parliament with a considerable risk of being defeated. In the United States, where a higher degree of transparency has always existed, Congress has over the years frequently—sometimes successfully—pressured the Federal Reserve to adjust its policies. Usually the complaints pertained to interest rates that were considered too high, or raised too quickly. American Presidents have also shown a penchant for pressuring the central bank, as related by its former chairman, Paul Volcker (2018). The best known example of such harassment is that by President Nixon, regularly summoning then Fed Chairman Arthur Burns to the White House to implore him to go slow on raising interest rates, despite an inflationary climate in the 1970s. Volcker also reveals that in 1984 President Reagan summoned him to the White House and let his then chief of staff, James Baker, tell Volcker that the President was ordering him not to raise interest rates before the upcoming election. Volcker, shocked by this aggressive attack on the Fed's independence, left without saying a word (Volcker 2018, 18, 19).

The Fed is usually considered to be a body 'independent within the government,' although this characterization has never found its way into any statute. It is often stated that the American Central Bank is a 'creature' of the US Congress which has the power to emasculate it. In this vein Sarah Binder and Mark Spiegel argue that the Fed is a political institution that is more vulnerable to getting its wings clipped than is usually realized (Binder and Spiegel 2017). It therefore needs to retain the support of a majority of members of Congress. A saving grace for the Fed is that many politicians are reluctant to strip the central bank of its autonomy for fear of getting blamed when the result is high inflation.

The other key player in the power struggle pertaining to the Fed is the American President. The Chairman of the Board of Governors of the Federal Reserve is appointed by the President for a term of four years, whereas the other governors enjoy a 14-year term. However, they often serve less than that. In such cases an opportunity arises to appoint board members that are known to share the general economic views of the President, which poses the danger of monetary policy that runs counter to the maintenance of stability. But there is a safeguard in that the nominated candidates need to be confirmed by the Senate. Crucially the choice of the head of the central bank is closely scrutinized through hearings of the

Committee on Financial Services whose members do not always vote along partisan lines. Yet the ultimate threat to the independence of the chairman is the alleged power of the President to remove him or her. But such a step requires 'cause,' another undefined concept. Conti-Brown (2016, 182) points out that according to the Fed's Statute, firing the Chairman would be in his/her capacity as governor. (There is no explicit mention of the chairman in this regard.) What is generally understood by most of those who study such matters is that 'cause' does not pertain to policy issues, but only to egregious behavior of the Fed Chairman (or other governors). Moreover, a removal based on cause has never taken place. And it is likely that a presidential decision to get rid of the head of the central bank would end up before the Supreme Court. However, this august body has become more politicized in recent years and a bi-partisan verdict might prove elusive. In a worst case scenario the central bank could become adrift under a leader who blindly follows the wishes of the President. With the Fed's credibility badly damaged, serious consequences could follow including foreign holders of US Treasury paper ($6.25 trillion, or 40 percent of the total outstanding) demanding higher interest rates or selling off their holdings (political motives could also play a role). There could also be a decline in confidence of financial markets in general and in the dollar. Ultimately the international monetary system could be affected, as occurred during the dollar crises of the 1970s.

Unrelenting Attacks

Since assuming office President Trump has repeatedly criticized the Fed for raising interest rates which in his view would be bad for the economy. In a next stage he insisted that the central bank should lower interest rates drastically. After a major tax cut enacted in 2017 that substantially increased the budget deficit, and with unemployment at record low rates of under 4 percent, most observers opined that as the economy was in danger of overheating, small but steady increases in interest rates was the appropriate policy response. In August 2018 the President started to attack Jerome Powell, the Fed Chairman, personally, adding that he was not sure he had picked the right person to head the central bank, stirring suspicions that he was thinking of firing Powell. His continued attacks and insults directed at the Fed served to heighten the tension. Trump's blatant accusations, including branding Powell as an 'enemy of the people,' were forcefully criticized by such luminaries as Lawrence Summers, who stated flatly that

'Fed bashing is foolish' and was undermining confidence which could actually push up interest rates significantly higher than the path then foreseen by the Fed (Summers 2018). A few members of Congress also publicly expressed their concern. Yet despite repeated slights and pressures on the Fed, the American Central Bank has as an institution been able to maintain its powerful position.

Elsewhere, many central banks experience a precarious future. For instance, in 2018 alone, a number of highly publicized attacks were aimed at monetary institutions of important emerging countries, eliciting strong reactions from markets. In Turkey President Erdogan repeatedly expressed strong displeasure at rising interest rates, claiming that higher interest rates caused inflation for which the Turkish central bank was responsible. To market participants it was clear that the Turkish economy was overheating leading to higher prices, a large current account deficit and massive capital outflows, all contributing to a precipitous drop of the Turkish lira. After markets reacted in a severely negative manner, the Turkish President apparently grudgingly accepted higher rates. In India, on its way to becoming an economic powerhouse and ill able to afford a blow to confidence, a serious conflict between Prime Minister Modi and the central bank of India broke out into the open, the Governor resigning as a result. Previously its former respected Governor, Raghuram Rajan, had resigned in a climate of growing animosity between the central bank and India's political leadership. Another instance of dangerous political meddling in an important emerging market country, the South African Reserve Bank came under fire. Its detractors hailed not only from the political leadership, but also included the supposedly neutral ombudsman. The predictable result was a swooning currency and a further erosion of already diminished confidence in the South African economy. In a reaction, the central bank Governor, Lesetja Kganyago, placed attacks on central banks in a broader context, warning that 'if politicians got their way on [central bank independence], they may just decide to go for the judiciary and then go for the next institution and then the next' (Bloomberg, 29 November, 2018).

Are Central Banks Too Powerful?

Following their successful operations during the Global Financial Crisis and their innovative policies in its wake, operating in the virtual absence of other policies to exit from the post-crisis malaise, central banks were described by former IMF official and CEO of a major investment firm, Mohamed El-Erian, as *the only game in town* (El-Erian 2016) an expression that struck a chord. He emphasized that the flipside of accolades for their earlier actions was criticism of the monetary institutions' role as virtually sole makers of macroeconomic policy and the power that flowed from it to central banks who were run by unelected officials. This is a legitimate question, but one that can be presented either in an uninformed and often aggressive way, or in nuanced terms. Focusing on the longer term, a debate concerning the optimal degree of central bank independence can be meaningful. The position of central banks is after all a crucial element in modern democracies and can inform views on the shape and role of central banks in coming years, and possibly, decades.

Politics Versus Economics

Based on experience over many years, it is clear that the role and independence of central banks is more of a political than an economic question. In light of the present nationalistic trend in a large number of countries and in the event that politicians from the far right (or conceivably from the far left) form governments or partake in government decisions, central bank's independence could be seriously undermined. Pressure to bring down interest rates at the wrong moment (coming elections are often a trigger), or to 'rethink' hiking interest rates when the economic case for doing so is clear, would lead to a loss of stability which in the longer run would damage growth and stoke inflation. In this regard the situation in the United States is crucial. If the Federal Reserve, the most important central bank in the world, bows to a political power play, a contagion effect is to be expected. Politicians in a wide range of countries could feel emboldened to follow the American example.

As regards the United Kingdom, the Bank of England *Act* of 1998 which bestowed operational independence on the central bank, 'leaves plenty of room for change,' according to *The Economist* (2 November 2019, 20). It notes that not only can the UK Treasury take over monetary policy for three months in 'extreme economic circumstances' (a decision to be taken by the government), but it can also add an objective pertaining to economic growth in tandem with the goal of price stability. The danger of a weakening of independence is much smaller with respect to the European Central Bank. With an executive board appointed on the basis of consensus among political leaders of the euro area countries, and with the board members accorded an eight-year non-renewable term and having to possess relevant experience for managing a central bank, the risk of 'packing' the institution with political favorites is practically negligible. Moreover, since the Council of the ECB is comprised of independent minded central bank governors of the national monetary institutions, the political situation in Europe would have to get seriously out of order before the ECB were to succumb to undue political interference. With respect to political pressure, the ECB has little to fear from the European Parliament, the official overseer of the ECB, as its actual power remains limited. Moreover, the ECB was founded on the basis of a treaty that would be extremely difficult to amend. In the event of a partial breakdown of the euro area (a considerable number of countries would continue to maintain a common currency), the ECB would continue as before, albeit in a slimmed down version.

Nonetheless, some serious observers have raised questions about the degree of independence enjoyed by (some) central banks. They posit that allowing a number of unelected officials to take far-reaching decisions represents a deficit of democracy. At the same time, the high degree of accountability practiced by many modern central banks has diminished concerns on this front, although some critics advocate an even higher degree of transparency. Another point of contention is the fear that central banks can be drawn into activities that go beyond their general remit. As we have seen, this became a hot political issue in the aftermath of the global financial crisis of 2007–08. Public and political sentiment against large bail-outs of financial institutions, especially those that are not part of the regular financial system (non-bank depository institutions) led to a legal prohibition for the Fed to financially support non-bank institutions, such as the insurance giant American Insurance Group, in the future. On a less controversial level, central banks are sometimes accused of straying beyond their mandate. A case in point is the opposition—especially in Germany—to what is considered to be quasi-monetary financing of budget deficits, such has been the case with respect to the ECB's large-scale financial support operations and its massive purchases of government bonds in the scope of QE. However, the German Constitutional Court has ruled that the ECB was not breaching the limits of its mandate laid down in its statute (see also Chap. 10).

Being dependent on shifts in political convictions creates an extra degree of uncertainty in the stance of monetary policy in the longer run. The problem does not so much lie with limited tweaking of legislation—as the world undergoes changes, some adjustments can be sensible—but in the possibility that a wave of ultra conservative views can place power in the hands of politicians who mistrust central banks and display a high degree of short-termism. While seeming unlikely at the time of writing, more nibbling away at central bank's independence, such as further restraining the Fed's ability to act as lender of last resort, may well occur.

A Fourth Branch of Government?

The reverse cannot be ruled out either. Moderately conservative observers could, in the fashion of the former German Central Bank, favor strengthening the autonomy of the protector of the stability of their currencies, creating a de facto fourth branch of government. In the early 1990s, when many governments were granting their central banks independence, it was sometimes suggested that since the leaders of central banks are analogous to Supreme Court judges, they should enjoy a similar degree of independence, thus constituting a de facto fourth branch of government (De Beaufort Wijnholds 1992). The position of the Swiss National Bank, whose independence is enshrined in the Swiss constitution, comes close to that model.

Elsewhere, the fourth branch model or the Swiss model, which provides very strong protection against attempts to undermine a central bank's independence, is unlikely to pass political muster in most countries. In his popular book, *In Fed We Trust*, David Wessel suggests that the global financial crisis of 2007–09 put the Federal Reserve (temporarily) in the position of a fourth branch of government (Wessel 2010). However, the Fed is too much beholden to Congress to consider this a more or less permanent state of affairs. Most governments and parliaments are likely to subscribe to the views of former Deputy Governor of the Bank of England, Paul Tucker, who argues that: 'Central banks are not … inherently a new fourth branch of government since they are subordinate, in different ways, to each of the higher-level branches of the state: delegation of statutory powers (legislature), nomination or appointment of agency leadership (executive) and adjudication of disputes under the law (courts)' (Tucker 2018). The upshot of these various positions is that the optimal degree of central bank independence differs among countries, just as the nature of their democracies is different (for instance, the United Kingdom does not have a written constitution), as well as the underlying priorities of a society (German stability orientation). In other words, in democratic societies, maintenance of a given degree of independence ultimately requires the support of the public.

While large-scale changes in the status of most central banks are unlikely in the near future, the money masters will not be in for an easy ride. They have in recent years become more visible to the public by virtue of their role in crisis management and their responsibility for not only the level of inflation, but also their influence on joblessness. The result is an increased scrutiny of monetary institutions. The general public, especially in the United States, may have gotten used to a combination of *sustained* low inflation (around 2 percent) coupled with low unemployment (below 4 percent). But it probably is not aware that, historically speaking, such a combination has seldom been achieved for a prolonged period and could at any time come to an end.

Monetary Policy

The core of central banking, monetary policy is one of the most important tools in modern economies. Its ultimate impact may not be as strong as that of fiscal policy, but its flexibility, as compared to the generally sluggish process of government spending and taxation, tends to place it in the forefront of economic policymaking. Central banks' intentions are therefore particularly closely watched. As to what constitutes optimal monetary policy, views continue to differ, although the gap between academic and central bank positions has become smaller, as was demonstrated in the beginning of this chapter. Still important differences of opinion have continued to exist between and within both camps. The long-standing debate known as 'rules versus discretion' is ongoing, albeit that in most central banks the supporters of discretion have gained the upper hand. Aiming to meet a monetary supply target, so prevalent in the 1970s and 1980s, has been replaced on a large scale by inflation targeting. The concept of a money supply has generally been relegated to the status of 'other indicators' in the determination of monetary policy decisions, with the important exception of the ECB where monetary analysis is accorded an explicit role. In the academic sphere, monetarism à la Friedman still has an active following among conservative academics and politicians, many of whom consider a fixed rule for monetary policy as a way to lessen the influence of the Federal Reserve. The famous Taylor rule (described in Chap. 9), in a variant that allows for an override of the rule by the central bank in extraordinary circumstances, can be seen as a middle way between discretionary monetary policymaking and the application of a fixed money supply target. Not only has Professor Taylor's approach been influential in monetary debates, it has also proved to be a useful teaching tool. But it has never been applied as a sole policy target by central banks.

A Need for New Approaches?

As the economic and financial environment tends to change over time, monetary policy has to adjust in order to maintain its grip on monetary conditions. The introduction of inflation targeting some 30 years ago and the more recent application of quantitative easing and forward guidance are prime examples of such adjustments. New approaches in inflation targeting and the development of innovative tools are likely to be developed in the coming years. A first step in that direction is that the Fed, the ECB and other central banks are reexamining their policies and engage in a public debate on monetary policy. This initiative is not only useful in itself, but also demonstrates a willingness of the central banks to listen to other voices.

An exchange on the best approach to inflation targeting is likely to develop along the following lines. Although IT has served most central banks well, there is a school of thought that considers maintaining a 2 percent fixed target as providing too little economic stimulus in a downturn. However, former Fed Chairman, Ben Bernanke, discards proposals to raise the target to 3 or 4percent, noting that the public will be very unhappy about such a move and that it would complicate planning for investment and other economic purposes. Hence, increasing the target would probably politically be a non-starter. Instead switching to an inflation target that is adjusted over time to take into account those periods that annual price increases fell short of the 2 percent goal (or vice versa) is under serious consideration. Supporters include John Williams, President of the New York Fed (Williams 2017). Known as price *level* targeting, it aims at keeping the very long-run average inflation rate at 2 percent and not let 'bygones be bygones' as under regular IT. In other words, while IT as practiced today does not 'play catch-up' for the years that inflation stays below 2 percent, price level targeting provides more room for economic stimulus by the central bank. By ensuring that interest rates can be maintained 'lower for longer,' the room for easing monetary policy would be increased. However, price level targeting would probably be hard to explain to the public and financial markets. Moreover, 'bygones are not bygones' under this approach implies that for years in which the target is exceeded, the leeway for future economic stimulus shrinks.

In order to avoid this obstacle, Bernanke has proposed a regime of *temporary price-level targeting* under which price-level targeting would only be applied during periods when the zero lower interest rate bound (ZLB) is in play. Thus the 'lower for longer' principle would be limited to instances when nominal interest rates reach zero. For other times the regular IT regime of a fixed 2 percent goal would be maintained. The main advantage of Bernanke's proposal, which he sees as a compromise solution, is that monetary policy would not have to be tightened when inflation shows an unexpected uptick during a time that the ZLB is in play. This ingenious policy instrument would, of course, also seem to require quite a bit of explanation, but that would be less difficult, according to Bernanke, as 'communication could remain entirely in terms of inflation goals, a concept with which the public and market participants are already familiar'.

Other, less sophisticated, but easier to understand proposals include moving away from a point target and introducing inflation target zones, thus adding flexibility to monetary policy. Adopting a symmetrical target of 1 to 3 percent could be a useful compromise solution, along the lines of the Bank of England's approach where the official target is 2 percent, but when inflation strays beyond a range of 1 to 3 percent, the Bank has to explain the reasons behind the missing the target in a letter to the Chancellor of the Exchequer. Another often advocated, but never implemented, suggestion is to target *nominal GDP*, thereby combining real economic growth and inflation. Problems with this idea include the dilemma of what to do when the target of, say, 5 percent is achieved while growth is zero percent and inflation, 5 percent (a severe case of stagflation). Measurement of the inflation component is another issue, since the GDP deflator can differ considerably from the much better known consumer price index. Also, public and market acceptance will require considerable education.

A broader question, raised by Paul Volcker and others, is whether an inflation target is actually necessary and why it should be 2 percent, which implies that, if sustained, the price level doubles in a little more than a generation (Volcker 2018, 224). Indeed, 2 percent annual inflation is not a scientifically derived number. Moreover, what is often overlooked is that what is targeted is changes in consumer prices only, whereas asset price inflation can at the same time be much higher. Several episodes of such a divergence have occurred, sometimes with disastrous outcomes, the events of 2007–09 being the prime example. A decade later, in many countries, both the stock market and house prices reached levels that are high by historical standards and are fueled by ultra-low interest rates. The borrowing public generally welcomes these increases in their wealth (which may of course be wiped out under different circumstances) and highly indebted governments that can borrow at practically no cost are equally satisfied with this state of affairs. (The lobby of savers and institutional investors has so far not had any discernable impact.) The result is an asymmetric burden placed on monetary policy to stimulate demand. The longer such a configuration lasts, the larger the danger to financial stability. A shift of central banks' main focus from the monetary area to that of the financial system appears to be overdue. And since protection through macroprudential policy of a safe and sound financial system cannot be fully relied on, as explained in Chap. 13, monetary policy should be unshackled from an exclusive concentration on achieving its inflation target, even if its falls short by a few decimal points. Claudio Borio, of the Bank for International Settlements, somewhat controversially, argues on the basis of historical data that fears of even modest deflation have been overblown. He posits that the view that deflation is always harmful in that it causes output to shrink because of a shortfall of demand is questionable. His extensive research, covering 140 years for 38 countries, finds only a weak link between output growth and deflation, except for the Great Depression, which he considers to be an outlier. His analysis implies that working with an IT of 2 percent need not be the optimal choice for every central bank in advanced countries. It is supported by the experience in recent years in the United States and the euro area that economic growth can remain satisfactory for a number of years, despite inflation remaining below 2 percent, and below but close to 2 percent for the euro area, as Fig. 14.1 shows. (It should be kept in mind that potential output growth in the United States is at least 1 percentage point higher than in the euro area.)

Rules Redux?

In a world where the private financial sector continues to undergo rapid changes and populist politicians increasingly denounce central banks' discretionary monetary policy, the preference for automatic rules could make

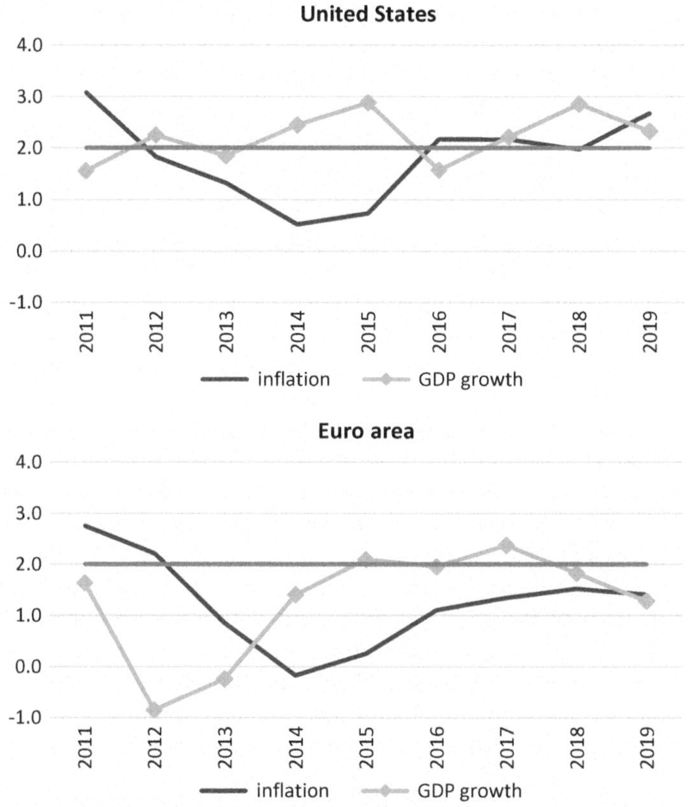

Fig. 14.1 Growth and inflation in the United States and euro area 2010–18. (Source: IMF, World Economic Outlook database (April 2019))

a comeback. The most likely candidate would be the Taylor rule. But there is also a school of supporters of a return to some form of 'pure' monetarism.

As illustrated in the box on monetary theory in Chap. 9, the Taylor rule, which performed well over many years, has more recently implied interest rate adjustments which would be unacceptable, such as significantly negative nominal rates. At the same time, adjusting the Taylor rule by giving the central bank the authority to override the rule under special circumstances, such as an oil price shock or an exchange rate crisis, is less extreme. Although such a feature would allow greater leeway for the central bank—and incidentally make it more independent again—it would very much depend on when an override is appropriate. Any override is bound to trigger contentious debates. Moreover, if the override is modest, the inflexibility of a rigid rule would remain and if the scope is very broad, the central bank would enjoy a practically discretionary environment.

Monetary rules, which its proponents believe would increase monetary stability and facilitate decision-making by businesses, households and financial markets, enjoy a degree of support from academics and politicians. They consider 'meeting to meeting' discretionary policymaking unsatisfactory and succeeded in garnering enough political support to have the US House of Representatives pass a bill in 2015 that would require the Fed to choose a monetary rule. It is unlikely, however, that this piece of legislation will come into effect anytime soon, particularly because of the shift in the composition of the House to a Democratic Party majority in 2018. While monetarists advocate a rule, they generally do not specify what that rule should be. For instance, Athanasios Orphanides, an academic and former central banker, argues extensively why a simple monetary rule is desirable, but does not make a suggestion as to what it should be (Orphanides 2018).

An obvious candidate for a simple rule, the Taylor rule aside, is for a path for growth of the money supply. But if there is no convincing evidence that the demand for money function is stable, a return of M1, M2 or M3 or the adoption of Divisia M4 (a very broad and weighted definition of money tracked by the Center for Financial Stability, a think tank in New York) to play a central role in central bank policymaking is hard to envisage. Still as a way of cross checking the economic outlook, monetary analysis can play a useful role, as is the case at the European Central Bank.

Whither Monetary Policy?

While monetary policy in advanced countries has been largely successful in the aftermath of the global financial crisis in avoiding economic stagnation, some doubts have arisen that a continuation of extremely loose monetary policy may have outlived its usefulness. It is increasingly argued that the negative effects after a decade of the application of unconventional tools have come to outweigh the positive effects. However, in two lengthy studies, ECB staffers conclude that the benefits of their institution's application of unconventional monetary policy are still larger than the associated costs (Hartmann and Smets 2018; Rostangno et al. 2019).

Looking at it from a different angle, the fact that the ECB, the Bank of Japan and various smaller central banks have not succeeded to reach their inflation targets after many years raises the question whether a change in course is called for. In the United States, the Fed succeeded in the course of 2019 to get close to its core inflation target while unemployment reached an unusually low level. This result was reached despite the Fed gradually increasing its policy interest rate to between 2.25 and 2.75 percent. Yet concern that a (mild) recession could be on the horizon, it lowered the Fed rate thrice with baby steps. Such tiny moves cannot be expected to have a discernable impact on growth, but serve basically as a signaling device ('we don't expect a real recession but we are extra vigilant'). An important drawback of this early warning move is that it lowers the room for a sizable cut when it is most needed, except if the Fed were to be willing to go into negative interest rate territory, which appears unlikely.

In his address to the American Economic Association in January 2020, Ben Bernanke has argued that the combination of quantitative easing and forward guidance has not only proved effective in staving off deflation, but can also under 'normal' circumstances in the United States—based on the assumption of a nominal neutral rate of interest rate of between 2 and 3 percent—be a useful and effective part of the monetary policy framework. Acknowledging that there are risks and costs to extended use of QE and forward guidance, Bernanke considers these to be modest for the most part. However, he sees 'more uncertainty between easy money, on one hand, and risks to financial stability, on the other,' in the form of a too risky search for yield by investors, the cause being irrational behavior or distorted institutional incentives. Therefore, '[v]igilance and appropriate policies, including macroprudential and regulatory policies, are essential' (Bernanke 2020). However, a few years earlier, Stanley Fischer, cast doubt as to the availability of effective macroprudential tools in the United States (Fischer 2017). There is a difficult trade-off to be made here between continuation of an accommodative monetary policy in light of a possible recession on the horizon, or of a new financial crisis in light of increased risk taking, higher debt levels and renewed asset price inflation.

The situation in Europe and Japan is different. Despite years of trying to bring inflation up to 2 percent, their policies of sticking to negative interest rates (and even lowering them further in some cases) and enormous bond buying programs have not delivered the sought-after result. Market participants, other observers and some central bankers themselves have suggested that monetary institutions are caught in a liquidity trap. Wall Street insider Mickey Levy argues that since there are several important non-monetary factors that are beyond the control of central banks, further easing is unlikely to provide significant economic stimulus. These factors include fears of an escalation of trade and currency wars, the uncertainty created by the Brexit drama in Europe, distortion of financial markets, especially in Japan, and solvency issues with respect to institutional investors, as well as a reduced profit outlook for banks (Levy 2019).

The ECB is not a monolithic bloc, and within its confines such sentiments are regularly expressed but not shared by a majority of the members of its governing council. In an unprecedented action, reflecting a serious internal split within the council, Klaas Knot, President of the Netherlands Bank, publicly reacted critically to the announcement on 12 September 2019 by the ECB Council that it was taking further measures given its concerns about the inflation outlook in the euro area. Knot described the package and especially the resumption of its asset purchase program, 'disproportionate to the present economic conditions' and expressed doubt as to its effectiveness. Furthermore, he flagged 'increasing signs of scarcity of low-risk assets, distorted pricing in financial markets and excessive risk-seeking behavior in the housing markets' (Knot 2019). Drawing attention to the (increasing) cost of a resumption of the ECB's bond-buying program in terms of threats to financial stability was most likely supported by several of his fellow council members.

The foregoing reflects a growing conviction that monetary policy in advanced countries is losing effectiveness and that governments should take over the task of fostering economic growth, not only by means of fiscal policy but also by introducing structural reforms. The room for fiscal expansion exists in a number of countries, especially in Europe. The governments of Germany, the Netherlands, the Nordic countries and some other smaller countries have significantly brought down their debt to GDP ratios and are running large current account surpluses on their balances of payments. Increasing government investment, particularly on infrastructure projects, can provide a welcome boost to overall demand. And since these countries can borrow (or replace maturing bonds) at zero or even somewhat lower interest rates, their debt service will gradually come down. While fresh borrowing will increase overall government debt, the debt/GDP ratio could decline if economic growth exceeds the level of interest rates. Such initiatives should ideally be supplemented by structural reforms which over time would increase growth rates.

Helicopter Money

A more radical means of monetary stimulus, which could be introduced when other instruments have failed, is known as 'helicopter money.' In 1968 Milton Friedman playfully suggested that if money were dropped from a helicopter, the resulting expansion of the money supply would directly influence the spending of households who would be the recipients of the bonanza (Friedman 1968). In later years helicopter money became a serious proposal; a central bank would make direct payments to households (in cash or by crediting their bank accounts) when the economy was experiencing a liquidity trap (a state where traditional monetary instruments are unable to overcome a recession). By increasing aggregate consumption, money from the sky could kick-start the stagnant economy. In 2002, Ben Bernanke suggested that helicopter money could be effective in staving off deflation with specific reference to the stagnating Japanese economy. The Japanese central bank did not follow his advice, but in the following years several academics and some central bankers expressed support for the helicopter approach. Among these were Willem Buiter, originally an academic economist who has held senior positions at the Bank of England and other financial institutions, and the influential journalist and author, Martin Wolf. The path chosen by major central banks to exit from the Great Recession, however, was implementing quantitative easing.

Central bankers have generally refrained from commenting on dropping money from the sky, while some, like former Fed chair Janet Yellen, see a role for it only under extreme circumstances. Reacting to a remark by then ECB President, Mario Draghi, that helicopter money is 'a very interesting concept,' Otmar Issing, former chief economist of the European Central Bank, described the notion of helicopter money a recipe for inflation. 'The idea of helicopter money [is] worrisome, even devastating. For it is nothing else but a bankruptcy declaration of monetary policy…A central bank that is throwing out money for free, will hardly be able to regain control of the printing press. This debate has spread out into the public; I see it as a total intellectual confusion' (Issing 2016). There is also some skepticism that helicopter money would be spent, the argument being confirmed by the results of a survey conducted by the Netherlands Bank in 2016. It is of course possible that surveys in other countries with a higher propensity to consume, such as the United States, would show different outcomes. There is also the possibility that if the public clamors for regular money drops and politicians answer the call, the central bank could become a dangerous money machine. Finally, there is the risk that by issuing helicopter money, which would not appear on the central bank's balance sheet as a liability, its equity (capital and internal reserves) could be wiped out, forcing governments to re-capitalize their monetary institutions and possibly by having taxpayers foot the bill.

Helicopter money should not be confused with quantitative easing. QE involves central banks creating liquidity by purchasing securities with the intention that the sellers (commercial banks) will use their enhanced liquidity position to extend more credit to the private sector which in turn is expected to stimulate aggregate demand. While helicopter money has the same goal, its route to such an outcome is a direct one, an immediate stimulus for households to spend the money.

A novel scheme to integrate a version of helicopter money with government finance has been proposed by Stanley Fischer and others (Bartsch et al. 2019). Since the authors consider monetary policy to be 'almost exhausted' and fiscal policy not 'nimble' enough to provide sufficient stimulus in the short term in a downturn, they advocate establishing a framework for coordination between the two macroeconomic instruments. Helicopter money as such is not proposed, given the likelihood that explicit permanent financing of fiscal stimulus, without 'explicit boundaries,' would open up the floodgates to uncontrolled government spending and could lead to runaway inflation. The solution suggested by the authors is to establish a standing emergency fiscal facility that would call for an unprecedented degree of coordination between central banks and the treasuries, made jointly responsible for reaching the central banks' inflation target when a recession materializes. Activation of the facility is to be determined by the central bank. When the target is reached and monetary policy space is restored, the facility will be terminated. The facility's size is to be determined by the central bank on the basis of an estimated direct injection of money that would be needed to reach the IT over the medium term. 'Going direct' will be performed by the central bank crediting private or public sector accounts with money, in fact subsidizing spending. The operation of the scheme will entail an increase in government debt, but as mentioned in the previous paragraph, need not be onerous when interest rates hover around zero. Under favorable circumstances, government debt to GDP ratios could even come down.

The authors are well aware of the political objections that can be expected when the proposal is launched in relevant forums. Central banks in particular are likely to be concerned by moving from the usual 'soft' cooperation with the treasury to 'hard' coordination. Pressure on central banks to activate the facility when they see no need to do so and to make 'going direct' permanent will be very strong and complicated by the fact that the treasury is in some way a co-decider. Independence of central banks, already under siege, could be seriously eroded.

Financial Stability

As we have seen, a major issue in modern central banking is the relationship between monetary policy focused on maintaining price stability and the pursuit of financial stability. In theory a conflict between the two goals can be resolved through the application of macroprudential policies. However, despite some successes, such policies have not been available everywhere and at all times. Excessive mortgage lending to households leading to rapid, unsustainable rises in house prices is a prime example of this lack of tools. In order to achieve a cooling off in the housing market and to avoid a crash with possible chain effects, the central bank can step on the monetary brake by raising interest rates, but such a general measure would not be welcome in times of low growth and high unemployment, as explained in Chap. 13. Leaning against the wind requires significant courage by central banks. Hence government action will be needed to prick the bubble, for instance by means of tax measures or placing a ceiling on the level of mortgages. But such interventions are likely to be unpopular with the electorate, causing politicians to waver until most of the damage has been done (the 'wait and see' bias mentioned in Chap. 13).

Were central banks to become less independent and more prone to political interference, the outcome could be unwanted inflation (above the target) as macroprudential measures would arguably be kept in the closet and leaning against the wind ruled out. Not only would risks to financial stability increase but the goal of price stability could become the secondary remit and low unemployment the main goal of monetary policy.

Going Cashless

Changes in payments habits of households could have far-reaching consequences for central banking in the coming years. Although suggestions of moving to a cashless society have been around for a long time, concrete developments have only surfaced in recent years. In many countries households have been making fewer payments with cash, as a result of the relative ease of obtaining debit and credit cards and using mobile phone applications. In addition to the spontaneous decline in the use of cash (banknotes) by the public, governments and action groups have taken initiatives to drastically reduce the use of paper money. In 2016 the Indian government declared that some large denomination banknotes would cease to be legal tender if not converted to newly issued notes within 60 days. Motives for the partial demonetization were to reduce black market transactions, broaden the tax base, combat illegal transactions and counterfeiting, as well as to promote digital payments. After an initial shock to the economy the results were somewhat successful, but do not seem to have brought about the fundamental adjustments in payments practices that the authorities were seeking.

The case for reducing the use of cash has also been made in the academic world. In his somewhat alarmingly titled book, *The Curse of Cash*, Harvard Professor Kenneth Rogoff argues that terminating the use of large-denomination banknotes in the United States, such as the US$100 and $50 bills—which represent the bulk of the nominal value of banknotes in circulation—while continuing to issue those of smaller denominations, would bring important benefits. Rogoff points out that such a policy would not only push back criminal activity and tax evasion in the underground economy but also increase the flexibility of monetary policy to stimulate the economy when needed. It would allow the Fed (and other central banks) to implement significant negative nominal interest rates in times of economic weakness by increasing the cost of keeping money in cash, since storing low-denomination banknotes would require much more space than stuffing $100 bills in suitcases (Rogoff 2016).

Meanwhile, changing payments habits in the United States (and elsewhere) by way of fewer transactions in cash have already led to a relative decline in the dollar banknote circulation. However, while the share of notes in the total US money supply (M1) of $3.7 trillion is about 45 percent (in 2018), a very large amount—estimated at close to $1 trillion—is held abroad, some of it circulating in countries that have made the US dollar their 'national' currency (Ecuador, Panama), but most of it likely serving as a means to conduct illegal transactions and tax evasion. And while the total US dollar bills in circulation, as reported by the Federal Reserve, is still growing apace, it is not known how much of this increase is the result of a greater use by the American public of other means of payment. As to the question of future growth of the total circulation of dollar bills, the Fed staff, somewhat surprisingly, expects the public's demand for currency to grow substantially from $1.7 trillion in 2018 to $2.5 trillion or more over the next decade, but declining as a ratio of M1(mentioned by Bernanke in 2016).

In such a scenario, terminating the issuance of $100 bills would satisfy Rogoff's plea. In the same vein of dealing with the problem of an excessive use of large denomination euro bank-notes, the European Central Bank has stopped printing new euro 500 bills.

In Sweden cash payments have declined dramatically, banknotes in circulation have fallen by over 50 percent in a decade, with the government actively supporting the trend. Because of the ease of using debit cards or phone apps and the reluctance of stores to accept cash, banks to handle cash and the rise in digital payments made among individuals for small amounts, the majority of the Swedish population is willing to go without cash, according to polls. The Governor of the Central Bank of Sweden, Stefan Ingves, observes that 'given that the role of a central bank is to manage the money supply, these developments potentially have wide-ranging consequences' Ingves 2016). With the digitization of payments advancing rapidly, central banks are studying whether they should issue digital money. Doing so could change the nature of monetary policy very significantly, depending on how the problem is addressed. Although of lesser importance, the decline in the use of banknotes will reduce the seigniorage, the income that central banks enjoy by issuing paper money which are in fact cost-free liabilities for these bodies. And as this source of revenue dries up drastically, central banks' financial independence could be undermined.

Another major challenge to central banks in the field of payments is the emergence of financial technology firms, as well as giant firms whose main business is not finance, but technology and whose sheer size and technological networks provide it with the potential to play a major role in payments and settlement. Given the importance of this 'new normal,' the following section explains how these firms can bring benefits in terms of higher efficiency and stronger competition, but also carry the risks of serious disruption and of undermining central banks' role in conducting monetary policy and in prudential supervision.

Fintech and Big Tech

While traditional means of payment, banknotes, checks and credit and debit cards are becoming less important, whole new payments *systems* are being introduced or designed. As payments systems are the wiring and plumbing of the global financial architecture, any disruption in their working can have serious consequences. Efficiency and security are therefore essential to ensure that payments are smoothly carried out, cleared and settled. Central banks have a large stake in avoiding breakdowns in this domain, but are not necessarily managers of payments systems. History provides many examples of such systems being run by commercial banks (clearing banks) and other specialized bodies, as described by Ugolini (2017). However, central banks' involvement plays a very important role in the United States (Fedwire), European Central Bank (Target 2) and elsewhere.

Box 14.1 China's New Payments System

Aaron Klein, a fellow at the Brookings Institution, has thoroughly analyzed the revolution in China's retail payment system (Klein 2019). Instead of relying on bank-based cards with chips, as in most other countries with well-developed banking systems, Chinese big tech firms (Alibaba and Tencent) have leapfrogged this stage and built systems based on digital wallets and QR codes (stands for Quick Response, a sophisticated successor of bar codes). A major consequence of these new methods of payment is a considerable loss of revenue for the Chinese banks. And while cash is still widely used—the highest denomination banknote is the equivalent of a mere \$15—making payments for higher priced items more cumbersome. The speed and efficiency of the new systems provide a strong incentive for the public to conduct retail, person to person and business transactions in general by using their smartphones which have become ubiquitous.

Some of the conclusions Klein draws are:

1. China's new payment system will continue to grow domestically and globally.

(*continued*)

Box 14.1 (continued)

2. The use of cutting edge technology facilitates the transition of the payment system away from banking and into technology and social media.
3. The strong incentives created by the transition from a banking based system to big tech firms are 'potentially concerning.' At issue are the room for anti-competitive behavior and breach of privacy. Klein states that 'it is not clear whether these concerns can and would be remedied by effective regulation.'
4. The Chinese system is unlikely to make headway in the United States, because the reward system connected to the existing card system is too lucrative; businesses may encounter difficulties in transitioning to a new system and generating a substantial reduction in costs; consumers are often inert; existing regulatory systems provide substantial protection through the bank-based system that may be lost by switching to the Chinese model.
5. However, Klein warns that '[t]he American legal and regulatory framework is not well prepared should payments move from banking to non-banking.' In other countries similar concerns exist.

Recently developed new payments systems, such as in China (Box 14.1), and fintech innovations, as well as efforts by big tech to introduce revolutionary changes in the way payments can be made outside the banking system, have captured widespread attention. Certain features of these innovations could loosen the grip of central banks on the money supply. The most far-reaching example is the proposal by Facebook to launch an artificial currency named the Libra. Reactions from official circles and economists have generally been critical, and, to the extent that such a system were to undermine monetary policy and lack regulatory oversight, governments are unlikely to allow it to function. With respect to other budding plans of big tech to offer financial services, the initial reaction of monetary and regulatory institutions seems to be more forthcoming, although cautionary.

Agustin Carstens, General Manager of the BIS, set out the issues with great clarity in a speech in December 2018. His main theme is that 'big tech firms' ' main advantage is that they can exploit existing customer networks and the massive quantities of data generated by their business lines.... Data give big firms the edge over competitors. But to public policymakers, this aspect represents one of the greatest challenges' (Carstens 2018). Commercial banks rely on a branch network through which they attract many small deposits which serve as the main source of their funding. Their lending is based on human decision-making. By contrast, big tech firms first extend a loan and subsequently fund them by raising money. No human interaction is involved in their lending which is based on predictive algorithms and machine learning techniques. Based on the same techniques loans can be cut off automatically.

While big tech's participation in the financial system can lead to more competition and innovation in the existing banking based system, it could also bring about excessive market concentration and systemic risks, as pointed out by Carstens. The exact role of big tech's involvement in the financial system needs to be fully analyzed in order to determine to what kind of regulatory oversight it should be subjected to. It is also of the essence that any developments toward the creation of parallel currencies should be investigated with great scrutiny, so as to avoid crippling monetary policy. Moreover, cooperation among central banks and other regulatory authorities regarding fintech and big tech is highly desirable, as has been recognized by the IMF and the World Bank, which drew up the Bali Fintech Agenda in 2018, among other initiatives, to work toward closing gaps in the legal frameworks between countries and to modernize data frameworks (International Monetary Fund and World Bank 2019).

The International Monetary System

Central banks are deeply involved in managing the international monetary system (IMS). There is no obvious reason to expect a change in this participation along with their governments. However, in the course of history, the IMS has undergone many changes and further shocks and drastic adjustments to the system not only cannot be ruled out but are likely to occur at some stage. Extreme proposals such as the adoption of a single global currency or a return to the classical gold standard are most unlikely to be adopted. A drastic increase in the role of special drawing rights (SDRs) in the IMS, at the expense of reserve currencies, while appearing improbable at present, could be a desirable solution in case of a collapse of the IMS caused, for instance, by a dollar crisis or a euro area break-up.

A more likely scenario for the future is an increased role of emerging and developing countries, and especially the BRICS, in the IMS. An early indication of such a development is the—still slow—rise of the role of the Chinese renminbi in the global financial system. The process of further increases in the quota share of emerging countries in the International Monetary Fund (and the share in the capital of the World Bank) is already underway and will lead to a stronger voice of these countries in shaping the future of the IMS. The European countries will lose some of their influence, especially if the members of the euro area continue to be unable to speak with one voice in resisting an amalgamation of their representation at the IMF. And under the (for now) unlikely scenario that the emerging and developing countries were to obtain a majority of the votes in the IMF, they are likely to push for a reduction of the number of executive directors and of members of the IMF from advanced countries and possibly on eliminating the veto right of the United States in that body. But since these amendments require 85 percent of the total voting power, such a development seems out of reach under normal circumstances.

Looking at a farther horizon, if major wars were to occur the world economy could be in ruins. The multilateral monetary, financial and trade system would be replaced by all-encompassing controls, and international trade and financial transactions would shrink dramatically. In essence, the world economy as we know it would cease to exist. Assuming that this would not be a war of total annihilation, but would involve all major powers, imports of essential goods would be settled in bilateral transactions, the scope of which is quite limited, as well as with gold or other scarce commodities. If the United States is still a functioning country, US dollars would also be a means of settlement, probably in cash given the risks of foreign assets being frozen and of cybercrime.

What role will be played by central banks in these scenarios that range from the plausible to the apocalyptical? There will always be a need for central banks of some kind, even under catastrophic conditions when the imperative would be to keep the economy going at some level above a primitive barter society. In a near-worst case scenario, the central bank could become the only money creating institution and its bank notes, to the extent they were still accepted, the only means of conducting domestic monetary transactions. (Gold holdings of individuals are likely to be modest in relation to the expected demand for cash.) In order to cope with such exigencies, central banks would need to have available large amounts of cash in their vaults ready to be issued at short notice. Such stashes do exist but the details are not made public.

As to settling international transactions, mostly trade, as financial systems are likely to be mostly paralyzed under extreme conditions, gold would be the asset of choice. Most central banks hold gold as part of their international reserves (in a number of cases a country's treasury is the undisputed owner of the yellow metal). The share of gold in international reserves shrank after the gold standard was abandoned and political tensions diminished, requiring a lesser need for a war chest and the fact that currency reserves yield returns, whereas gold bears no interest. However, the demonetization of officially held gold, much discussed at the time of the introduction of SDRs, was never complete. While several central banks in Europe sold considerable amounts of gold in the years after the breakdown of the Bretton Woods system, monetary institutions in other parts of the world added to their gold stocks. More recently such purchases have gradually risen and delivery not as usual taken for safekeeping at the Federal Reserve Bank of New York, the Bank of England and some other (normally) safe locations. Furthermore, a number of central banks have repatriated part of their official gold, probably fearing that their foreign exchange reserves can be frozen in a conflict, or inspired by the resurgence of nationalism.

Cooperation Among Central Banks

There is a long history of central bank cooperation which has made important contributions to the smooth functioning of the international monetary and financial system, including extending bridge or longer-term financing, maintaining a continuing dialogue concerning policy matters, and sometimes—in crisis conditions—joint interest rate movements. The central bank fraternity tends to be close-knit, especially among advanced countries, but those from other parts of the world have joined up in increasing numbers, demonstrated by the strong growth of the membership of the Bank for International Settlements. And the central banks of rising economic powerhouses such as China and India have become prominent members of what was once a more or less closed club of Western institutions.

Absent catastrophic events, such as mentioned in the previous section, global political tensions are likely to affect central bank cooperation to a lesser extent than between governments. As most members of the fraternity are to a greater or lesser extent independent from their governments, they tend to refrain from conducting politics among themselves, to the benefit of monetary and financial stability. For instance, while they cannot prevent governments from resorting to protectionism, they can issue (collective) warnings about the dangers of such measures and attempt to counteract their nefarious effects on financial stability. The biggest threat to this state of affairs would be the loss of independence of the individual members of the central bank community. Close cooperation with the International Monetary Fund on halting protectionism and currency manipulation can also form a buffer against nationalist tendencies in international economic relations.

Climate Change

Science and empirical evidence have led to the widespread recognition that climate change, if unchecked, will bring about profound—and possibly disastrous—changes in the way humans live. It is up to governments to prevent a worsening of this development in the short run, for instance by imposing carbon taxes, as well as to deal with its consequences in the longer run, not only through fiscal policy, but perhaps more importantly by outright prohibitions, such as against burning coal, and by drastically reducing the use of oil. The effects of climate change as we know now can be manifold, such as severe to extreme physical damage from natural disasters, rupture of energy supplies, communications breakdowns, disruption of transportation systems, failed crops and mass migration, all of which will be very costly. As a consequence, the international financial system could suffer severe shocks. Here is where the role of central banks as guardians of financial stability comes in.

Central banks have recognized that they have a role to play as a stabilizing force, especially if one looks beyond the short-term. Leading the way in the discussion of how official monetary institutions could contribute to a lessening of the fall-out of climate change, the Governor of the Bank of England, Mark Carney, stated in 2015 that 'challenges currently posed by climate change pale in significance compared to with what might come' (Carney 2015). Soon other central bankers took up the theme, while recognizing how difficult it is to arrive at workable solutions to a threat of which the magnitude and tipping points are unknown.

The effects of climate change can affect all core activities of central banks. In recent years there has been a strong surge in research and activities to better integrate climate change in the daily functioning of central banks. An important initiative for international cooperation was launched at the Paris One Planet Summit of 2017. The Central Banks and Supervisors Network for Greening the Financial System (NGFS) consists of a group of central banks, supervisors and international institutions who exchange experiences, share best practices and contribute to the development of environment and climate risk management in the financial sector. In a short period, the NGFS has acquired a central role in the debate on the effects of climate change on the financial sector (Elderson 2019). Based on its work, the NGFS has published a progress report with a call for action and recommendations (NGFS 2019).

* * *

As very powerful institutions, central banks are under constant scrutiny, sometimes praised for taking resolute action, such as keeping the global financial system afloat during the crisis of 2008–09, but at other times criticized for being too powerful. Most economic policymakers, as well as investors and firms are of the view that strong monetary institutions are essential to avoid political interference and short-termism. But the optimal degree of independence is not necessarily the same for all countries and must be seen against the background of each country's political framework and the maturity of its economy. Independence as enjoyed by the former German Bundesbank and the present-day European Central Bank—unique in its supranational framework—is not a feasible option for most central banks. This is not to say that the majority of central banks have achieved the degree of autonomy that could be considered optimal under their political system. In fact, there is room for strengthening the central banks' positions vis-à-vis their governments in several advanced countries and many developing nations. It has to be kept in mind, however, that independence is not set in stone in most cases and that efforts are needed to maintain a high level of monetary leeway. Therefore the world's monetary authorities need to continue adapting to changing circumstances and to effectively communicate their policy decisions to politicians and the public, as well as providing a degree of forward guidance to financial markets. Accountability, including clear and comprehensive communication, goes hand in hand with independence in today's world. The various challenges that monetary institutions could face in the near and longer term future were analyzed in the final chapter. It is of the essence for a smooth operation of the global economy that the main players will be allowed to react freely to meet these challenges. Their strategy should neither be to react meekly to criticism nor attempt to extend their power beyond the monetary and financial domain and to maintain a balanced working relationship with their governments. They should heed the warning of former Governor of the Bank of England, Mervyn King, that: 'the greatest threat to the future and independence of central banks comes from the danger of promising too much' (King 2016, xxi). To which can be added that central banks should focus on their core tasks and avoid entering into areas that belong to fiscal policy. Failing that, monetary policy unnecessarily risks to be politicized.

References

Alesina, Alberto and Lawrence Summers: "Central bank Independence and Macroeconomic Performance", *Journal of Money, Credit and Banking*, May, 1993, 251–62.

Bartsch, Elga et al: "Dealing with the Next Downturn: From Unconventional Monetary Policy to Unprecedented Policy Coordination" *Black Rock Investment Institute*, New York, August 2019.

Bernanke, Ben: *The Courage to Act: A Memoir of a Crisis and its Aftermath*, W.W. Norton, New York, 2015.

Bernanke, Ben: "Shrinking the Fed's Balance Sheet", The Brookings Institution, 26 January, 2017.

Bernanke, Ben: "The New Tools of Monetary Policy", presidential *Address*, The American Economic Association, 4 January 2020.

Binder, Sarah and Mark Spiegel: *The Myth of Independence: How Congress Governs the Federal Reserve*, Princeton University Press, Princeton NJ, 2017.

Blanchard, Olivier: "Shall we reject the Natural Rate Hypothesis?" Peterson Institute for International Economics, 21 November 2017.

Blinder, Alan: *The Quiet Revolution: Central Banking Goes Modern,* Yale University Press, New Haven, 2004.

Blinder, Alan: *Advice and Dissent: Why America Suffers when Economics and Politics Collide*, Basic Books, New York, 2017.

Carney, Mark: *Speech* before Insurance Market Participants, Lloyds Bank, London, 2015.

Carstens, Agustin: "Big Tech in Finance: New Challenges for Public Policy" *Keynote Address*: FT Banking Summit, 4 December 2018.

Cerrutti, Eugenio, Stijn Claessens and Luc Laeven: "The Use and Effectiveness of Macroprudential Policies", International Monetary Fund, *Working Paper* no 15/61, 2015.

Conti-Brown, Peter: *The Power and Independence of the Federal Reserve*, Princeton University Press, 2016.

Couere, Benoit: "Independence and Accountability in a Changing World", *Introductory Remarks* at the Transparency International EU Event, Brussels, 28 March, 2017.

De Beaufort Wijnholds, Onno: "Of Captains, Pilots and Judges: The World Wide Movement toward Central Bank Independence", *Inaugural Lecture*, University of Groningen, September, 1992.

Dincer, Nergiz and Barry Eichengreen: "Central Bank Transparency and Independence", *International Journal of Central Banking*, March 2014, 189–253.

Economist, The: "Downing Street Calling", 2 November 2019, 20.

Elderson, Frank: *Opening remarks* at the NGFS Conference, Paris 17 April, 2019.

El Erian, Mohamed: *The Only Game in Town: Central Banks, Instability and Avoiding the Next Collapse*, Random House, New York, 2016.

Fischer, Stanley (B): "The Independent Bank of England – 20 Years on" *Remarks* at a conference sponsored by the Bank of England, 28 September, 2017.

Fischer, Stanley: "Monetary Policy Expectations and Surprises", *Speech*, Columbia University, New York, 17 April 2017.

Friedman, Milton: "The Role of Monetary Policy", presidential *Address*, American Economic Association, 1968.

Greenspan Alan: Testimony before United Sates Congress, February 2005.

Hartmann, Phillip and Frank Smets: "The First Twenty Years of the European Central Bank", *ECB Working Paper* No 2219, December, 2018.

Ingves, Stefan: "Going Cashless", *Finance and Development*, Washington DC, June 2016.

International Monetary Fund and World Bank Group: "Fintech: The Experience So Far", *Joint Paper*, Washington DC, May 17, 2019.

Issing, Otmar: Interview, *Frankfurter Algemeine Zeitung*, 22 March 2016.

Kganyago, Lesetja: Quoted from *Bloomberg*, New York, 28 November, 2018.

King, Mervyn: *The End of Alchemy: Money, Banking, and the Future of the Global Economy*, W.W. Norton, New York, 2016.

Klein, Aaron: "Is China's New Payment System the Future?" *Report*, The Brookings Institution, June 2019.

Knot, Klaas: "Comments on ECB Policy Measures" *Press Release* by the Netherlands Bank, 13 September 2019.

Levy, Mickey: "Monetary Policy Realities facing the ECB, Fed and BoJ: More Easing won't Stimulate Economies", *Center for Financial Stability*, New York, 29 July 2019.

Long, Heather: "Americans Urge Federal Reserve to Boost Economy", *Washington Post*, 30 October, 2019.

Lucas, Robert: "Central Banking: Is Science Replacing Art?" in European Central Bank, (ed) *Monetary Policy: A Journey from Theory to Practice*, Frankfurt, 2007.
Marsh, David: *The Most Powerful Bank: Inside Germany's Bundesbank,* Times Books, New York, 1992.
Minsky, Hyman: "Can 'It' Happen Again?" in *Essays on Instability and Finance,* M.E. Sharpe, Armonk NY, 1982.
Network for Greening the Financial System: *A Call for Action: Climate Change as a Source of Financial Risk,* Paris, 2019.
Orphanides, Athanasios: "Improving Monetary Policy by Adopting a Simple Rule" in James Dorn (ed), *Monetary Policy in an Uncertain World: Ten Years after the Crisis*, Cato Institute, Washington DC, 2018, 237–44.
Paul, Ron: *End the Fed*, Grand Central Publishing, New York, 2009.
Powell, Jerome: "Changing Market Structures and Implications for Monetary Policy" *Speech* at Federal Reserve Bank of Kansas City Symposium, Jackson Hole, Wyoming, 24 August, 2018.
Rogoff, Kenneth: *The Curse of Cash,* Princeton University Press, Princeton NJ, 2016.
Rostangno, Massimo et al: "A Tale of Two Decades: the ECB's Monetary Policy at 20", European Central Bank *Working* Paper *Series,* No 2346, December 2019.
Shiller, Robert: *Narrative Economics: How Stories Go Viral & Drive* Major *Economic Events*, Princeton University Press, Princeton NJ, 2019.
Shiller, Robert: *Foreword* in Alan Blinder, *The Quiet Revolution*, Yale University Press, New Haven & London, 2004, XIV.
Summers, Lawrence: "Fed Bashing is Foolish", *Washington Post*, 6 November 2018.
Tucker, Paul: *Unelected Power: The Quest for Legitimacy in Central Banking and the Regulatory State*, Princeton University Press, Princeton NJ, 2018.
Ugolini, Stefano: *The Evolution of Central Banking: History and Theory,* Palgrave Macmillan, Basingstoke, 2017.
Volcker, Paul with Christine Harper: *Keeping at it: The Quest for Sound Money and Good Government*, Public Affairs, New York, 2018.
Wessel, David, *In Fed We Trust: How the Federal Reserve Became the Fourth Branch of Government,* Three Rivers Press, New York, 2010.
Williams, John: "Inflation Level Targeting", Brookings Institution, Washington DC, 2017.
Yellen, Janet: "What's (not) up with Inflation?" *Remarks* made at a panel discussion, The Brookings Institution, Washington DC 3 October, 2019.

Author Index

O. de Beaufort Wijnholds, *The Money Masters*,
https://doi.org/10.1007/978-3-030-40041-5

Subject Index

O. de Beaufort Wijnholds, *The Money Masters*,
https://doi.org/10.1007/978-3-030-40041-5

F

U

W

The manufacturer's authorised representative in the EU is Springer Nature Customer Service Centre GmbH, Europaplatz 3, 69115 Heidelberg, Germany. If you have any concerns regarding our products, please contact ProductSafety@springernature.com

Printed and bound by CPI Group (UK) Ltd, Croydon, CR0 4YY

30/09/2026

02225644-0011